Delivering
Police Services
Effectively

Advances in Police Theory and Practice Series

Series Editor: Dilip K. Das

Delivering Police Services Effectively
Garth den Heyer

Civilian Oversight of Police: Advancing Accountability in Law Enforcement
Tim Prenzler and Garth den Heyer

Collaborative Policing: Police, Academics, Professionals, and Communities Working Together for Education, Training, and Program Implementation
Peter C. Kratcoski and Maximilian Edelbacher

Corruption, Fraud, Organized Crime, and the Shadow Economy
Maximilian Edelbacher, Peter C. Kratcoski, and Bojan Dobovšek

Policing in Israel: Studying Crime Control, Community Policing, and Counterterrorism
Tal Jonathan-Zamir, David Weisburd, and Badi Hasisi

Policing Terrorism: Research Studies into Police Counterterrorism Investigations
David Lowe

Policing in Hong Kong: History and Reform
Kam C. Wong

Cold Cases: Evaluation Models with Follow-up Strategies for Investigators, Second Edition
James M. Adcock and Sarah L. Stein

Crime Linkage: Theory, Research, and Practice
Jessica Woodhams and Craig Bennell

Police Investigative Interviews and Interpreting: Context, Challenges, and Strategies
Sedat Mulayim, Miranda Lai, and Caroline Norma

Policing White Collar Crime: Characteristics of White Collar Criminals
Petter Gottschalk

Honor-Based Violence: Policing and Prevention
Karl Anton Roberts, Gerry Campbell, and Glen Lloyd

Policing and the Mentally Ill: International Perspectives
Duncan Chappell

Security Governance, Policing, and Local Capacity
Jan Froestad with Clifford D. Shearing

Policing in Hong Kong: History and Reform
Kam C. Wong

Police Performance Appraisals: A Comparative Perspective
Serdar Kenan Gul and Paul O'Connell

Los Angeles Police Department Meltdown: The Fall of the Professional-Reform Model of Policing
James Lasley

Financial Crimes: A Global Threat
Maximilian Edelbacher, Peter Kratcoski, and Michael Theil

Police Integrity Management in Australia: Global Lessons for Combating Police Misconduct
Louise Porter and Tim Prenzler

The Crime Numbers Game: Management by Manipulation
John A. Eterno and Eli B. Silverman

The International Trafficking of Human Organs: A Multidisciplinary Perspective
Leonard Territo and Rande Matteson

Police Reform in China
Kam C. Wong

Mission-Based Policing
John P. Crank, Dawn M. Irlbeck, Rebecca K. Murray, and Mark Sundermeier

The New Khaki: The Evolving Nature of Policing in India
Arvind Verma

Cold Cases: An Evaluation Model with Follow-up Strategies for Investigators
James M. Adcock and Sarah L. Stein

Policing Organized Crime: Intelligence Strategy Implementation
Petter Gottschalk

Security in Post-Conflict Africa: The Role of Nonstate Policing
Bruce Baker

Community Policing and Peacekeeping
Peter Grabosky

Community Policing: International Patterns and Comparative Perspectives
Dominique Wisler and Ihekwoaba D. Onwudiwe

Police Corruption: Preventing Misconduct and Maintaining Integrity
Tim Prenzler

Delivering Police Services Effectively

Garth den Heyer
Police Foundation
Washington, DC, USA

CRC Press
Taylor & Francis Group
Boca Raton London New York

CRC Press is an imprint of the
Taylor & Francis Group, an **informa** business

CRC Press
Taylor & Francis Group
6000 Broken Sound Parkway NW, Suite 300
Boca Raton, FL 33487-2742

First issued in paperback 2019

© 2017 by Taylor & Francis Group, LLC
CRC Press is an imprint of Taylor & Francis Group, an Informa business

No claim to original U.S. Government works

ISBN-13: 978-1-4987-4234-4 (hbk)
ISBN-13: 978-0-367-87471-1 (pbk)

Library of Congress Cataloging-in-Publication Data

Names: Heyer, Garth den, author.
Title: Delivering police services effectively / Garth den Heyer.
Description: 1 Edition. | Boca Raton : CRC Press, 2016. | Series: Advances in police theory and practice ; 27 | Includes bibliographical references.
Identifiers: LCCN 2016008147 | ISBN 9781498742344
Subjects: LCSH: Criminal justice, Administration of. | Organizational change.
Classification: LCC HV7419 .H49 2016 | DDC 363.2068--dc23
LC record available at https://lccn.loc.gov/2016008147

Visit the Taylor & Francis Web site at
http://www.taylorandfrancis.com

and the CRC Press Web site at
http://www.crcpress.com

Contents

Series Preface   xiii
Foreword   xv
About the Author   xix
Acknowledgments   xxi

Section I
THE THEORY OF POLICE REFORM TO ACHIEVE EFFICIENT AND EFFECTIVE SERVICE DELIVERY

1   Introduction   3

Demand for Police Services   4
Conclusion   7

2   Defining Methods for Improving Police Services   9

Introduction   9
Efficiency and Effectiveness of Service Delivery   9
Understanding Costs   12
Defining Consolidation   14
Conclusion   15

3   Theory of Government and Police Reform   17

Introduction   17
Theory of Government Funding   20
Theory of Modern Police Reform   21
Theory of Local Government Reform, Regionalization, and
Mergers   24
Theory of Police Agency Regionalization and Mergers   27
Conclusion   29

**4   Historical Approaches to Improving Police
     Service Delivery**   **31**

Introduction   31
Government Approach to Reform 1980–2000   32
Factors That Led to Police Reform 1980–2000   33
Value for Money and Planning, Programming,
and Budgeting   33
Rise in the Number of Regionalizations, Consolidations,
and Mergers   34
Rise of New Public Management   37
Conclusion   40

**5   Late-Twentieth-Century Approaches to
     Improving Police Service Delivery**   **41**

Introduction   41
Factors That Influenced the Improvement in Service Delivery
Strategies in the Late-Twentieth-Century   42
Performance Measurement, Organizational Structures, and
Service Delivery   43
Effects That New Public Management Has Had on Police
Agencies   46
Value for Money   47
Organizational Structure   49
Performance Measurement   52
Compstat   55
Intelligence-Led Policing   56
Civilianization of Sworn Positions   58
Civilianization in the United States   60
Civilianization in Canada   61
Civilianization in the United Kingdom   63
Outsourcing, Alliances, and Police Interagency Collaboration   64
Mergers, Amalgamations, and Regionalization   69
Regionalization in the United Kingdom   72
Use of Technology   74
Conclusion   75

Section II
STRATEGIES EMPLOYED TO IMPROVE SERVICE DELIVERY IN AUSTRALIA, CANADA, ENGLAND AND WALES, NEW ZEALAND, AND THE UNITED STATES

6 **Strategies Employed to Improve Service Delivery in Australia**   **79**

Introduction 79
Changes to the Australian Public Service and Police 80
New South Wales Police Force Case Study 84
Queensland Police Service Case Study 85
Conclusion 87

7 **Strategies Employed to Improve Service Delivery in Canada**   **89**

Introduction 89
Canadian Police 90
Rationalization of Police Agencies and Police Services 90
Regionalization of Canadian Police Agencies 92
Case Studies of the Regionalization of the Canadian Police 94
   British Columbia Province 94
   Greater Vancouver Region 95
   Ontario Province 98
   Halifax City 99
Conclusion 100

8 **Strategies Employed to Improve Service Delivery in England and Wales**   **101**

Introduction 101
Brief History of Police Reform in England and Wales 102
Structure and Size of the Police Service in England and Wales 103
Efficiency and Effectiveness of Police Service 106
Difficulty of Merging Police Services 109
Five Reports That Have Examined Police Effectiveness 109

Her Majesty's Inspectorate of Constabulary (2004)
Modernizing the Police Service: A Thematic Inspection
of Workforce Modernization—The Role, Management,
and Development of Police Staff in the Police Service of
England and Wales   110
Her Majesty's Inspectorate of Constabulary (2005) Closing
the Gap: A Review of the "Fitness for Purpose" of the
Current Structure of Policing in England and Wales   110
Her Majesty's Inspectorate of Constabulary (2010) Valuing
the Police: Policing in an Age of Austerity   113
Her Majesty's Inspectorate of Constabulary (2011)
Adapting to Austerity   114
Policy Exchange (2011) Cost of Cops: Manpower and
Deployment in Policing   115
Conclusion   115

**9   Strategies Employed to Improve Service
      Delivery in New Zealand   117**

Introduction   117
New Zealand Reforms   118
The First Phase: A Performance and Accountability Framework   119
The Second Phase: Reorientation   119
New Zealand Police   120
Response of the New Zealand Police to the Environment   120
New Zealand Police Corporate Planning (A New Approach to
Objectives and Outputs)   121
New Zealand Police: Strategic Planning   122
Policing Excellence Program   124
Conclusion   125

**10   Strategies Employed to Improve Service
      Delivery in the United States   127**

Introduction   127
Economy   128
Management   129
Community-Oriented Policing   130
Staffing of Police Agencies   130
Amalgamation, Mergers, and Regionalization   131
Inconsistencies of Consolidations   132
Ambiguities of Regionalization   134
Examples of Consolidation and Regionalization   136
Consolidation of Police Agencies in Pennsylvania   137

Consolidation of Police Agencies in Other States   140
Conclusion   140
Part 2: Conclusion   141

Section III
CASE STUDIES

**11   Establishment of Police Scotland: A Reform to
Increase Effectiveness   145**

Introduction   145
Background to the Reform   146
History of Policing in Scotland   147
Governance of Police prior to April 1, 2013: "Tripartite
Structure"   149
Major Issues Leading to the Reform   152
Case for Change   156
    Financial Backdrop   156
    Sustainable Policing Project   157
    Police Reform Program: Outline Business Case   159
    Consultation on the Future of Policing in Scotland 162
    The Reform Bill   163
Methodology   163
Results   165
    Why Was a Merger of All Police Forces Adopted? What
    Were the Main Drivers?   165
    What Alternatives to a Merger Were Considered?   166
    What Activities and Budget Analyses Were Undertaken to
    Plan for and Implement the Merger?   166
    Has There Been Any Change in the Efficiency and
    Effectiveness of the Delivery of Services by the New Police
    Service of Scotland?   167
Discussion   170
    Policy Analysis Framework   172
Conclusion   174

**12   Ghosts of Policing Strategies Past: Is the New
Zealand Police "Prevention First" Strategy
Historic, Contemporary, or of the Future?   175**

Introduction   175
A Framework for Analyzing the New Zealand Police Change
Management Programs   176

New Zealand Public Sector Reforms (1984–1990)   178
Initial Response by the New Zealand Police to the
Environment of the Late 1980s   179
Creation of Policing 2000   183
Investment in Technology   184
Profound Change in Culture   184
Post 2000 New Zealand Police Organizational Change
Programs   185
    Policing Excellence   185
    Prevention First   186
    Discussion   190
Comparison of Policing 2000, Policing Excellence, and
Prevention First   191
Has the Service Delivery of the New Zealand Police Improved
as a Result of Policing 2000, Policing Excellence, and
Prevention First?   194
Conclusion   195

**13   Increasing Service Delivery Efficiency in
      Camden County Police Department, New Jersey   197**

Introduction   197
Background   198
Proposal to Establish the CCPD   205
Establishing the CCPD   207
CCPD Draft Plan   209
CCPD Metro in 2014   212
CCPD's Performance 2012–2014   213
2013 Performance   214
2014 Performance   214
CCPD Metro Approach to Crime Prevention   215
Conclusion   217

14   Conclusion   219

References   223
Index   241

Series Preface

While the literature on police and allied subjects is growing exponentially, its impact on day-to-day policing remains small. The two worlds of research and practice of policing remain disconnected even though cooperation between the two is growing. A major reason is that the two groups speak in different languages. The research work is published in hard-to-access journals and presented in a manner that is difficult to comprehend for a layperson. On the other hand, police practitioners tend not to mix with researchers and remain secretive about their work. Consequently, there is little dialogue between the two and almost no attempt to learn from one another. Dialogue across the globe, among researchers and practitioners situated in different continents, is of course even more limited.

I attempted to address this problem by starting the IPES, www.ipes.info, where a common platform has brought the two together. IPES is now in its 17th year. The annual meetings, which constitute the major annual events of the organization, have been hosted in all parts of the world. Several publications have come out of these deliberations, and a new collaborative community of scholars and police officers has been created whose membership runs into several hundreds.

Another attempt was to begin a new journal, aptly called *Police Practice and Research: An International Journal*, PPR, to open the gate to practitioners to share their work and experiences. The journal has attempted to focus on issues that help bring the two onto a single platform. It is certainly evidence of growing collaboration between police research and practice that PPR, which began with four issues a year, expanded into five issues in its fourth year and is now issued six times a year.

Clearly, these attempts, despite their success, remain limited. Conferences and journal publications do help create a body of knowledge and an association of police activists but cannot address substantial issues in depth. The limitations of time and space preclude larger discussions and more authoritative expositions that can provide stronger and broader links between the two worlds.

It is this realization of the increasing dialogue between police research and practice that has encouraged many of us—my close colleagues and I connected closely with IPES and PPR across the world—to conceive and implement a new attempt in this direction. The result is a book series, *Advances in Police Theory and Practice*, that endeavors to attract writers from all parts of the world. Further, the attempt is to find practitioner contributors. The objective is to make the series a serious contribution to our knowledge of the police and to improve police practices. The focus is not only in work that describes the best and successful police practices but also one that challenges current paradigms and breaks new ground to prepare a police for the twenty-first century. The series seeks comparative analysis that highlights achievements in distant parts of the world as well as one that encourages an in-depth examination of specific problems confronting a particular police force.

It is hoped that through this series it will be possible to accelerate the process of building knowledge about policing and help bridge the gap between the two worlds—the world of police research and police practice. This is an invitation to police scholars and practitioners across the world to come and join in this venture.

Dilip K. Das, PhD
Founding President
International Police Executive Symposium, IPES, www.ipes.info

Founding Editor-in-Chief, *Police Practice and Research: An International Journal*, PPR, www.tandf.co.uk/journals

Foreword

Economic crises have profound implications for crime, disorder, and attitudes toward policing. Upon writing of the economic collapse of the 1970s and 1980s, policing scholar Robert Reiner noted how in the United Kingdom this led to increased inequality and social exclusion, drove up crime, and politicized law and order. But what about the current economic crisis that has its origins in the global financial collapse of 2007? There is already strong evidence that this is increasing social and economic inequality and leading to differences in communities' exposure to crime and disorder. But is it also posing significant challenges for police organizations? After many years of ever-increasing police budgets, the current economic crisis and the ensuing "age of austerity" are bringing about fundamental shifts in the policies, practices, and structures of policing. This is new and uncharted territory for police organizations. The recent history of spending on policing has been one of sustained and significant growth. Public spending on policing in the United States more than quadrupled between 1982 and 2006, while in Britain, the amount of money invested in policing by central and local government each year since 1994 had more than doubled by 2008/2009. Faced now with significant cuts in their budgets, police leaders are under considerable pressure to take decisions about how to manage their resources effectively and improve the efficiency of policing. As a former UK chief police officer, Peter Neyroud has observed that for many police organizations across the globe, this is both an age of austerity and an era of reform.

Against this background, this excellent book provides a very timely and detailed analysis of the complex challenges police organizations now face. It addresses a fundamental question: How can police forces continue to deliver efficient and effective services as their budgets are reduced and yet the demands that they face, from being responsive and accessible to local communities to being capable of tackling new forms of criminality, show no signs of diminishing? The range of radical options being embraced by police organizations in different parts of the globe is indicative of the scale of the challenges they face. Expanding the use of technology, changing the composition of the police workforce, introducing new forms of public management, and merging and amalgamating police districts and forces are all strategic choices that have to be made against the background of continuing austerity. In some places, these reforms are being driven internally by police leaders; in other areas, the pressure for change is from bodies external to police forces, often from audit and inspection organizations or governments.

This book provides an outstanding analysis of these issues. It brings a refreshing clarity of perspective based on careful consideration of different theoretical frameworks and wide-ranging empirical evidence. Indeed, one of the real strengths of the analysis presented here is the geographical scope of the study. Case studies drawn from the United States, Europe, and New Zealand ensure that the arguments are grounded in strong empirical evidence and also provide fascinating insights into similarities and differences in approach that can only emerge from this kind of comparative research. In the United States, for example, policing remains largely decentralized, diverse, and locally funded with local police organizations having a high degree of autonomy. By contrast, in Europe, policing is strongly influenced by a complex relationship between central and local government creating a mosaic of different forms of contemporary restructuring, ranging from the formation of national police organizations to the reenforcing of localism. Through a compelling and thought-provoking narrative, this book shows how particular frameworks and ideas have been adopted and adapted in different settings in the search for more efficient and effective policing. Another unique strength of this book is that it is written by someone who is able to bring the insights of both a practitioner with significant operational policing experience and a researcher who has traveled widely, experiencing policing in different settings and contexts, and who is comfortable dealing with theoretical and empirical issues. Like all good texts, this book generates more questions than it is able to answer and in so doing helps set an agenda for future work in this area. Significant issues that emerge from this analysis include the following: What is the type and style of leadership required to deal with an increasingly complex economic and political environment? What impacts do the search for ever greater efficiency and effectiveness have on citizens' perceptions of police legitimacy and their trust and confidence in police organizations? And given that the police are faced with problems that are rarely just policing issues, but require partnership and collaboration, what are the interdependencies and interconnections between changes to policing and the restructuring of other agencies in fields such as social work, health, and education who also face difficult challenges associated with declining budgets?

This book then is very much a key reference point within the continuing discussion and debate about the future character, shape, and restructuring of public police organizations. The long-term effects of the global financial crisis in terms of unemployment and social exclusion, poverty, and inequality are all likely to drive up crime, and so the police will continue to face increasing pressures on their resources while public expectations of service delivery remain high and the demands the police face grow in complexity. Garth den

Heyer has provided an exceptionally clear, evidence-based analysis of how police organizations are navigating these challenges of providing an efficient and effective response to the problems of crime and disorder in an increasingly unequal world.

Professor Nicholas R. Fyfe
Director, Scottish Institute for Policing Research and Associate Dean, School of Social Sciences, University of Dundee, Dundee, United Kingdom

About the Author

Garth den Heyer is a senior research fellow with the Police Foundation and a lecturer at Walden University, Minneapolis, Minnesota. He is also an associate with the Scottish Institute of Policing Research. His main research interests are policing, militarization and the security gap, and service delivery effectiveness; policy development, strategic thinking, and reform; operational leadership and the police role in peacekeeping; countering terrorism; organized crime; and transitioning and postconflict nations.

Acknowledgments

In late August 2012, while on a cruise from Boston to Montreal, I received confirmation that I had been awarded a research grant from the Office of Community Oriented Policing Services (2012-CK-WX-K017) to undertake a national and international comparative assessment of the cost-reducing strategies that have been adopted by police agencies to maintain the effective and efficient delivery of services. Part of this research included developing and drafting an extensive literature review of cost-reducing strategies. This book has evolved from the original literature review. I thank the COPS Office for the opportunity to undertake the research.

I am indebted to Karen Amendola and Earl Hamilton from the Police Foundation for their guidance and support. I am also extremely grateful to Nick Fyfe from the Scottish Institute of Policing Research who spent a significant amount of his time in the summer of 2014 discussing the issues explored in this book.

I am also tremendously grateful to my wife, Vicki, for her assistance and support.

This book is dedicated to my two grandsons, Liam and Joshua, who give me great joy.

The Theory of
Police Reform to
Achieve Efficient
and Effective
Service Delivery

I

Introduction

1

Commencing in late 2007, the world suffered the worst economic and financial crisis in 70 years (Domitrovic, 2013), resulting in a significant loss of revenue for central and local governments. The contraction of state and local government funding had a negative impact on the funding of police agencies, which influenced how police services would be delivered. By 2014, eight city governments in the United States had declared bankruptcy (governing.com, 2015) and more than 10,000 police officers had been laid off (COPS, 2011), while in the United Kingdom, more than 20,000 police officers lost their jobs (Morris, 2010). The actual number of police officers who lost their jobs during this period has not been confirmed, but despite laying off large numbers of staff, police agencies were pressured to further reduce staff numbers and spending. Not only did agencies have to operate with reduced numbers of staff and less funding, but increasing public demand for police services compounded the problem further.

With reduced levels of funding, police agencies have found it difficult to maintain their service delivery levels and to deliver special programs, such as Community Policing (Wilson & Grammich, 2012). As a response, many police managers have relied on historical strategies to reduce organizational costs, such as terminating the employment of some staff members and leaving vacancies unfilled, while others have implemented only short-term organizational change, such as reducing the availability of patrol officers' overtime.

Instead of relying on traditional cost-saving measures, police agencies need to identify alternate strategies if they are to operate within their funding levels and be able to offer the services that the government and the public expect. Unfortunately, there is no off-the-shelf option for absorbing budget cuts while preventing or responding to crime (Schieder, Spence, & Mansourian, 2012). Furthermore, there is little research available that documents the benefits that may be gained from adopting alternative cost-saving strategies. Given the extent and the projected longevity of the financial crisis, simply trying to outlast decreasing levels of funding is not a long-term option for police agencies (Cohen McCullough & Spence, 2012).

Her Majesty's Inspectorate of Constabulary (2011) recommended that police adapt to the new operating environment as soon as possible so that the confidence of the public is maintained and that the level of crime stays on the current, downward trend. The alternative is to continue as always, which will see funding allocations reduce and personnel and service levels decrease.

The United States National League of Cities maintained that it would take years for cities and counties in the United States to benefit from the effects of any recovery from the recession. Other researchers have warned that it may be a long time before budgets return to pre-2008 levels, in real dollar terms or purchasing power (Cohen McCullough & Spence, 2012; Sustainable Policing Project, 2011). These predictions emphasize the importance of examining alternative ways to deliver efficient and effective services when funding has been reduced.

The new operating environment can be viewed either positively or negatively by police managers. The constrained environment offers an opportunity for police to innovate and to improve the efficiency and effectiveness of its service delivery. Many agencies are evaluating the organizational structures that they use and are examining alternative management methods, such as agency consolidation, regionalization and amalgamation, organizational centralization/decentralization, New Public Management (NPM), enhanced performance management, and civilianization, in an effort to reduce agency costs. These methods form the basis of a new, open-minded approach, as it is acknowledged that the status quo can no longer remain (Thomson, 2012).

Owing to the lack of available, relevant literature, organizations may find it difficult to identify suitable, alternative strategies to improve their service delivery and performance. What is needed is well-documented, comprehensive, evaluations of police agency change programs. Where literature pertaining to police restructuring is available, the results of the research are often conflicting. For policing to advance as a profession, there is a need for scholars and practitioners to evaluate policing processes and for the findings to be examined, analyzed, and shared.

Demand for Police Services

The principal concern of police during periods of decreasing levels of funding is how to manage crime and deliver services in response to the occurrence of crime. New methods that will improve the efficiency and effectiveness of service delivery and the economical use of resources during periods of decreasing levels of funding are required. There are three elements that police managers need to take into account when identifying strategies that would be suitable for improving the delivery of service and reducing police operating costs:

1. Crime can and needs to be more effectively controlled.
2. Police resources can be used more effectively, and they must be better utilized if the crime control problem is to be addressed.
3. Pursuing a policy agenda that works toward a new form of police agency can realize a more effective utilization of police resources (Farmer, 1984).

While police can effectively control or reduce crime (see Bayley, 1998; Eck & Maguire, 2000; Mazerolle, Soole, & Rombouts, 2007; Sherman et al., 1997; Weisburd & Eck, 2004), Farmer (1984), however, claimed that what is needed to improve the control of crime is "a new form of police agency" (p. 1). Interpreting Farmer's statement is difficult, but by setting the statement in the context of 1984, what Farmer was probably meaning was, not that new police agencies per se are required, but rather new frameworks and control mechanisms to improve service delivery and performance within an agency are needed. Farmer (1984) clarified his claim by maintaining that what is needed to improve the control of crime is "new understandings and improved practice in the utilization of police resources. The use and misuse of police resources—or police resource allocation—is a vitally important issue for crime control, as it is for police policy-making and management" (pp. 1–2).

A major issue that should be kept in mind when discussing the relationship between police and the incidence of crime is that crime cannot be completely eliminated by increasing the number of police officers. Increasing the number of police officers when attempting to reduce the level of crime may result in a diminishing level of return. As an agency increases the number of police officers, at a certain point, the increase starts to yield a smaller reduction in crime (Heaton, 2010). Schieder et al. (2012) agreed that police do have an effect on the level of crime, but they raise two fundamental questions:

1. Would decreasing the number of officers result in an increase in crime and, if so, what would be the extent of the increase?
2. Is there a percentage in the decrease of staffing to which a department can still maintain its effectiveness but beyond which law and order cannot be realistically controlled? (Schieder et al., 2012)

These two questions confirm that new perspectives are needed to examine the efficiency and the effectiveness of police service delivery and to determine whether the current level of service will meet the future needs of society. In order to determine whether the current level of service will meet the future needs of society, an examination and analysis of the performance and the workload of the police may provide an avenue for understanding whether the structures and the organizational models employed are capable of adapting to future demand (Wilson, 2012). This knowledge will enable the police to structure their agencies accordingly to meet future demand.

The demand for police services has increased over time, resulting in the significant expansion of the role of the police. Two factors have influenced the increase in demand. The first is the extent to which the role of the police extends beyond traditional crime fighting, and the second is that the responsibilities of the police now include community policing, homeland security, and investigating transnational crime. The increase in the demand for police services is not expected to diminish in the foreseeable future, which means that police agencies must be prepared to reorganize their structures and their resources to meet the increase in demand. Agencies have attempted to change their role and meet the increase in demand for services in several ways, such as

1. Reprioritizing functions and reallocating resources to account for new responsibilities that do not come with commensurate resources
2. Delaying response and reducing or eliminating special units
3. Introducing cameras and other technology to carry out the roles that officers might have otherwise fulfilled (Wilson, 2012)

Research conducted by Melekian (2012a) supported the conclusions of Wilson and added that four operational areas have been affected by the change in demand: increased reliance on the use of technology; increased use of civilians both as employees and as volunteers; consolidation among agencies, either of core services or in the form of agency mergers; and alternative forms of response to nonemergency calls. Three situational factors have arisen as a result of the change in demand, and these factors have converged with the four operational areas affected by the change in demand, compounding the managerial challenges for police agencies. The three situational factors are as follows:

1. The constriction of the economy, which has reduced the availability of funding for police agencies. Reduced funding often results in a reduction in the number of sworn officers available to handle patrol duties.
2. A new generation of police officers who wish to be more directly and creatively engaged in their work.
3. Recognition by law enforcement leaders that patrol is the link between the agency and the community (Loveday, 1995a; Melekian, 2012a).

Murphy (2002) maintained that the police response to the increase in the demand for service has been a combination of both traditional and new management thinking. Traditional police managers have looked for strategies within conventional policing models that are grounded in the 1970s thinking to respond to the increase in the demand for police services. However, the management methods that were used for maintaining service delivery during the 1960s and 1970s are no longer sufficient or practical (Kocher, 2012). While traditional managers have tended to justify or develop existing service delivery approaches and management structures, innovative managers have examined more modern strategies, which include private-sector initiatives and NPM models and have adopted service delivery approaches and strategies that aim to increase organizational and operational efficiencies and effectiveness (Murphy, 2002).

Conclusion

Every police agency has its own individuality, but when examined from a distance, the commonalities among police agencies are more striking than the individual differences (Farmer, 1984). Farmer's view is particularly poignant when agencies are responding to an increase in the demand for police services and to the fiscally restraining environment. Although police agencies are different, they are also very similar, and a successful cost-reducing strategy adopted by one agency could be adapted by other agencies to suit their specific circumstances. While there have been significant improvements in policing since the 1960s, Burack (2012) claimed that police agencies will need to be better managers of their resources, improve the efficiency and effectiveness of their service delivery, and ensure that public funds are spent wisely if they are to provide value for the taxpayer.

Police managers need to explore new approaches to delivering services and measuring their performance if they are to operate within their funding allocation, and ideally, they should not rely on historical strategies to reduce their operating costs, such as decreasing staff numbers. There is no off-the-shelf answer to solve budgetary problems and nor is there "a one-size fits all solution to either preventing or responding to crime across communities and crime types" (Schieder et al., 2012, p. 10).

Agencies need to implement comprehensive, dynamic, and flexible management and performance frameworks if they are to successfully adapt to further changes in the operating environment.

This book examines the cost-reducing strategies that police agencies have adopted in order to maintain the effective and efficient delivery of services and discusses the strategies that relate to managerial and organizational structural reform within the policing programs of Community-Oriented Policing, Problem-Oriented Policing, and intelligence-led policing. While there may be a current phenomenon of police agencies searching for alternative approaches to improve service delivery, the search for improving police performance and the better utilization of resources actually started in the 1980s in a number of different locations around the world.

This book comprises 14 chapters. Following the introduction and a discussion of definitions, the theory and the history of government and police reform are presented in Chapters 3 and 4. Chapter 5 presents the late-twentieth-century approaches to improving police service delivery. Chapters 6 through 10 discuss the initiatives that are currently being undertaken to reform police in Australia, Canada, England and Wales, New Zealand, and the United States. Section III of this book presents three case studies that examine the strategies that have been undertaken in Scotland, New Zealand, and Camden, New Jersey, to improve the efficiency and effectiveness of police service delivery. These case studies demonstrate that the approaches taken to reform police agencies have all been very different.

The first case study examines the reasons for establishing a national police agency. The second case study evaluates and compares three extensive change management programs that were implemented by the New Zealand Police to improve the efficiency and the effectiveness of its delivery of services. The final case study examines the approach taken by a financially strapped city and county to reduce its operating costs.

The book concludes with a discussion of the challenges that police face when undertaking major reform. To increase the likelihood of a successful reform program, it is evident that police managers need to have a clear understanding of their responsibilities and the role of police and where they fit in the bigger picture of government and governance.

Defining Methods for Improving Police Services

2

Introduction

The terminology used in the literature that relates to police agencies undertaking organizational reform or restructuring in order to decrease costs or to improve service delivery effectiveness is extremely confusing. This confusion is compounded when comparing American policing literature with international literature as a number of American researchers use the terms "consolidation," "amalgamation," "merger," "regionalization," and "integration" interchangeably or for specific forms of organizational reform. In one American example, researchers (Wilson, Weiss, & Grammich, 2012) defined consolidation as the merging of the local police and fire department to form one local emergency agency. In comparison, researchers in the United Kingdom used the term "consolidation" to refer to the merging of agencies that provide the same function, for example, policing (the merging of two police agencies) (Loveday, 2007). The discussion throughout this book will use the term "consolidation" in relation to the merging and reform of police agencies only.

This chapter defines and discusses the terms "efficiency" and "effectiveness," "amalgamation," "consolidation," "merger," and "regionalization" in the context of police reform. The major terms used in describing consolidation in police reform conclude the remainder of the chapter and form the basis for the discussion that follows.

Efficiency and Effectiveness of Service Delivery

As a result of the 2007 economic crisis and the subsequent constraints on police agency budgets, police managers have attempted to improve agency efficiency by cutting costs and improving agency performance without using any additional resources. However, determining the appropriate performance measurements and how an agency's performance should be measured is problematic. Reviewing an individual police agency's performance or comparing the performance of a number of police agencies is difficult, as very few service delivery measurement matrices exist, and the majority of agencies still rely on quantitative performance measures, such as the number of calls for service, the number of crimes reported, and the number of crimes cleared. Relying principally on quantitative performance measures, such as the number of reported crimes is not ideal, as police perform many other functions that are not related to the occurrence of crime. Police agencies that rely solely on the number of crimes reported to measure their performance are not measuring the delivery of their services comprehensively. Instead of using quantitative data to measure service delivery performance, it is recommended that organizational outputs and social outcomes be used. An organizational output is defined as the amount of service or product that is produced by an agency and a social outcome is defined as something that follows as a result or consequence of the production of an output in a society (Boston, 1991).

In economic literature, productivity is generally measured in terms of output obtained for a given input and is widely defined as encompassing both effectiveness and efficiency (Cloninger & Sartorius, 1979; Hatry, 1975). However, the terms "effectiveness" and "efficiency" are frequently misused in relation to police work, with police officers attempting to prove their effectiveness by pointing to their efficiency in specific areas (den Heyer, 2009). Distinguishing between effectiveness and efficiency is necessary when examining the service performance of a police agency, as an organization may indeed be efficient, but unless its activities accomplish the desired output or outcome, it cannot be regarded as being completely effective. Similarly, an organization may be deemed effective, but it may not be operating at minimal cost, or if its inputs are wasted when converting to output, it cannot be regarded as being efficient (den Heyer, 2009).

Another area of confusion relating to effectiveness is the difference between "police effectiveness" and "crime control effectiveness" (Skogan & Frydel, 2003). The term "police effectiveness" is defined as including measures of performance, which pertain to those areas of police productivity that are capable of being measured, for example, recorded crime, the number of arrests, and resolution rates. On the other hand, "crime control effectiveness" is defined as including those less tangible areas of activity, which are difficult, if not impossible, to measure, such as crime prevention, social assistance, and the maintenance of public order (Fisk, 1974). As a result, a situation could arise in which police effectiveness increases without a commensurate increase in crime control.

The delivery of an effective service is extremely important for police managers because research has identified "that much of the effectiveness of police depends on the specific type of policing that they employ and the specific activities that they undertake" (Schieder, Spence, & Mansourian, 2012, p. 12). This is a significant observation in regard to Community Policing because the results of Schieder's research indicate that the police–citizen relationship is circular. The impact that police have on local crime is affected by its ability to respond, the resources that are available, and its relationship with the community. However, the community will only work with the police if they have confidence in the police.

The police–community relationship is especially important when improving the effectiveness of police service delivery. There is robust research that demonstrates that offending is geographically concentrated (Braga & Weisburd, 2010), and if offending is to be addressed, then approaches or responses must be tailored within the context of the community. The community approach emphasizes that the concentrated and focused use of police resources is particularly important in times of declining levels of funding (Schieder et al., 2012), as police managers will need to balance organizational, operational, and service delivery priorities with the needs and priorities of the community.

The number of responses to nonemergency calls is a major variable, which influences the effectiveness of police agencies. Such responses take up the bulk of an officer's directed time (Melekian, 2012b). However, because responses to nonemergency calls are important to citizens and are often used to establish relationships with the community, the majority of agencies are reluctant to consider alternative responses to these kinds of calls or requests for assistance. If the service that police agencies deliver is to improve, true changes in the methods and approaches to the delivery of patrol services will need to occur (Melekian, 2012b).

One aspect of policing that is changing is the number of civilian personnel employed. In a 2011 survey of police chiefs, conducted by the Police Executive Research Forum, more than half of the respondents stated that they would reduce the number of civilian personnel employed before they would reduce the number of police officers employed (Police Executive Research Forum, 2011). However, decreasing the number of civilian staff employed will not necessarily increase the effectiveness of the service delivered by an agency. This is because it may be necessary to use police officers to perform the work that was previously undertaken by civilian personnel, leading to a reduction in the number of officers available for patrol and for carrying out investigations. Any reduction in the number of police officers available for patrol or to undertake investigations will lead to a decrease in an agency's capability to deliver police services and in the efficiency and effectiveness of the service delivered. The sworn to civilian ratio also affects the efficiency and effectiveness of the service delivered.

Measuring the level of the service delivered and how it is delivered are two methods that may be used to assess an agency's efficiency and effectiveness. The performance of the majority of police agencies is assessed by an evaluation of statistical data, which is used to represent various outputs. The statistical approach to police performance measurement has gained acceptance through the introduction of Compstat-type frameworks and processes. Although Compstat and its derivatives, CitiStat and StateStat, are capable of measuring and recording a police agency's quantitative outputs, they do not measure the quality of the service provided (Fuentes, 2012).

The definitions of efficiency and effectiveness that will be used in the discussion throughout this book are as follows:

1. Efficiency—the ratio of effective or useful output to the total input in any system. It indicates the degree to which, for example, police hours or other input resources, which have been designated to perform particular activities, do in fact, do so. The inputs into any system could consist of hours, staff, or funding.
2. Effectiveness—the capacity to produce a desired effect or purpose without regard to costs or other inputs. When something is deemed to be effective, it means that it has achieved an intended or expected outcome, such as a police agency achieving the objectives that have been documented in its annual plan.

Understanding Costs

There is a widespread lack of understanding of the costs involved in providing police services and how these costs compare with the outcomes that are to be achieved. Costs cannot be linked to an improvement of a specific process or the delivery of an outcome if there is poor knowledge of the meaning of and the influence of costs. If there is poor knowledge of costs, police agencies will not be able to make comprehensive and sustainable operational cost reductions and, instead, could implement 1D actions, such as across-the-board cuts in staff numbers, compensation, or services that are deemed to be noncore or nonessential (Kaplan & Porter, 2011).

An inability to measure costs and an unawareness of the costs involved in delivering individual police services have led to a cross-subsidization between services. Cross-subsidization has caused major distortions in the supply and the efficiency of service delivery and occurs when the profits from one area of an organization are used to pay for the costs of another area of an organization, which is unable to provide services as a result of a lack of resources or funding (Kaplan & Porter, 2011). The inability to accurately measure and compare the costs associated with outputs and outcomes is one of the main reasons why police managers struggle with understanding where the strategic side of a police organization meets with the operational side.

The weakness in understanding the costs involved in policing or providing police services can also impact a police organization at the division or unit management level. Kaplan and Porter (2011) emphasized that a cost measurement framework that is incapable of measuring the cost of producing outputs means that effective and efficient police division or unit managers go unrewarded, while inefficient managers are not motivated to improve.

Fortunately, there are methods that may be adopted to accurately measure costs, which will enable comparisons to be made across organizational outputs and social outcomes. Measuring police agency costs should not be based on the number of different services provided, or the volume of services delivered, but on the value of the service (Kaplan & Porter, 2011). To correctly estimate the value, costs and outputs need to be measured at the offence or offender level (Kaplan & Porter, 2011). Kaplan and Porter (2011) suggested that aggregating an accurate cost measurement system with a structured measurement of outputs and outcomes will assist in improving the achievement of outcomes while decreasing costs, which will subsequently result in an improvement in the service delivered. A model for delivering a high level of service and improving value is presented in Table 2.1.

With an accurate cost measurement system in place, police managers will be able to identify and "target their cost reductions in areas where real improvements in resource utilization and process efficiencies" can be made

Table 2.1 Service Delivery Value Improvement Model

Value Improvement Elements[a]	Explanation
Eliminate unnecessary process variations and processes that do not add value—look for areas of rationalization/synergies.	There are significant variations in the processes, tools, equipment, and materials used by divisions/units performing the same service.
Improve resource capacity utilization/ decrease low resource utilization.	This applies to human and physical resources.
Identification of and greater visibility into areas where substantial and expensive unused capacity exists.	This information will identify the root causes of costs.
Decrease the storage of specialized equipment for "just in case."	This needs to be a practical assessment and police agencies need to maintain a contingency.
Deliver the right processes at the right locations.	Through the accurate measurement of the costs of delivering services, police are able to see opportunities to perform correctly resourced and lower-cost services.
Match officer skills to the process.	Resource utilization can be improved by examining whether all of the services performed by personnel require their level of expertise and training.
Speed up handling of nonemergency calls/ offences.	Police have multiple opportunities to reduce handling time for nonemergency calls/ offenses, for example, phone reporting.
Optimize over the full life cycle of an offence/crime.	Reduction of duplication of handling aspects of crime investigation and prosecution.

Source: Author.
[a] Adapted from Kaplan and Porter (2011).

(Kaplan & Porter, 2011, p. 63). This may enable police agencies to spend less without having to decrease their service levels or compromise the quality of the service delivered. The ability to measure costs and outputs will enable police leaders to obtain more accurate and relevant information in relation to their operational and administrative costs. Kaplan and Porter (2011) maintained that accurately measuring costs and outputs is the most significant tool available for reforming the economics of police service delivery.

Defining Consolidation

There are four terms that are often used interchangeably when discussing the combining of police agencies: "consolidation," "merger," "regionalization," and "integration." Although the definition of each term is similar, they are subtlety different and are used to explain specific types of organizational reform. A definition of each term is presented in Table 2.2.

Using the word "consolidation" is a principal problem when defining police organizational reform. Consolidation is a word used by economists to describe the act, the process, or the state of being consolidated. Consolidated in this context is defined as the combining or the merging of two or more commercial interests or corporations (or elements) to perform a common or related function (Oxford Online Dictionaries, 2013). A point of note is that this definition does not include a reference to either of the components, effectiveness or efficiency.

The term "consolidation" is often used by researchers and economists when referring to structural organizational reform that may have been undertaken to improve the efficiency of police and public safety services. According to Wilson et al. (2012), there are three forms of consolidation that describe the integration of police and fire services into a single agency:

1. Nominal—executive functions are consolidated under a single chief executive but there is no integration of services.

Table 2.2   Four Interchangeable Consolidation Terms and Definitions

Term	Definition
Amalgamation	The process of combining or uniting multiple entities into one form
Merger	The union of two or more organizations
Regionalization	The forming of a region, especially for administrative purposes
Integration	The act of combining or adding parts to make a unified whole

Source: Oxford Online Dictionaries, http://www.oxforddictionaries.com/, 2013.

2. Partial—partial integration of services. Not all former staff are cross-trained; some retain separate functional roles. However, administrative personnel are fully consolidated.
3. Full—full integration of services, cross-trained staff, and consolidated management and command.

A fourth form of consolidation integration that was identified by Wilson and Grammich (2012) is

4. Functional—services are not integrated, nor are staff cross-trained, but the individual agencies may share facilities or training and dispatch resources.

The definition of the word "consolidation" was used in a more traditional sense by the Pennsylvania Governor's Center for Local Government Services in their report on the Southern York County Regional Police and the Borough of Stewartstown. The Center identified that the consolidation of police services included the abolishment of police boundaries and that the "individual be consolidated into one regional police department encompassing all political jurisdictions" (Pennsylvania Governor's Center for Local Government Services, 2012, p. 7).

There are eight approaches to consolidation that police agencies may consider adopting to improve the efficiency and effectiveness of their service delivery at the local, city, or state level. The eight approaches are presented in Table 2.3.

Conclusion

Each approach to consolidation may comprise any of the four forms that were identified by Wilson et al. (2012) and Wilson and Grammich (2012). The four forms provide a useful framework for any discussion on the consolidation reform of police agencies. The four forms of consolidation have been defined and are listed as follows:

1. Nominal—joint management structure, but agencies remain and operate separately.
2. Partial—some services of parts of agencies are integrated.
3. Full—full integration.
4. Functional—sharing of support services or buildings.

Table 2.3 Eight Approaches to Consolidation

Form of Consolidation	Definition
Shared services[a]	Two or more agencies combine specifically defined administrative or functional services or units. These could be human resource services, accounting, communications, dispatch, specialist squads, the use of buildings, or the administration and storage of records.
Local merger[a]	Two or more separate police agencies join to form a single larger or new organization.
Regionalization[a]	A number of jurisdictional-based agencies combine to form one large geographically based agency.
Amalgamation	The action, process, or result of combining or uniting two or more police agencies.
Contracting services[a]	A formal contract to pay for law enforcement services provided by one jurisdiction to another or others.
Outsourcing	A formal contract for administrative or support services provided by non–law enforcement agencies.
Civilianization	The replacement of sworn officers by nonsworn staff in nonoperational technical or administrative positions.
Internal consolidation	The internal combining or elimination of operational or support units.

Source: Author.
[a] Adapted from New Jersey State Association of Chiefs of Police (2007).

It is these four forms of consolidation that will be referred to in the remainder of this book.

The following chapter presents the theory and components of government and police reform and will provide a framework, which will enable the changes that have been made to police agencies in an effort to improve police service delivery since the 1980s to be understood.

Theory of Government and Police Reform

3

This chapter examines the theories of government and police reform, which have provided the basis for improving managerial accountability and delivering efficient and effective service. Five principal areas of governmental and police reform will be discussed. The theory of government funding and the theory of government finance within the context of the Rational Systems School of Management will be discussed initially. The theory of police reform and the theories associated with regionalization and the merging of government organizations will be examined in the second and third sections of the chapter. The final section discusses the theory of merging police agencies.

Introduction

The economy of a western democracy, by convention, is divided between the private and public sectors (Hughes, 1994). The private and public sectors are usually perceived as being distinct and separate, but Hughes (1994) claimed that distinguishing the economy as being divided into two mutually exclusive sectors may be incorrect. This is because the modern capitalist economy is a completely mixed system in which the public- and the private-sector forces interact, and therefore, the economic system is neither public nor private, but a mixture of both (Hughes, 1994).

The public sector is usually perceived as being that part of the economy that exists to provide advice to the government, coordinate government transactions, and provide goods and services to the public (Boston, 1991). According to Hughes (1994), the public sector is "engaged in providing services (and in some cases, goods) whose scope and variety are determined not by the direct wishes of the consumers, but by the decisions of government bodies, that is, in a democracy, by the representatives of the citizens" (p. 90). The sector performs a multitude of roles and handles a large number of problems. However, the roles of government agencies are often quite separate from one another and are frequently in conflict with central government policy and with the private industry.

While economies may be viewed as being public or private, in the majority of western democracies, a large proportion of Gross National Product is derived from the public sector (Boston, 1991). The composition of the "mix" or the extent to which governments provide goods and services and how the mix is structured varies from country to country and varies across time. According to Rutherford (1983), developed mixed economies comprise four basic types of public sector organizations:

1. Central or federal government—responsible for the redistributive function of the state, managing the economy, and supervising and coordinating public agencies. It is also responsible for providing services that must be, or can most efficiently be, provided at the national level. These are usually public goods, such as national defense and the administration of justice.
2. Local government—responsible for providing a flexible system, which is capable of responding to local requirements in relation to the level and the nature of the services requested.
3. Regional or national agencies that are established to provide a single service or a limited range of services.
4. State-owned enterprises. These are industrial concerns, run along commercial lines, but under state control.

For as long as there have been public organizations, there have been calls for the examination of their policies and procedures. While these calls have usually been for political reasons, they can also result from the financial mismanagement by agency executives or because the sector has become too large or threatening to elected representatives. The call for government agency reform has led to the formation of the Rational Systems perspective; that financial management should be the concern of the employees of an agency, whether they are financial specialists or not (Boston, 1991). The responsibility delegated to employees for the financial management and the services provided by an agency is supported by law in many countries. Government agency executives and senior managers in New Zealand, for example, have a statutory responsibility for ensuring that their organizations are controlled in such a way as to ensure that all expenditures of public money are made with due regard to economy and in the avoidance of waste and extravagance (Pallot, 1991).

To meet their statutory obligations, public-sector agencies may need to undertake organizational and financial reform. Three of the reasons why this may be necessary are as follows:

1. Service or policy incompleteness—problems that reflect that an agency's system is incomplete in some form or area. However, incompleteness does not suggest inherent difficulties.
2. Policy or process implementation—problems that relate to how policies, processes, or systems have been implemented.

3. Inherent—problems inherent in the restructuring of an agency, but not necessarily in other parts or systems of the agency (Gill, 2000).

There are two further reasons why an agency may be found to be in need of reform. The first is that over time, public-sector agencies may become complacent in the standard of service that they deliver and the public may call for their reform. Gorringe (2001), however, claimed that it can be expected that any public-sector management system will be criticized over time. This is not because the underlying government service model is broken but results from individual tastes and society changing over time and from the identification of more efficient methods for delivering service.

The second reason for the need for public-sector reform, which has been described as being cyclical, is because of the absence of any agreed public-sector management principles or values and because, over time, government attention shifts between social objectives that are often not achievable in the short term (Ayto, 2011). Inevitably, as a government solves or alleviates one problem, others are exacerbated and new challenges are identified. The continual circle of new challenges means that "[p]ublic sector management is a race without a finish line" (Gill, 2000, p. 65). Gill (2000) holds a similar, but earlier, view as Ayto (2011) and explained that as one management issue is resolved, it is replaced by a new generation of even more comprehensive and complex issues. This continual cycle may be similar to that which is experienced in the private sector, but the public sector has one further complicating element: political interference.

Political interference along with an absence of public-sector management principles or values (Ayto, 2011) is the primary reason for the debate as to the form that public-sector management should take. There is also debate as to whether the management of the public sector is different from that of the private sector. The question is whether public-sector management should consist of the same characteristics as the private sector and whether it should be expected to achieve the same objectives (Ackroyd, Hughes, & Soothill, 1989).

Ackroyd et al. (1989) maintained that the supporters of the view that public-sector management is the same as private-sector management have not "fully [considered] the forces shaping public-service management as a set of distinctive practices or the prospects for refining and developing them" (p. 604). The management of the public sector involves a very different set of actions from the management of the private sector.

An examination of public-sector organizations reveals that its individual structures, processes, and policies have been developed as an adaption to successful practice, and the structure of a public service agency signifies and represents the confluence of two relationships (Ackroyd et al., 1989). The first relationship is between the receiver or the customer of the government service and the government agency providing the goods and services.

The New Zealand Government, for example, assumes a dual role, as both the purchaser and the supplier of public goods and services. The second relationship is between the elected political controller and the management of an agency (Ackroyd et al., 1989). There is a contractual relationship between the politician and an agency's chief executive, for example, the Chief of Police, with the executive being accountable to the politician.

Public sector management may be characterized by its individual structural concepts or elements. Gill (2000) described the elements of public-sector management as the three "Ss" and three "Ps":

1. Strategy
2. Structure
3. Systems
4. People
5. Performance
6. Politics

This model has been described as being designed on the principles of clarity and simplicity and has strengths in its unity of vision, coherence, and its encompassing nature (Gill, 2000). The concept of strategy is the key component of the model as it drives the other concepts, including financial management. Conceiving the public service as being constructed from these six elements is beneficial, as they can be used as the building blocks for organizational reform.

In comparison to private-sector management, public-sector management is different owing to the likelihood of political influence and that improvement in service delivery can only come from logical, mutually reinforcing strategies that take into account the will of local politicians and the desires of the community.

Theory of Government Funding

Government expenditure refers to the spending by a government sector and includes the purchase of final goods and services, or Gross Domestic Product, and Transfer payments. Government expenditure also refers to the funding of the government sector. The government sector uses the allocation of funds to undertake key functions that enable the sector and the individual agencies to operate and produce a product or deliver a service.

The financial management of a public sector is an area of the Rational Systems School of Management in which an emphasis is placed on the achievement of acceptable financial outcomes (Pallot, 1991). The Rational Systems School is founded on the perspective that organizations are instruments that attain specific goals (Baron & Greenberg, 1990). Within the

Rational Systems, finance is a management process model that comprises three objectives to ensure that an agency's budget is

1. Made available at the appropriate time so that managers can manage.
2. Made available for the annual budget period.
3. Used in the most effective, efficient, and economical way. This means that resources are allocated to the most beneficial programs and are utilized to an optimum level in order to provide the greatest benefit for the least cost, or to provide cost-effective, quality service (Pallot, 1991).

The financial system of a government consists of a number of components, which enable a government agency to translate strategy into deliverable actions, and promotes informed decision-making and for the chief executive officer to be held financially accountable. The individual components are coordinated during the implementation of an agency's strategic plan and its annual business plan, which enables a responsive and efficient service to be delivered (The Treasury, 1996). The annual business plan describes an agency's outputs and documents the expense involved in delivering individual outputs.

When delivering agency outputs, there are five main areas of expenditure:

1. Current expenditure on inputs, including labor and raw materials, to be used in the production of goods and services
2. Capital expenditure on fixed assets needed in the production of goods and services
3. Grants and subsidies paid in cash to individuals and corporations
4. Loans to individuals and corporations, normally at noncommercial rates of interest, for purposes that are regarded as having social benefits
5. Interest on the state's outstanding debt (Rutherford, 1983)

Government agencies tend to be structured in a manner that ensures accountability for the achievement of specific activities or outputs (Rutherford, 1983). Accountability is an aspect of the legal framework, which establishes detailed and prescriptive rules as to how an agency is to operate and the authority given to an individual manager. However, the legal framework is often restrictive in "the objectives that may be pursued and the methods that may be used" (Rutherford, 1983, p. 9).

Theory of Modern Police Reform

The economic, political, and social changes of the 1980s, along with the introduction of Reaganomics and the doctrines of the New Right

Government of Dame Margaret Thatcher, all had a major influence on policing. The objective of these governments was to reduce government spending and improve the efficiency of the service delivered by government agencies. These objectives and the following five factors had an impact on the need for police reform:

1. The role of modern governmental thinking (Rose & Miller, 1992)
2. Recurring state fiscal crises (Spitzer & Scull, 1977)
3. Urban geography (Jones & Newburn, 1999; Shearing & Stenning, 1983)
4. The natural proclivities of capitalism (Rigakos, 2000, 2002)
5. Globalization, an increase in the occurrence of transnational crime, terrorism, and demand for police services (den Heyer, 2011)

The social, economic, and political environment of the 1980s and the factors mentioned earlier resulted in political pressure being placed on the public sector, including policing, to do more with less and to be more accountable for the use of public funds (Gillespie, 2006; Loveday, 1995a). In response, public-sector managers critiqued their organizational structures, budgets, and service delivery processes to see whether improvements could be made (Gorringe, 2001). While police management did undertake a number of reviews, they did not make any substantial inroads into the way that they delivered their services. In 2006, Her Majesty's Treasury released a report on the productivity of police, which claimed that the management of police budgets and human resources fell short of best practice (Her Majesty's Treasury, 2006). The report also observed that police management did not appear to understand the connection between operational performance and value for money. The report described the relationship as being "two sides of the same coin" (Her Majesty's Treasury, 2006, p. 2).

During this period, police resources were not being used efficiently, which was a consequence of failing to develop a benchmarking framework that was capable of measuring the productivity of police staff and the effective deployment of resources. An effective delivery of service relies on the efficient deployment of resources, and it is the efficient deployment of resources that is the most important performance benchmark that a police agency can use.

To improve the efficiency and the effectiveness of government agency service delivery and to measure agency performance, New Public Management (NPM) was introduced to a number of western nations during the 1980s and the 1990s. The introduction of NPM in the 1990s formed the basis for police reform initiatives in the United Kingdom, New Zealand, and Australia. Bayley and Shearing (1996) described the process of reform in the organization and the administration of police agencies as revolutionary. The reforms had a compounding effect on the management of the public sector, and, in particular, the police, and transformed police services into a commodity that subsequently resulted in the privatization of some areas (Lithopoulos & Rigakos, 2005).

The introduction of NPM into police agencies by the New Zealand, UK, and Australian governments was a strategy that furnished agencies with an accountability and performance framework and sought to improve leadership skills and management practices (den Heyer, 2011; Loveday, 1995b). NPM is fundamental to the system of an organization and to the methods and the administration of how an organization delivers its services. In order to be able to successfully implement NPM, an agency needs to identify its core service delivery functions.

Identifying an agency's core functions enables a "social-market" approach to be created between the purchaser (government) and the provider (police agency) of services. A government, for example, purchases a number of hours of service from a police agency, the payment of which, in turn, becomes the police agency's source of funding. The main advantage of a social-market approach, where a government purchases a service that was delivered by a government agency, is that there is a clear separation between the purchaser and the service provider. According to Loveday (1995b), "[t]he social market approach seeks to ensure that the consumer (the purchaser) of services rather than the provider of services determines what is produced, by whom and when" (Loveday, 1995b, p. 289). A social-market structure ensures that NPM, as a comprehensive organizational approach, can work with police service delivery methods, such as Community Policing.

The central components of a social-market approach include the following:

1. A rational financial framework
2. Clearly defined service delivery outputs
3. A purchaser/provider split
4. A contract between the provider and the purchaser
5. Customer choice and input into an agency's service delivery direction and outputs
6. A performance management framework
7. Appropriately trained and qualified management personnel
8. An independent inspection and audit process (Loveday, 1995b)

NPM and the social-market approach demand clearly defined, measureable outputs that link an organization's financial system to a desired outcome of a government.

Theory of Local Government Reform, Regionalization, and Mergers

The oldest local government reform school of thought is known as Traditional, Reform, or Traditional Reform (Trueblood & Honadle, 1994). This school of thought can be traced back to the late 1800s when its supporters examined the tendency of American cities to create suburbs, which led to "fragmented" government (Trueblood & Honadle, 1994). Since the early 1960s, the Public Choice Government Reform school of thought has replaced the Traditional school of thought, and to date, it still dominates the reform debate (Trueblood & Honadle, 1994).

Public choice theory has had a major influence on modern thinking and the development of political science, public policy, and public administration (Boston, 1991). A number of different terms have been used to describe public choice theory, including social choice theory, rational choice theory, the economics of politics, and the Virginia School. The main principle of the theory was that people were believed to be rational and dominated by self-interest (Gorringe, 2001). The theory also sought to minimize the role of the state, limit the discretionary power of politicians, and curb the functions of government (Boston, 1991). It was believed that politicians had abused their power and that power could be minimized through the restructuring of budgets and performance arrangements (Pallot, 1991). As a result of the belief that this theory is correct, government agencies that have implemented NPM have separated their policy-making functions from the delivery of their service.

Modern research, based on the public choice theory, maintains that any government reform program should include "(1) the preferences of citizens and other actors in the system; (2) the nature of the good or service desired; and (3) the structure of the institutions through which demands are expressed and production decisions made" (Bish, 2001, p. 5). These three elements should be considered when proposing the regionalization of a local government agency or when developing any reform plan. While these elements may determine that an amalgamation of municipalities or government agencies is the appropriate option, Bish (2001) claimed that this is flawed thinking and is driven by a desire to centralize the control of organizations. This view is supported by others who maintain that the advantages of a centralized government have been overemphasized and overstated (La Grange, 1987).

Historically, only large-sized, professionally organized government agencies were viewed as being able to provide efficient public services and govern appropriately, while smaller-sized governments and government agencies were considered to be unprofessional, uncoordinated, and inefficient (Bish, 2001). However, smaller-sized municipalities and agencies are often more efficient and flexible in delivering services than larger-sized agencies, which casts doubt on the financial assumptions typically used to strengthen and defend amalgamations (Bish, 2001). The cost of governing smaller-sized municipalities in metropolitan areas is generally lower (Bish, 2001). While the cost of producing one service unit is lower in a smaller-sized municipality, this does not necessarily translate to smaller-sized municipalities being more efficient producers of services than larger-sized municipalities (Bish, 2001). The cost of production appears to rise with the size of the municipality or agency for three reasons:

1. Larger-sized cities provide more services. They may, for example, provide daytime services for commuters and shoppers and evening services for entertainment.
2. Larger-sized municipalities often undertake more activities than smaller-sized ones. They may, for example, provide more welfare or support-type services.
3. There are diseconomies of scale in producing some services (Bish, 2001).

Bish (2001) maintained that two conclusions may be drawn from the cost to size research. The first is that the size of a municipality is not the primary determinant of costs (Bish, 2001). This is because governments may outsource areas of its service delivery requirements to the private industry. A municipality may, for example, be responsible for the collection of trash, yet the trash is physically collected by a local, privately owned, trash company. The second conclusion is that while larger-sized municipalities may cost more to operate, it is not clear as to the proportion that the various cost-increasing influences contribute to higher costs (Bish, 2001).

La Grange (1987) claimed that there is no guarantee that any proposed amalgamation or regionalization of agencies will increase the coordination and efficiency of the services delivered in a geographical area and noted that larger-sized agencies may be inefficient due to internal disputes and arguments over budgets and resources, leading to the inefficient allocation of resources. Another argument against regionalization and amalgamation is that larger-sized monopoly councils or agencies that are responsible for a large geographical area are often not capable of dealing with the range of issues that larger jurisdictions appear to highlight (Bish, 2001). Bish (2001) also claimed that the diversity of metropolitan areas, the need for close relationships with the public, and having the ability to handle a variety of issues at a local level are some of the reasons why some large monopoly councils are incapable of governing. Research has indicated that a single organization cannot accomplish all of the tasks that are asked of it (Bish, 2001).

Supporters of regionalization and amalgamations claim, however, that smaller-sized, individual councils and agencies are inefficient and more expensive to administer than larger-sized councils and agencies. The supporters base these claims on five main propositions:

1. A consolidated government is more efficient and effective than several smaller-sized governments. This is because costs can be managed in large-sized agencies and may be reduced through the elimination of duplicated services, personnel, and equipment. Furthermore, a larger-sized unit may also be able to take advantage of economies of scale or lower per-unit costs of government services.
2. Consolidation helps eliminate spillovers or externality effects. Many government services benefit citizens in contiguous areas, who neither pay for a service nor share in the effort involved in its delivery. Spillover effects can be eliminated if the taxing jurisdiction is coterminous with the service jurisdiction.
3. The environment for decision-making and long-range planning is improved. A single government in an area is better able to coordinate policies and decisions than several separate governments.
4. Consolidated governments, with only one governing body, are easier for citizens to understand, use, and contact.
5. Consolidation matches area needs with area resources. Tax burdens within a community are equalized from the creation of a government that more clearly corresponds to regional area needs (Trueblood & Honadle, 1994).

Two methods that determine the scale at which local government activity is produced most efficiently have been identified. However, neither of the two methods provide a definitive conclusion upon which a planning decision can be based (Bish, 2001). The first method is the engineering/accounting approach, in which the unit costs for each agency's outputs are calculated with an optimum agency size being determined in relation to the different levels of capital investment (Bish). The second method is the statistical estimation of the "average cost of production curve to determine the lowest cost range" (Bish, p. 12). There are, however, a number of problems with both of these methods. First, the studies assume that the agencies included in Bish's research are delivering services efficiently. Second, while the level of service delivered by an agency may be able to be measured, the quality of the service may not, and as a result, the majority of efficiency studies use "population-served output measures" (Bish, 2001, p. 12). In the case of police agencies, these studies are usually developed on more than basic population measures (Bish, 2001). Studies usually assess the structure of an agency by using a number of different qualitative and quantitative evaluation methods.

One evaluation method, for example, examined the conversion of an individual agency's inputs into outputs to assess the different methods of organizing policing in metropolitan areas (Parks, 1985).

Both determination scale methods have been used to determine economies of scale not only at the organization level but also within an organization. Both determination methods indicate that economies of scale exist for a particular internal activity (Bish, 1999). However, the local conditions of a particular or specific organizational activity or service "are much more important than the inherent characteristics of the particular activity" (Bish, 2001, p. 14).

Organizational economies of scale are only one-half of the service delivery efficiency equation. The second half of the equation is that organizations need to have an incentive to be efficient (Bish, 2001), as many agencies in the public sector will not implement strategies to improve efficiencies unless there is an incentive. Normally, there is only a drive for efficiency after it has been imposed on an agency, usually as a result of a government decreasing its funding.

Theory of Police Agency Regionalization and Mergers

Councils and municipal governments often consider regionalizing or consolidating their police agencies and services to ease economic burdens. However, the regionalization or consolidation of police agencies or services is not the only strategic option for every municipality experiencing financial problems, as regionalization can take a number of different forms, be of various sizes, and can differ from community to community (Krimmel, 1997). Although the regionalization of police agencies can be adapted to suit specific communities, the concept of having varying levels of economies of scale appears to depend on the size of the municipality. Douglas and Tweeten (1971), for example, found a U-shaped cost curve with the lowest point being with municipalities with populations between 250,000 and 500,000, while Beaton (1974) found economies of size only for very-small-sized cities with populations of less than 2000.

Two problems have been experienced when implementing a consolidation program. One is how to merge several smaller-sized agencies into one larger-sized agency (La Grange, 1987), and another is that there may be some reluctance from local politicians to implement a consolidation program from the fear that they may lose control of local police agencies. As a result, any attempt to regionalize police agencies may be derailed (Krimmel, 1997). The reasons for the hesitance to consolidate differ with each individual community, as each police agency is subtlety different, and there is no one-size-fits-all model or a cookie cutter approach that determines how to structure an agency (New Jersey State Association of Chiefs of Police, 2007).

A number of reasons can be found in the literature as to why local communities should not consider regionalizing their police departments. La Grange (1987) considered the principal reason as to why police agency consolidation is not an option for all communities is because not all mergers provide benefits to small, rural communities. Early research suggested that the quality of the police service delivered by many small- to medium-sized departments is actually better than the quality of service delivered by many of the larger-sized departments (Ostrom, Parks, & Whittaker, 1973; Parks, 1985; Rogers & Lipsey, 1974). Researchers have identified four major areas of contention in regionalizing police agencies. These are as follows:

1. The community will have less input into its local police agency.
2. There will be fewer patrol officers in the community.
3. Larger-sized police agencies are not more efficient or economical.
4. Public satisfaction with urban police services varies inversely with the size of the municipality (Lithopoulos & Rigakos, 2005; Pachon & Lovrich, 1977).

However, supporters of regionalized police agencies and services may argue that larger-sized police agencies offer better services through

1. Reduced agency operational costs.
2. Equitable distribution of police resources.
3. Increased cooperation between officers in contiguous jurisdictions.
4. Increased specialization of officers.
5. Better trained officers with higher levels of professionalization.
6. Lower personnel turnover.
7. Operational economies of scale.
8. The elimination of duplication of effort by several smaller-sized police agencies.
9. A larger-sized agency can take advantage of centralized record-keeping systems, crime laboratories, or other specialized services not readily available to smaller-sized police agencies.
10. Increased purchasing power.
11. Efficiency gains in the hiring of officers (Krimmel, 1997; Lithopoulos & Rigakos, 2005; Pachon & Lovrich, 1977).

It is difficult to evaluate whether consolidated police agencies are actually more efficient and effective than nonconsolidated police agencies as research has not yet been conducted in this area of police management. Another difficulty in identifying the benefits of consolidation is that the majority of reports proposing consolidation were produced after an amalgamation "was a fait accompli and tended to rationalize rather than criticize its impacts" (Lithopoulos & Rigakos, 2005, p. 339).

Krimmel (1997) conducted a comprehensive evaluation of the consolidation of eight police agencies in the 1972 Northern York County Regional Police Department, Pennsylvania (NYCRPD), and found that the NYCRPD had 28% less total costs and 25% less cost per officer than similar nonconsolidated police agencies. However, the cost per officer was 13% higher in the NYCRPD (Krimmel, 1997). Krimmel (1997) also noted that the cost per crime incident was 50% less and the cost per call was 70% less.

The police chief of the NYCRPD supported the consolidation and claimed that the new regionalized structure provided a sound basis from which to deliver more effective police services by eliminating duplication (Krimmel, 1997).

Conclusion

A number of issues are evident when attempting to analyze or evaluate police service delivery improvement programs. The problems range from the ability to measure the efficiency of police service delivery, the shallowness of existing research, and the lack of robust theory and empirical analysis. The lack of theory means that it is difficult to identify performance measures that enable policy makers and researchers to measure whether police agencies are delivering services that are socially efficient and effective (Rutherford, 1983).

A number of comprehensive evaluations have concluded that consolidation efforts to improve service delivery have had both positive and negative results. However, there are two important elements that impact consolidation programs. The first is that larger-sized municipalities generally subsidize suburban policing services, and second, larger-sized central city areas have different types of policing issues than smaller-sized towns and rural areas (Pachon & Lovrich, 1977). Pachon and Lovrich (1977) also emphasized that any difference in police expenditure between a central city and a suburb is "more of a reflection of the differing socioeconomic characteristics of these two inter-dependent metropolitan subsystems than a result of their relative sizes" and that there is even some evidence to suggest that "if all things were equal" in cities and suburbs of differing sizes, the larger jurisdictions "would produce more economical and more satisfying police services" (p. 45).

To summarize, each consolidation is different and smaller-sized police agencies do not "ensure inefficiency and waste any more than centralized (large-sized) government ensures proficiency and parsimony" (La Grange, 1987, p. 12).

Police agencies in the future will differ in structure and process from those that exist today. More consolidation programs will take place and more services will be outsourced. To ensure that police agencies are able to adapt, police managers need to adopt flexible structures and processes and establish service-delivery approaches that maintain the confidence of the public.

Historical Approaches to Improving Police Service Delivery

4

Introduction

In 1999, the UK Home Office Police Research Group claimed in their report "Applying Economic Evaluation to Policing Activity" that there was "a growing need for the police to make resource allocation decisions transparent, to evaluate outputs and outcomes, and to demonstrate that resources are being used to generate the best returns" (Stockdale, Whitehead, & Gresham, 1999, p. v). As the researchers have alluded, it is important that a value is assigned to an agency's inputs, outputs, and outcomes. To enable police to be able to assign a measurable value to its service delivery inputs, outputs, and outcomes, Stockdale et al. (1999) suggested three processes. The processes referred to are determining performance indicators, cost-effectiveness analysis,* and cost–benefit analysis.† These processes provide a practical framework that will make resource allocations transparent, enable outputs and outcomes to be evaluated, and demonstrate that resources are being used to generate the best returns. However, there is a limitation to this approach. An accurate economic evaluation cannot be applied to any change in the functional areas of police service delivery as it cannot take into account all of the variables that are involved in evaluating a police service, and therefore, as a consequence, an accurate measurable value cannot be assigned.

A problem that has become evident when examining police service delivery is that there is an intellectual time lag (Amin, Gills, Palan, & Taylor, 1994). A time lag occurs because scholars have focused more on crime-related policing issues rather than on the efficiency and the effectiveness of the service that police deliver. Few studies have been conducted, especially comparative studies of the strategic and managerial processes and systems that police use.

Further problems with taking an economic approach to conducting research into policing are the highly fragmented system of law enforcement, the lack of standards and coordination between police agencies, and the inefficiency

---

* Cost-effectiveness analysis (CEA) is a form of economic analysis that compares the relative costs and outcomes (effects) of two or more courses of action.
† Cost–benefit analysis (CBA), sometimes called benefit–cost analysis (BCA), is a systematic approach to estimating the strengths and weaknesses of alternatives.

of police operations (La Grange, 1987). These problems were originally identified by the President's Commission on Law Enforcement (1967) and by subsequent committees: Advisory Commission on Intergovernmental Relations
(1971), Committee for Economic Development (1972), and the National
Advisory Commission on Criminal Justice Standards and Goals (1973). All of
these groups recommended that police services be consolidated "to enhance
the quality and efficiency of police response" (La Grange, 1987, p. 7).

This chapter reviews the literature that relates to the recent approaches
taken by governments and police agencies in Australia, Canada, New Zealand,
the United Kingdom, and the United States to improve the efficiency and effectiveness of their service delivery. The history of the approaches taken, such as
organizational consolidation and New Public Management (NPM), and how
they relate to the provision of police service delivery will also be discussed.

Government Approach to Reform 1980–2000

Dissatisfaction with the efficiency and the effectiveness of government agencies was common in many countries during the early 1970s (Boston, 1987).
Of particular concern was their poor economic performance and their lack
of accountability (Boston, 1987; Deane, 1986). In the late 1970s, further problems were encountered. There were concerns about the traditional way that
government agencies were being managed and that they were being operated without any clear organizational performance objectives to direct them
(Deane, 1986). The absence of objectives resulted from the confusion of the
role and the function of each government agency (Deane, 1986), as each
agency was a mixture of commercial, social, and regulatory functions, which
also offered policy advice. It became evident over time that further problems
lay in the disproportionate layers of management, excessive paperwork, the
inability to keep expenditure under control, and the inability of agencies to
cope with change.

As a response, new organizational structures and procedures, management systems, incentive structures, and financial control mechanisms were
introduced (Boston, 1987). The aim of introducing these initiatives was to
improve the efficiency in which resources were used (in both operational and
allocative terms) and to increase the accountability of the public service to
the government (Boston, 1987). Managerial strategies used by the private sector were introduced to government agencies as it was believed that the private
sector was more efficient, and such methods would increase the effectiveness
of government agencies. However, it was found that the introduction of such
strategies had little success (Littlechild, 1983), and it became acceptable for
public enterprises to display an element of inefficiency, owing to the fact that

the majority of government agencies provided services that the private sector could not economically provide (Littlechild, 1983).

Some of the changes that were made to the methods of management and to the structures of public-sector agencies were particularly comprehensive, and, in the case of New Zealand, "were without question, the most significant reforms since the creation of a permanent, unified, politically neutral, meritocratic career service in 1912" and would rank as "one of the most comprehensive reorganizations of the public sector initiated anywhere" (Boston, 1987, p. 424).

Factors That Led to Police Reform 1980–2000

The usual approach to reform that police agencies adopted during the twentieth century was to consolidate forces by way of amalgamation, and their response to any new demands made of them was by way of specialization (Loveday, 1995b). Police forces, especially in the United Kingdom, were encouraged to amalgamate to form larger-sized operational units, initiate specialized functions, narrow the span of control, and extend organizational hierarchies.

Officer specialization became an accepted practice between the World Wars (Loveday, 1995b). During the 1950s and 1960s, the practice grew significantly in response to the advances made in technology, the perception that the role of the police had become more complex, and the increase in the demand for police services. The specialized nature of the role of a number of officers and units reduced the span of control and resulted in more effective management.

In the United States, the Task Force Report, the Police/the President's Commission on Law Enforcement and Administration of Justice (1967), was the first to raise the issue of the efficiency and the effectiveness of police agency service delivery. The Task Force noted that formal "cooperation or consolidation was an essential ingredient to improve the quality of law enforcement". However, Ostrom (1973) contended that the Task Force had made no attempt to define the term "improving the quality of law enforcement" (p. 94), nor had they indicated as to how any improvements should be measured.

Value for Money and Planning, Programming, and Budgeting

Another issue that was raised by the President's Task Force was in relation to the cost of delivering police agency services. In one of the strongest statements made by the Task Force, they proclaimed that "police agencies should not enter into agreements unless they provide the same level of service at a reduced cost or improve the service at a cost which is justified" (cited in Martin, 1997, p. 92). A proviso that was made to this statement was that consolidation should be the preferred approach for police agencies only when there was complete consolidation by the governments involved (Martin, 1997).

According to Drake and Simpler (2004), the initiatives identified by the Task Force formed the basis for the interest taken in police force efficiency and for the advancement of management best practice, which lead to the strategic approach of Value for Money (VFM) that was conceived by the Government of the United Kingdom. The concept of VFM could be traced to the accounting methods of planning, programming, and budgeting (PPB) that was adopted by government agencies in the United Kingdom between 1969 and 1974 (Drake & Simpler, 2004).

The PPB methodology was readily accepted by police managers in the United Kingdom, who found traditional management methods difficult. The PPB methodology enabled police managers to identify a value for resources by measuring inputs and outputs. According to Drake and Simpler (2004), the growth and the expansion of the police forces in the United Kingdom was credited to the implementation of PPB. However, the popularity of PPB was lost in the late 1970s, as it was found to be impractical owing to the absence of a robust framework that identified and measured police service delivery inputs and outputs (Drake & Simpler, 2004).

The first official document in the United Kingdom that discussed the effectiveness of police force service delivery was the 1983 Home Office Circular 114/83 "Efficiency, Effectiveness and Economy." The circular established the framework for police forces to increase their service delivery effectiveness and described in plain language what the UK forces had to do in order to achieve the three Es, which were described by the Home Office as Efficiency, Effectiveness, and Economy (O'Byrne, 2001).

Rise in the Number of Regionalizations, Consolidations, and Mergers

The large number of local police agencies in the United States and the inefficiency and duplication of police services had been of concern from at least the late 1940s (Smith, 1949, cited in Farmer, 1978, 1984; Ostrom, Parks, & Whitaker, 1978). In 1949, Smith noted that

[t]here is therefore no such thing in the United States as a police system, nor even a set of police systems within any reasonably accurate sense of the term. Our so-called systems are mere collections of police units having some

similarity of authority, organization, or jurisdiction; but they lack any systematic relationship to each other.

Cited in Ostrom et al. (1978, p. 111)

This view was repeated nearly 20 years later by the President's Commission on Law Enforcement and Administration of Justice, who summarized the policing situation as

[t]he machinery of law enforcement in this country is fragmented, complicated and frequently overlapping. America is essentially a nation of small police forces, each operating independently within the limits of its jurisdictions. The boundaries that define and limit police operations do not hinder the movement of criminals, of course. They can and do take advantage of ancient political and geographic boundaries, which often give them sanctuary from effective police activities.

Cited in Ostrom et al. (1978, p. 111)

An inherent assumption within these two statements is that local agencies are duplicating each other's work. However, in 1978, this assumption was refuted by Ostrom et al. (1978). Ostrom et al. found that more than "eighty-six per cent of local patrol agencies in the 80 Standard Metropolitan Statistical Areas that were examined, reported that they assisted other police departments outside their jurisdiction" (p. 137). They also found that almost all local police agencies provided assistance to, and received assistance from, other agencies (Ostrom et al., 1978).

One approach taken to reduce expenditure in local government and police agencies is the amalgamation or regionalization (Murphy, 2002), of specific services or of individual agencies. The amalgamation or regionalization of services or agencies is proposed on the theory of reducing expenditure while maintaining services and increasing service delivery effectiveness. A reduction in expenditure and an increase in effectiveness are theoretically achieved from the creation of an economy of scale and from an organizational structure that reduces operational, personnel, and administrative costs (Murphy, 2002).

The regionalization of smaller-sized local police agencies is believed to reduce operational and administrative duplication, add to agency professionalism, and increase the efficient use of limited resources. Similarly, the amalgamation or regionalization of larger-sized police agencies can create new operational, personnel, and administrative efficiencies and make the provision of specialized services and technologies possible. Murphy (2002) advocated that the amalgamation or regionalization of police agencies or specific police services should deliver a well-managed organization that is capable of allocating its resources more efficiently. The advantages and disadvantages of

Table 4.1   Advantages and Disadvantages of Local Police Agency Amalgamations, Regionalizations, or Mergers

Advantages	Disadvantages
1. Improved safety of the public and officers	1. The cost of undertaking amalgamation
2. Standardization of equipment and supplies	2. Generally, there is a period of management restructuring
3. Standardization of the communication and information systems	3. Management of personnel issues
4. Centralization of dispatch systems	4. Alleged loss of local identity
5. Improved crime analysis, solution, and prevention	5. Alleged difference in policing styles or organizational cultures
6. Rationalization of office space requirements and capital expenditures	6. Need to establish an appropriate accountability and reporting structure to the city or county
7. Ability to do more strategic regional planning and to keep abreast of innovations and technology	
8. Better ability to achieve employment equity goals and to provide bilingual services	
9. Ability to offer high and uniform standard of training	
10. Establishment of a single court liaison section at the courthouse	
11. Reduction in the number of police services boards	
12. Clarification of accountability and liability	
13. Increased capability to create specialist squads, such as drugs and gangs	

Source: Author.

local police agency amalgamations, regionalization, and mergers have been summarized and are presented in Table 4.1.

Governments have not amalgamated or merged local police agencies in a continuous manner. The United Kingdom, for example, went through two distinct phases (one in the late 1940s and another in the late 1960s) of amalgamating or merging police forces and commenced a third phase (in 2005), but owing to extensive protest, the government reversed its merger policy (Loveday, 2006a).

Canada has implemented the most amalgamations and mergers of local police agencies. Amalgamations and mergers have taken place in Canada in two major phases (pre-1980 and post-2000). A large number of mergers commenced prior to 1980, but none were implemented between 1980 and 1997. Amalgamations and mergers were favored during the 1960s and 1970s, and this was when the majority of regional police forces in Ontario were established. Ontario furthered the concept of amalgamations with the view that amalgamated police agencies delivered a more efficient and effective service by eliminating duplication and reduced operating costs (Martin, 1997).

Martin (1997) maintained that the reason that there were no amalgamations or mergers of police agencies between 1980 and 1997 in Canada was due to the introduction of Community Policing. This was because the introduction of Community Policing was a new approach to service delivery, and it was feared that it could be at risk if a regionalization of police agencies program was reintroduced (Martin, 1997). Since 2000, however, Canada has returned to the policy of regionalization and there have been a large number of mergers, especially at the township level (Murphy, 2002).

The regionalization of police agencies in the United States has been very different from the regionalization programs that have been established in the United Kingdom and Canada. The United States appears to have viewed local police mergers with suspicion, and very few mergers have been undertaken. This perception has been compounded by the opinion that local police mergers can weaken community involvement through the distancing of the process of police goal setting and direction from a local to a regional level, and, in the process, lessening police accountability to the community that they serve (Martin, 1997).

Rise of New Public Management

In the majority of western nation states, public-sector agencies grew in number, size, and complexity throughout the twentieth century (Hughes, 1994). The 1970s saw a movement away from the larger, interventionist role of government agencies (Hughes, 1994). The smaller government philosophy gathered momentum with the election of the Thatcher Government in the United Kingdom in 1979 and with the Reagan Administration in the United States in 1980. This coalesced in the 1980s with a number of changes made to the form of government agencies, which included extensive reductions in agency funding, efficiency drives, and the introduction of a number of different forms of privatization (Hughes, 1994). The political emphasis that was placed upon the public sector was to do more with less and the public wanted the public sector to be more accountable for the use of public funds and to deliver better and more focused services (Gillespie, 2006; Loveday, 1995a).

A doctrine of new government agency management emerged during this period, especially in New Zealand and the United Kingdom, in which an increased focus was placed on service delivery outcomes (Moynihan, 2006). It was believed that if agencies placed an emphasis on service-delivery outcomes, then in return, "governments would enjoy dramatic performance improvement and results-based accountability" (Moynihan, 2006, p. 77).

This new approach to government management was called NPM, which was based on five theoretical microeconomic frameworks: public choice theory, principal agent theory, transaction cost theory, technical rational theory, and institutional theory (Bale & Dale, 1998; Boston, 1991). In the policing context, NPM encompassed the following nine features:

1. Decentralization of managerial control
2. Controls that focus on outputs and outcomes rather than on inputs and procedures
3. The development of a strategic plan that is linked to the annual corporate planning process
4. Defining and setting of organizational and individual aims and objectives on an annual basis
5. The development of personal and organizational performance indicators
6. The development and implementation of a comprehensive corporate planning framework
7. The development and implementation of a personal appraisal process
8. Linking organizational strategies and delivery objectives to positions
9. The development and implementation of managerial reviews and performance evaluation frameworks (Boston 1991; Butterfield, Edwards, & Woodall, 2004)

Despite the pressure for western nations to review their bureaucracies, the adoption of NPM was uneven across governments and across sectors within governments. NPM was, for example, more readily accepted in New Zealand and the United Kingdom than it was in the United States and within the education, health, and welfare services than within police forces and agencies. The United States only partially accepted the results-oriented doctrine, with state governments selecting only certain parts, such as strategic planning and performance measurement, but ignoring those aspects that could have enhanced managerial authority (Moynihan, 2006). Moynihan (2006) maintained that state governments in the United States undermined "the logic that promised high performance improvements" (p. 77).

The situation was similar in a number of European nations. These countries adopted only selected features of NPM, while others embraced a managerial ethic without introducing NPM completely (Butterfield et al., 2004). Introducing NPM to European police forces appears to have had minimal impact (Gillespie, 2006).

There are a number of reasons for the differing acceptance rates. The first reason could have been the different fiscal crises that each western nation

experienced during the 1980s. These crises included a period of rapid infla-
tion, and, in the case of Germany, it also included a number of social problems associated with the end of the Cold War. Leishman, Cope, and Starie
(1995) noted that another reason may have been that the introduction of
NPM was in "response to a set of special social conditions developing in the
long period of peace in the developed countries since the [S]econd [W]orld
[W]ar, and the unique period of economic growth which accompanied it"
(p. 27). The period from the end of the war until the early 1980s affected
individual countries differently, and the response of each country to the economic conditions was different owing to the resources and capabilities that
each country possessed.

The introduction of NPM has been successful in enhancing public sector organizational effectiveness and efficiency in the United Kingdom and in
New Zealand, and while the principles of NPM were supported by managers in other western nations, the strategy was slow to be introduced in these
countries. Acceptance of NPM depended upon the management capabilities
of the managers concerned and the level of organizational efficiency prior to
the reform being undertaken (Bale & Dale, 1998).

The performance framework contained within the NPM was readily
accepted by the majority of police agencies within New Zealand, Australia,
and the United Kingdom. The approach was very similar to the earlier strategy
of Policing by Objectives (Golding & Savage, 2008). Objective setting included
a planning cycle and goal setting within an assessment process (Golding &
Savage, 2008). However, it fell out of favor because the approach was not well
accepted by police managers, and at that time, there was more of a focus on
issues relating to crime, such as the increase in the availability of hard drugs.

Police management benefits from the utilization of an NPM performance
framework. It allows police to encapsulate high-level objectives and relevant
performance indicators. Adopting this approach in conjunction with a com-
pilation of comprehensive performance indicators has resulted in significant achievements being made. The adoption of NPM by countries such as
New Zealand, Australia, and the United Kingdom enabled their police agencies to measure and compare the performance of their organizations with
the performance of other police organizations and enabled comparisons to
be made over time (den Heyer, 2011).

The appropriateness of the use of some of the components of NPM by
police agencies has caused rigorous debate, especially in regard to the adoption of private-sector business principles. The contention has been based on
the view that police agencies are vastly different from the private sector, and
as a result, the adoption of private-sector attitudes and theories is therefore
inappropriate (Butterfield et al., 2004). It was believed that the differences
between the operating environment of the private sector, its business goals
and objectives, and its structures and values are so different from those of the

police, that it would be impossible to implement such managerial techniques successfully within police, and that the level of change required to implement the reform would be too complex (Butterfield et al., 2004).

As Boston (1991) noted, some supporters of NPM assumed that some of the components of private-sector management could be introduced into the public sector because of the number of similarities between the sectors. However, the public and private sectors are very different in a number of functions and form, and it is wrong to assume a priori that private-sector management practices are necessarily better than those used in the public sector (Boston, 1991).

Conclusion

The past 40 years have seen extensive change in the political and the operating environment of police agencies. These changes have often been fundamental, rapid, and imposed by governments. As a result, police managers and executives have had to continually examine alternative methods to maintain service delivery levels while keeping within their diminishing funding levels. Police are acutely aware that any decrease in agency funding, no matter how small, could lead to a decline in the number of officers and staff employed and to the abolition of special units and services (Kocher, 2012).

In the search for alternative service delivery methods, many police agencies have amalgamated or merged or have introduced NPM or components of NPM. There is a limitation in our understanding of these new management approaches, and there have been few independent evaluations of the claims that larger-sized police agencies are better than smaller-sized agencies and that amalgamations, mergers, or NPM decreases organizational costs or that they increase efficiency and service delivery effectiveness.

Late-Twentieth-Century Approaches to Improving Police Service Delivery

5

Introduction

In early 2010, the newly appointed director of the Office of Community Oriented Policing Services for the U.S. Department of Justice Bernard Melekian claimed that there were four components of policing that needed to change to ensure the survival of American policing: a change in the way that police deliver their services, the use of technology, the use of volunteers, and the introduction of the regionalization/consolidation of police agencies (Thomson, 2012). While these four components were identified in the context of U.S. policing, they apply equally to policing in any western democracy. The four components that Melekian identified, in concert with the complexity of law enforcement, public safety, and homeland security, have created a need for local police agencies to transform their structures and methods of service delivery to improve efficiency and effectiveness. The drive to improve the delivery of service means that police agencies need to examine how they can deliver their services using fewer resources. Agencies need to use fewer resources when government funding has been reduced, and if agencies are to maintain their service delivery levels, they need to use resources more efficiently and effectively. Without the appropriate level of resources, "do more with less" often means that agencies need to divert existing resources from noncore services and prioritize calls for service.

In order to maintain the level of service delivered using fewer resources, police agencies must cut operating and personnel costs. To achieve this, police agencies need to make informed decisions and choices about where and how to make savings. Agencies need to have the knowledge of where potential gains may be made and the advantages and disadvantages of the efficiency options that they select.

However, some police agencies may be unable to take advantage of the efficiency options available, owing to the complacency that has developed from experiencing a sustained period of growth in funding allocations. In some cases, agencies may have an "ingrained culture" of complacency, which hinders the identification and the introduction of modern management techniques that allow resources to be deployed more effectively.

According to Loveday and McClory (2007):

> This cultural environment, and its accompanying structural deficiencies, is undermining police performance at a time when forces must balance the demands of neighbourhood policing, fight serious crime that may cross force boundaries (Level 2 crime) and offences that cross national borders, including terrorism (Level 3 crime). In the absence of mergers, achieving the desired balance of resources will require collaboration between forces and this, together with the correct strategic balance between local policing and cross-border crime fighting, must be taken into account when developing reform policies. It is as much a financial matter as a strategic one. (pp. 6–7)

Since the early 1980s, in response to the changing demands of society and government, police agencies in advanced liberal democracies have undergone a series of strategic and managerial reforms and have restructured their organizations to improve service delivery and transparency. Agencies have drawn on the principles of new public management (NPM), which focus on performance measurement processes and frameworks to improve organizational efficiency. These changes motivated Cope, Leishman, and Starie (1997) to claim that a new policing order had emerged. This chapter discusses the factors that influenced the design and development of strategies to improve service delivery in the late twentieth century and examines the concept of effective service delivery.

Factors That Influenced the Improvement in Service Delivery Strategies in the Late-Twentieth-Century

The rigidity of police organizational structures and the globalization of crime have had an influence on the development and the improvement of police service delivery. Despite maintaining the use of historical structures, forms, and functions, the organization of policing in the twentieth century has evolved in response to the introduction of new technology, the types and forms of crime, the drive to be more efficient and effective, and the need to be more transparent and accountable. Later complexities, such as 9/11 and the late-2007 worldwide financial crisis, have imposed even more extensive and far-reaching changes than any other previous change levers.

Reiss (1992), however, claimed that the basic structure of police organizations has undergone very little change since the beginning of the twentieth century. The problem with this observation is that it pertains to only one area of policing in the United States, the policing system. What Reiss meant is that there has been no change in local, geographically based policing in the United States or in the large number of small-sized agencies that make up this system. Aside from the policing system, numerous elements associated with policing in the United States have undergone extensive change since the early 1980s. These changes have been in response to the identification and the development of a number of new approaches to police service delivery and include the introduction of Community Policing and Compstat.

While extensive change has taken place since the early 1980s, it has been difficult for many police agencies to introduce change owing to the history of local policing being closely related to the political history of the city or area of which it is a part. History impacts on the type of structure that is established in a local police agency and, in turn, can hinder the ability of managers to implement change. The history of local police agencies can affect an agency's relationship with other agencies, and local police agencies often have little formal integration with state and federal police agencies. As the world becomes more entwined and global, the decentralized system of policing and the large number of police agencies in the United States leaves the country and the rest of the world in a vulnerable position, to which criminals are able to use to their advantage.

Performance Measurement, Organizational Structures, and Service Delivery

The effectiveness of police service delivery is highly complex and extremely controversial and is influenced by performance measurement, organizational structure, and governance. For an agency to be able to measure its performance and evaluate its service delivery, a performance measurement framework needs to be established. A performance measurement framework enables management to determine the level of service that an organization is to deliver, how employees will contribute to that service, and the amount of service that each employee should deliver.

A performance measurement framework should include both quantitative and qualitative methods to evaluate the performance of an organization and its employees. The method to evaluate a police agency should include the examination of the level of service delivered and should comprise more than organizational or employee outputs. Using quantitative and qualitative methods would provide a more comprehensive and balanced framework to measure the performance of a police agency, rather than using the number of reported crimes in a geographical area, which is a commonly used, but insufficient method. As well as measuring an agency's progress toward the achievement of its specified outputs and government outcomes, a comprehensive performance framework needs to include a measurement of community satisfaction with the services delivered by the police and the public's sense of security.

A robust performance measurement framework and the acceptance of a management culture will enable an agency to be managed as a composite system.

A performance management system should comprise a number of supporting elements, of which have been listed as follows. The inclusion of supporting elements in a performance measurement framework will assist in identifying the various options that may enhance service delivery efficiency and effectiveness. The supporting elements include the following:

- Planning and performance management: planning for short-, mid-, and long-term strategic, operational, and tactical objectives to ensure that the organization vision and focus are aligned. The plans include identified success factors, a regular performance review process, and enhanced organizational performance improvement procedures.
- Resource management: the identification, provision, and efficient management of resources, including personnel, facilities, equipment, finance, and information.
- Core product/service management: identifying, measuring, challenging, and continually improving the core competencies of the agency. These competencies include patrol, investigations, and all support services.
- Measurement, analysis, and improvement of systems and processes: ensuring that customer input is sought and valued and that service levels are consistent and are regularly satisfied, performance is evaluated and improved, internal performance auditing beyond compliance audits is conducted, and corrective action techniques are used that ultimately repair the cause of problems so that reoccurrence is eliminated.
- Knowledge/quality management: creating an environment that fosters individual and organizational learning and growth, ensures continuity, and reduces the challenges related to succession planning (Frazier, 2012).

However, measuring the performance of police agencies and the achievement of outcomes is difficult. It is more difficult than measuring the performance and the achievement of outcomes in the private sector because police objectives are often inconsistent and police are often held accountable for social outcomes that they cannot control. This is especially problematic when comparing preimprovement service delivery outputs with postimprovement service delivery outputs. Lithopoulos and Rigakos (2005) claimed that complications arise because of the difficulty in defining and measuring the effectiveness of police service delivery owing to the role and the objectives of police agencies being ambiguous and changing over time. At the same time, society is undergoing change, which also makes measuring the performance of a police agency difficult. When these difficulties are combined with the police culture of conservatism and their slowness to adapt to change, police agencies find themselves one step behind in their ability to improve their service delivery.

The shape and size of an organization's structure is another area that should be examined when endeavoring to enhance an agency's service delivery. Previous research has indicated that the shape of an organization's structure relates to the size–efficiency relationship of an agency (Drake & Simper, 2000).

The structure of an organization is heavily influenced by the hierarchical structure and the span of control that is in place. To maintain effective control of staff and to ensure that staff share an agency's strategic vision and are providing a quality service, the agency will need to have a narrow span of control. The supervision of staff is important as their performance and behavior are important factors in improving the efficiency and the effectiveness of the service delivered.

How an organization's resources are deployed and utilized is also important. The efficient use of resources supports an organization's hierarchical structure and enables it to achieve its objectives. Policing is labor-intensive, and personnel salaries and benefits usually comprise more than 80% of an agency's annual budget (Murphy, 2002). The allocation and deployment of resources, especially uniform officer resources, become critical when agency funding is reduced. If an agency is facing a decreasing level of resources and is not able to significantly increase organizational efficiency and effectiveness, it often has little choice but to limit or cut nonemergency or nonessential services. Murphy (2002) suggested that one option that is available to increase the efficiency and the effectiveness of an agency when experiencing a decrease in the level of resources, such as the number of patrol staff, is to implement a response criterion for calls from the public and a process of differential response or a public call prioritization system.

An improvement in the management of personnel is the most obvious approach to improving service delivery. Also of importance is the use of new technology, which can provide support to management and enhance the deployment of agency personnel.

The final element that should be examined to improve police agency governance and the management of service delivery is private-industry values and strategies (Murphy, 2002). Private-industry values and strategies are based on the motive of making a profit and delivering a high standard of service. It is for these reasons that private-industry practices often conflict with the social character of policing. Policing is a profession in its own right, and private-industry practices and strategies should be examined to identify what may be learned and how these lessons may be adapted to improve policing. Strategies and practices borrowed from the private sector should not be taken as a template to be applied without adaption but should be examined for their applicability in policing. Taking such an approach when introducing new methods to policing will enable agencies to further develop strategies to suit their own specific needs. In the long term, adapting the strategies used in the private sector may result in a more professionalized police service.

The future success of policing is in the ability of agencies to appreciate the benefits of adopting new service delivery and management enhancement methods and ensuring that any development and implementation of service delivery strategies strengthen the police–citizen relationship. The development and implementation of new service delivery strategies are complex and need to go beyond adopting a single improvement program, such as introducing a call prioritization system, without considering the impact that the introduction may have on other areas of the organization.

Effects That New Public Management Has Had on Police Agencies

During the 1960s and 1970s, the reputation of the police in the United States, the United Kingdom, Canada, and Australia was not held in high regard by the public, with allegations of police wrongdoing and unsatisfactory behavior, which resulted in calls for police reform (Dixon & Kouzmin, 1994). Police wrongdoing and unsatisfactory behavior were not the only reasons for the appeal for police reform, the police were also viewed as being inefficient, and it was hoped that reform would bring about changes that would improve accountability and efficiency. As a response, Community-Oriented Policing was introduced in the hope that police decision-making would become more transparent and that the police–community relationship would improve. As well as introducing Community Policing, during the 1980s, the UK, New Zealand, and Australian police all implemented various aspects of NPM to increase organizational accountability and efficiency.

NPM, from a practical perspective, is a management approach where an emphasis is placed on improving organizational performance (Hoque, Arends, & Alexander, 2004). A focus on improving performance creates the need for a performance framework, which provides a structure for an agency's activities to be monitored and evaluated through the application of modern management and accounting tools and techniques (Hoque et al., 2004). Modern accounting tools and techniques usually include comprehensive budgeting procedures, accrual accounting systems, and financial reporting.

Some claim that NPM is not a management tool but a description of a series of public-sector reforms and innovations that occurred in the United Kingdom, New Zealand, and Australia in the 1980s. These critics claim that NPM is really an enhanced form of public sector administration (Hoque et al., 2004). The definition of administration in this context is that it is a bureaucratic public system, "characterized by a rigid adherence to rules and regulations, compliance, stability, predictability, input orientation, and inefficiency" (Hoque et al., 2004, p. 79). Another view of police reform cited by Hoque et al. (2004) is that police may only be implementing NPM and other efficiency reforms to legitimize their standing with citizens, government, and the media.

The introduction of NPM in most countries has been supported by the introduction of managing for outcomes, accrual accounting, and zero-based budgeting, which has led to the development of business planning processes, budget forecasting, and a focus on government social outcomes (Hoque et al., 2004). This strategic realignment of how police manage has fundamentally changed the financial focus and how police activities are funded. Rather than funding programs, police are funded on managing and achieving outputs and outcomes (Hoque et al., 2004).

To successfully introduce NPM, the number of levels in a hierarchical structure in an organization needs to be carefully considered. The trend in the UK, New Zealand, and Australian police agencies has been to flatten the organizational structure in response to the myth that "flatter is better" (Hilmer & Donaldson, 1995, p. 22). The myth that flatter organizational structures are better is based on the belief that flatter structures decrease costs and improve communication and customer service (Vickers & Kouzmin, 2001). However, the "flatter is better" myth does not necessarily apply to police agencies. Flatter structures were implemented when the New Zealand Police merged with the New Zealand Traffic Safety Service and then again in a second round of restructuring six years after the merger. Middle and senior management positions were removed from the organizational structure, but these positions were later reestablished and actually increased in number, owing to an increase in planning, reporting, and legislative requirements (New Zealand Institute of Economic Research, 2007).

NPM has bought many positive changes to the management of police agencies. However, police were slower than other government departments to realize the benefits of the new form of management, as police managers were not comfortable with the economic ideals and because the majority of these managers did not have the training or experience in strategic planning, leadership, and budgeting (Vickers & Kouzmin, 2001).

Value for Money

Public spending on policing in England and Wales rose significantly at the same time that crime was escalating during the 1980s and 1990s (Neyroud, n.d.), which gave the impression that police were inefficient and ineffective.

The perceived lack of police performance during this period led to the development of a number of initiatives to better measure the outcomes achieved by the police, and these, together with the best value approaches introduced in England and Wales, resulted in the development of the value for money (VFM) strategy (Neyroud).

VFM can be described as a strategy within NPM, and it became part of the policing vocabulary in England and Wales with the release of the UK Home Office Circular number 114 in 1983 (Neyroud, n.d.). The circular linked the performance of police staff "specifically to the ability to demonstrate value for money," which was summarized as "efficiency and effectiveness" (Home Office, 1983). The principal components of VFM were described by the Her Majesty's Inspectorate of Constabulary in 1998 as follows:

- An appropriate level of service is provided at a reduced cost.
- An improved level of service is provided at the same cost (increased demand met, quality enhanced).
- New areas of work are undertaken without the need for additional resources.
- Adjustment/reappraisal occurs to take account of static or reducing expenditure and any changes in the operational environment (Her Majesty's Inspectorate of Constabulary, 1998).

VFM should not be seen as a single strategy, but as part of a package to improve the efficiency and the effectiveness of a police agency's service delivery. According to the Her Majesty's Inspectorate of Constabulary (1998), VFM is not an "absolute condition" but, in practice, "is synonymous with effective [personnel and organizational] management" (p. 7). The achievement of VFM is intrinsically linked to the quality of the service delivered, the attaining of organizational objectives, and the "efficient, effective and targeted use of resources" (Her Majesty's Inspectorate of Constabulary, 1998, p. 8).

The benefit of VFM, as with NPM, is that there is no specific method for ensuring its achievement, as circumstances pertaining to each organization are different. Location-specific circumstances can be a benefit or a barrier during the introduction of, or the achievement of, VFM (Her Majesty's Inspectorate of Constabulary, 1998). According to the Her Majesty's Inspectorate of Constabulary (1998), there are six variables that differentiate organizations:

1. The local environment (internal and external)
2. Socioeconomic and demographic characteristics
3. Local needs and policies
4. Local customs and practices

5. The availability of skilled staff
6. The history of funding by governments

These variables are not static, which means that police managers must constantly review the services that their agency delivers and the performance and adaptability of their staff. As with the majority of organizational management approaches, the implementation and the achievement of VFM require dynamic processes and leadership skills (Her Majesty's Inspectorate of Constabulary, 1998). Police agencies in England and Wales that successfully implemented VFM exhibited the following characteristics:

- Proactive management
- Empowerment of staff
- Clear objectives are set
- Effective planning
- The ability to convert plans into effective actions
- The analysis and costing of processes
- Closely monitored service delivery
- Periodic review
- Comparative analysis and benchmarking (Her Majesty's Inspectorate of Constabulary, 1998)

Difficulties in achieving VFM may be experienced as a number of operational inefficiencies that are related to the cost of delivering services may be outside the control of a police agency (Drake & Simpler, 2004). The noncontrol of agency efficiencies arises, according to Drake and Simpler (2004), especially in larger-sized agencies, because input prices are often higher in larger-sized cities. As a result, larger-sized agencies may not be able to easily control the efficiency in which their services are delivered.

Organizational Structure

Examining the structure of an organization is one option to improve the efficiency and the effectiveness of service delivery. To ensure that local police agencies are able to improve their service delivery and respond to the changes in the environment, agencies must have flexible and dynamic organizational structures, hierarchies, and systems. While paramilitary bureaucratic structures and approaches may have served their purpose in managing patrol and investigative officers, they are not well suited for modern governance practices (Kraska, 1996; Schafer, 2012).

Police agencies are structured along very bureaucratic lines, which are renowned for their inflexibility, lack of innovation and creativity, and for resisting change (Moore & Stephens, 1991; Schafer, 2012). It is for these reasons that it has been suggested on numerous occasions, that the bureaucratic paramilitary model of policing is no longer viable (Etter, 1993; Vickers & Kouzmin, 2001). While the paramilitary structure will be needed for emergencies and for other operational responses in a rapidly changing, technologically based world, agencies that retain their bureaucratic organizational structures and fail to implement strategies to improve their service delivery efficiency and effectiveness risk being unable to deliver core services. As a consequence, agencies that are not able to address their core missions could have organizational structural changes imposed on them by municipal government or investigative commissions.

Improvements in efficiency and effectiveness can be achieved by reducing the support and the administrative costs of an agency. Personnel costs may consume more than 80% of a police agency's annual budget (Loveday, 1995b). This means that any reduction in the number of personnel transfers immediately to a cost saving, but it does not necessarily improve the effectiveness of the service delivered by an agency. An agency's effectiveness can only be improved if the savings that are made from reducing support and administrative personnel are redirected into patrol or investigative personnel. It is the work undertaken by patrol or investigative personnel that contributes to an agency's outputs, not the work of support or administrative staff. Support or administrative staff contribute to the overhead costs of an organization.

In 1990, the UK Audit Commission noted that one of the major problems with police organizational structures is that they tend to "drift into top-heaviness" (Audit Commission, 1990, p. 9). As a result of the top-heaviness of police forces and that larger-sized policing units tend to become bureaucratic, the Audit Commission recommended that the chain of command in police agencies be reduced, especially in the more senior ranks, and that the savings be reappropriated to employ more officers for street patrol (Loveday, 1995b).

However, agencies need to be able to strike a balance when implementing a flatter organizational structure. A flatter hierarchical structure that empowers lower-level managers needs to retain the organization's capability and resilience to ensure that it is able to respond to large-scale emergency incidents. Police agencies in recent times have instituted flatter structures and implemented decentralization programs that have devolved operational decision-making to lower-level managers, but to ensure organizational coordination, the formulation of strategy should remain centralized. Cope et al. (1997) described police agencies that implement flatter structures as introducing components of centralized and decentralized management simultaneously.

Lower-level managers need to be made accountable and be given the responsibility of managing resources in a flatter structure, but controls or assurance factors need to be put into place to provide senior managers and executive officers with the confidence that outputs are being delivered. Flatter structures also assume that lower-level managers have the skills to manage (Vickers & Kouzmin, 2001). It is for these reasons that flatter structures in police agencies may have an impact on the delivery of services and on the outcomes that are to be achieved (Vickers & Kouzmin, 2001).

When reviewing the size and the shape of the organizational structure of an agency, a complicating factor is that the consideration of the public's expectations of what the police should be doing is included in an agency's Community Policing program. The expectations of the public subsequently influence the size and the shape of an agency's hierarchical structure. This is because the introduction of Community Policing in the 1990s legitimized the expansion of many police agencies, which subsequently raised the public's expectation for an active police response to community problems (Murphy, 2002).

The organizational structures and approaches adopted prior to implementing Community Policing were difficult to sustain, as they were often dysfunctional owing to a lack of organizational coordination. As the majority of agencies found themselves needing to operate with diminishing levels of resources, they focused more on delivering essential core services at the expense of delivering Community Policing. Focusing on the delivery of core, essential services is a method that has been adopted by police agencies as a means to use existing resources more effectively to meet public demand.

How an agency is structured also affects the availability and the presence of police patrols. The availability of police on the street was an important component of Her Majesty's Inspectorate of Constabulary's assessment of the UK police forces. The 2004 Her Majesty's Inspectorate of Constabulary assessment report noted that the UK police forces, as currently organized and structured, were not fit for purpose and that police patrol and security services were inadequate (Loveday, 2008). The report recommended that the police service make "more effective use" of force personnel if they were to professionalize the service (Loveday, 2008).

To improve the professionalization of service delivery, police must investigate new personnel management systems, new methods of recruitment and training, and new administrative frameworks and processes to create flexible organizational structures that will meet the challenges of the new environment. The modernization of organizational structures will create resilience through "a range of initiatives that seek to improve performance, efficiency and frontline policing" (Loveday & McClory, 2007, p. 22). The term "resilience" has been defined by the UK Home Office as "the capacity of a system, potentially exposed to hazards, to adapt, by resisting or changing in order to reach and maintain an acceptable level of functioning and structure" (Loveday & McClory, 2007, p. 23).

Another component of an organizational structure that should be examined to improve the efficiency and effectiveness of an agency's service delivery is criminal investigations. Previous literature has suggested that if detectives are managed by creating identifiable goals and objectives, the length of time involved in solving crime cases may be reduced (Brandl & Frank, 1994; Eck, 1983, 1992). Crime reduction strategies and the level of an agency's service delivery can be further improved by including detectives and analysts in Community Policing initiatives. The involvement of detectives and analysts in Community Policing increases the likelihood of the gathering of information from the public and assists in problem solving and the deployment of patrol staff (Eck, 1999; Lacasse, 1986; Loizzo, 1994; Walker & Katz, 2008).

Including detectives in wider policing and improving their management and deployment are important, not only to increase an agency's effectiveness, but because it forms a basis for responding to the globalization of crime. It is also important when an agency is considering implementing an intelligence-led approach to service delivery (Liederbach, Fritsch, & Womack, 2011).

Police agencies vary in size and structure, and any change to the structure of a local police agency must take into account how the local government and municipality are structured. This is to ensure that relationships are maintained and that the implementation of Community Policing is efficient and effective.

Performance Measurement

One of the main reasons that police agencies undertake an NPM reform program is so that a performance management system that enables managers to measure the delivery of an organization's services can be implemented (den Heyer, 2011). Implementing an NPM program is a deliberate action taken to improve the efficiency and the effectiveness of an agency and promotes accountable and improved delivery of service (den Heyer, 2011). Ayto (2011) credited the performance management aspect of NPM with supporting better decision-making by police managers.

The introduction of NPM will enable managers to move away from a focus on rules for the use of resources toward a focus on accomplishments that are likely to enhance agency performance and the achievement of specified objectives and outputs. A focus on using resources to achieve outputs will result in the availability of better quality performance information, which enables better management and resource decisions to be made. The benefit of introducing NPM is that it provides performance information to management so that they can make better decisions about the organization's resources and how these resources can be used. NPM also provides an incentive to individuals whose performance is being monitored, as it is capable of guiding their current and future performance efforts. However, the availability of performance information is not an end in itself (Ayto, 2011), as such information is only one factor that is necessary for the effective management of an organization.

The establishment of a management framework for better decision-making will ensure that there is a strategic relationship with the performance management system. This relationship has four essential and mutually reinforcing elements:

1. Specifies clear objectives (the desired performance of an organization)
2. Gives managers the authority to act (freedom to manage)
3. Provides incentives for individuals to perform
4. Provides reliable information of results (actual performance) (Ayto, 2011)

An NPM performance management system in a police agency usually includes the following seven components:

1. The development of a strategic plan that is linked to the annual corporate planning process
2. Defining and setting of organizational and individual aims and objectives on an annual basis
3. The development of personal and organizational performance indicators
4. The development and implementation of a comprehensive corporate planning framework
5. The development and implementation of a personal appraisal process
6. Linking organizational strategies and delivery objectives to individual positions
7. The development and implementation of management reviews and performance evaluation frameworks (Boston, 1991; Butterfield, Edwards & Woodall, 2004)

The development of an extensive organizational performance measurement and management system, which includes all of these components, will minimize nine of the major performance difficulties that were experienced by the UK police. The difficulties experienced were as follows:

1. The nature of policing itself
2. The police culture

3. Ethical behavior and attitudes
4. The difficulty in establishing a causal link between organizational inputs and outputs with outcomes
5. The lack of performance management skills
6. The lack of an agreed database
7. The lack of input and financial data for activity-based costing
8. The over-reliance on partnerships with other public agencies
9. Obscure priorities and messages given by external stakeholders (O'Byrne, 2001, p. 93)

The performance of an organization can be measured by examining whether it has achieved its objectives. The measurement of the performance can be ratified through an audit or evaluation process. Performance can also be measured by relating annual corporate plans to outcomes and the achievement of annual performance indictors justifies the use of resources and enables the efficiency of an organization to be assessed. Performance indicators, the strategic plan, and the corporate plan are all linked using this approach (Butterfield et al., 2004). The performance specifications in an NPM program clearly define what each police manager and staff member should achieve by outlining what each person is expected to deliver. Performance indicators can be used to monitor their performance. An NPM program provides a better accountability framework by correcting vague or unachievable performance specifications that are often used in the public sector.

An NPM performance management system ensures that costs are identified and assigned to the appropriate service delivery component or output. The emphasis on performance ensures that managers do not focus solely upon the financial aspects of management and upon legal compliance but instead concentrate on managing resources efficiently and effectively (Pallot, 1991). As noted by Pallot (1991), it soon became apparent after NPM was introduced to the UK and the New Zealand police, that NPM was a combination of both financial and general management and that the two were so entwined that it was difficult to separate them.

The accounting system is the major component used to comprehensively evaluate the performance of an organization. To enable an accurate evaluation of the performance of an organization to be completed and for any improvement in service delivery efficiency and effectiveness to be measured, police agencies need to use accrual accounting instead of a cash-based accounting system. Accrual accounting is able to capture all of the expenditure for a defined period, enabling the organization to recognize revenue and expenses when they are incurred, rather than at the completion of a cash transaction.

In order for the police to be able to measure its organizational performance, the performance framework needs to be a combination of both output and outcome objectives. However, outcomes refer to an end state and the end goals for police are not always obvious (Marnoch, 2009). Furthermore, outcome measures have a number of weaknesses when they are used to evaluate the management of police organizations. Outcome measures are not a direct measure of managerial value, as police, in order to achieve an outcome, usually require the input from a number of different agencies across the public sector.

How police agencies perform is related to how they use their resources, which are limited. This means that if an agency is to improve its service delivery effectiveness, it must focus on delivering the same level of service using less resources or deliver more service using the same amount of resources (Boyd, Geoghegan, & Gibbs, 2011). The adoption of a comprehensive and robust performance management system that includes the seven NPM performance components that were discussed earlier will provide the basis for a police agency to continuously review and improve its performance and better utilize its resources.

Whatever performance indicators are used and despite the difficulty in evaluating police performance or service delivery effectiveness, the ethos of performance management (Golding & Savage, 2008) has now become firmly established in the management practices of police agencies in most western nations and usually forms the basis for decision-making and strategic direction.

Compstat

Compstat is the most prominent and widely accepted police performance management system used in the United States. Compstat has been widely accepted because it has been perceived as being able to assist an agency achieve its mission and objectives (Police Executive Research Forum, 2013b).

Compstat is a strategic management system that reduces crime by decentralizing decision-making to middle managers. It aids in reducing crime by holding managers accountable for their performance and by increasing the capacity of an organization to identify, understand, and monitor its response to crime (Willis, 2011). Compstat's strategic emphasis suggests that an agency will need to constantly scan its operating environment, identify any problems, make the appropriate adjustments, and respond to crime efficiently and effectively (Willis, Mastrofski, & Weisburd, 2007). This means that any response to crime will be able to be measured, coordinated, and controlled using an appropriate allocation of resources.

Compstat has an advantage over other police performance systems, and its adoption is especially beneficial for those agencies that are trying to improve their service delivery effectiveness. It can be adapted to respond to local problems and takes into account the resources available at the time of the response. It is believed that Compstat is compatible with a Community

Policing program (Willis, 2011); however, there has been very little research conducted on the impact of implementing both Compstat and Community Policing. Willis (2011) claimed that any research that has been undertaken on agencies that have introduced both Compstat and Community Policing found that the programs "work independently, with each having little effect on the other" (p. 655). This is because Compstat focuses on problem solving at a strategic level but empowers officers to find solutions to local problems. By implementing both Compstat and Community Policing in unison, agencies will have a more robust management task and coordination structure, which has a community focus.

Willis (2011) claimed that a major problem with Compstat is that instead of it being used as a performance measurement tool, it is used as a crime reduction program. However, according to the Police Executive Research Forum (2013b), Compstat can be used to evaluate crime levels as well as to measure the aspects of an agency's performance. Some agencies use Compstat to monitor officer overtime, officers' use of force, and complaints made against police. Compstat is also used to manage the budgets of both an organization and an individual unit and to ensure that managers are held accountable.

The major benefit of Compstat is that it is adaptable and can be made to include those elements of which are important to an agency. The introduction and the adaption of Compstat by an agency will not be the final state, as Compstat not only meets an agency's current needs but is also capable of evolving to meet an agency's future needs. To ensure that an agency remains effective, Compstat and its supporting frameworks and processes will require constant examination and adjustment. The Los Angeles Police Department, for example, is now using a system called "Compstat Plus," which incorporates three additional substrategies: uses detailed diagnostic exercises to identify and assist underperforming areas, promotes dialog among stakeholders to assess the results of diagnostic exercises, and creates a plan of action, which involves key stakeholders (Police Executive Research Forum, 2013b).

Compstat and its supporting processes will keep evolving, especially as advances in technology are made. The continuing improvement in information systems and computer technology will increase the ability of police agencies to identify crime problems and enable resources to be coordinated and deployed. To take advantage of the advances made in technology and the availability of better quality information, agencies will need to invest in crime analysis tools and the employment of crime analysts.

Intelligence-Led Policing

Intelligence-led policing (ILP) is an approach that is used throughout an organization and may be used to improve the efficiency and the effectiveness of a police agency's service delivery. Although it has been described as being the delivery process of the UK National Intelligence Model, it is principally a police reform movement (den Heyer, 2008). The concept of ILP is based on the theory that police should be less reactive and more proactive in their approach to the occurrence of crime. The basis of ILP is that it assumes that the criminal environment is a permanent feature of the police operating environment. According to Glensor and Peak (2012), ILP is a "collaborative law enforcement approach combining problem-solving policing, information sharing, and police accountability, with enhanced intelligence operations" (p. 14).

The development of ILP evolved from "the supposed failure of the police to address the systemic sources of crime and crime patterns" (Tilley, 2003, p. 313). Historically, police performance was viewed as being poor. This perception was based on the fact that there were low clearance rates for a number of crimes and that the police were not capable of analyzing why crime occurred. To address this, the police introduced methods such as ILP and Hot Spot policing to increase clearance rates with an expectation that these methods would also improve the efficiency and the effectiveness of its delivery of service.

The major benefit of ILP is that it is closely associated with Problem-Oriented Policing (POP) (Goldstein, 1990). They are both tactics that can support a broader policing paradigm, such as Community Policing (Glensor & Peak, 2012). Eck and Spelman (1987) noted that a number of police intelligence units use the POP methodology scan, analysis, respond, and assess (SARA) as a structure for resource prioritization and, as such, complements ILP. The ILP approach in turn defines a process for setting priorities and provides a framework in which problem solving can be applied. This means that an evidential base is critical both to POP in the analysis and response stages and to ILP in the selection of crime reduction strategies. Furthermore, the use of POP and SARA can provide a "case management–oriented" focus for targeting offenders or crime hotspots via intelligence.

According to Glensor and Peak (2012), ILP, Community-Oriented Policing, and POP "are not separate and distinct entities and strategies," but advance the "evolution of community oriented policing and problem solving to address 21st century challenges of crime and disorder" (p. 14). If the broader policing philosophy of Community-Oriented Policing together with the service delivery approach of POP is implemented simultaneously in a police agency, the framework will provide the context for ILP (Laycock, 2001). This is an important point; although the mechanism for ILP may be sound, it may be introduced to situations where the context is not appropriate for that style of policing. This means that if police agencies are looking at introducing ILP, they need to ensure that the organization has a clear understanding of the impact that ILP will have on its service delivery.

Civilianization of Sworn Positions

A large number of police agencies have implemented civilianization programs in order to reduce agency operating costs. The potential benefits of implementing such a reform program may offer much more than just the savings that may be achieved through outsourcing (Loveday, 2015). Replacing sworn officers with civilians has been found to lower costs, primarily from paying lower salaries and other personnel benefits and from the reduction in training requirements (Schwartz, Vaughn, Walker, & Wholey, 1975). Civilianization has also been viewed as part of the movement toward professionalizing policing and has been a key component of Community Policing (Griffiths, Palmer, Weeks, & Polydore, 2006).

Civilianization can take many forms. It is mainly used to replace sworn, uniformed staff in administrative or support positions with civilian staff, or to augment the patrol capacity of an agency by deploying civilian staff in uniform to perform patrol duties. The aim of civilianization is to reduce an agency's operating costs and improve its level of service delivery.

Police agencies rely extensively on civilians to perform a variety of roles (Reaves & Goldberg, 1998). Civilians are usually employed by an agency as communication room call takers or dispatchers, specialist operations support (crime scene technicians, fingerprint officers, forensic laboratory scientists), forensic computer analysts, and legal advisors (Forst, 2000). In sheriff's departments, more than a third of all civilians support jail operations (Reaves & Smith, 1995). The level of civilianization in an agency may depend on a number of factors, such as the police union may be strong in a department or in an agency or an agency may have not considered expanding the positions and making them available for civilian employees.

A number of policing or law enforcement roles have become so specialized that agencies have become increasingly reliant on civilians to fulfill these roles. These specialist roles, such as forensic computer technicians, financial crime analysts, and legal advisors, require specific educational and practical qualifications that are often difficult for sworn officers to obtain. It can also be difficult for sworn staff to gain the experience needed to meet the requirements of a profession. This means that agencies may have no alternative other than to employ civilians for specific roles if they wish to keep the skilled role within the agency. The alternative is to outsource the skilled role to a specialized private company.

The majority of police agencies around the world initially resisted the opportunity to implement a civilianization program when it was first suggested in the 1960s and 1970s. The majority of police officers viewed support or office-bound roles as inferior, and not real police work, but this resistance had largely disappeared by the 1980s and 1990s, as civilians gained credibility and proved that they were capable of undertaking the roles for which they were employed (Forst, 2000).

The impact that civilianization has on how police operate and how it affects the efficiency and effectiveness of an agency's service delivery is unknown (Police Executive Research Forum, 2013a), nor is its effect on the culture of a police agency known. According to the Police Executive Research Forum (2013a), a civilianization program has the potential to improve an agency's efficiency and effectiveness by diversifying an agency's workforce skills and by redirecting the deployment of sworn officers to patrol. It has been suggested that civilians can increase the effectiveness of service delivery and can professionalize some functions by relieving sworn officers from administrative duties (Forst, 2000; Loveday, 1995b, 2006b, 2007, 2008). The suggestion is based on the belief that a civilian who is appointed to a position will have the appropriate technical training, skills, and experience for the role. However, this supposition is extremely hard to prove, as no research has been undertaken to examine whether or how a civilianization program increases the efficiency or effectiveness of an agency's service delivery.

To assess the level to which an agency can implement a civilianization program, an agency needs to complete a workload study or an analysis of the organization and determine the target service levels to be achieved, the costs involved, and the potential savings to be made. When an agency has this information, there are two ways to gauge the limit to which an agency can implement a civilianization program. The first approach involves a comprehensive review and examination of positions, duties, and roles within an organization. This process will identify those positions that should be solely civilian, civilian or sworn, or solely sworn. The second approach is to review the ratio of civilian staff employed to sworn staff. A higher ratio indicates that an agency has a higher number of sworn to civilian staff and that the agency could have a number of administrative roles that could be better performed by civilian staff. The second approach focuses on analyzing the personnel mix, but more from an administrative and operational support perspective, rather than from a service delivery-level perspective.

Civilianization is often not accepted, and in some instances, lacks credibility with sworn officers, resulting in some tradition-bound executives being reluctant to appoint civilian staff to support functions. However, according to Forst (2000), it has become clear over time that civilian staff perform specific specialized roles more effectively than sworn officers. This is because civilian staff are usually trained as specialists for the position for which they are employed, whereas sworn officers are trained as generalists in policing and law enforcement.

Civilianization in the United States

Police agencies in the United States have implemented civilianization cautiously, principally by employing civilian staff to replace police personnel who hold office-bound jobs, such as, in radio or communication centers. In 1950, the proportion of civilian employees holding law enforcement positions was 7.5%, which almost doubled to 13.9% by 1970 (United States Department of Justice, 1951, 1971). From 1971 to 1990, the percentage of nonsworn police personnel employed almost doubled again, reaching 26.7% (United States Department of Justice, 1991). Hawley (2004) claimed that the average percentage growth in the number of civilian employees was 12% in the 31 largest agencies between 1991 and 1993, compared to only a 3% increase in the number of sworn employees and a 4% increase overall. In 2006, statistics showed that the trend of employing civilian staff had slowed to 30.8% of the workforce in police agencies (Police Executive Research Forum, 2013a; United States Department of Justice, 2007).

Civilians were initially employed more in larger-sized metropolitan police agencies than in smaller-sized agencies (Schwartz et al., 1975), and they tended to be employed more widely in the west than in the east (Reaves & Goldberg, 1998). Civilians were also employed in greater proportions in municipal and county departments than in state police agencies (Reaves & Smith, 1995).

It has been suggested that the increase in the number of civilian staff employed by U.S. police agencies may be due to the introduction of and the acceptance of Community Policing in the 1980s (Police Executive Research Forum, 2013a; Reaves & Goldberg, 1998). However, others have suggested that decreasing agency budgets and increases in crime in the 1970s contributed to the increase in the number of civilian staff employed (Palmer & Cherney, 2001). Another view as to the reason for the increase in the number of civilian staff employed since the 1980s, held by the Police Executive Forum (2013a), which evaluated the introduction of civilianization by police agencies that had received funding from the Byrne Grant Program, is that grant recipient organizations sought to increase their service delivery by adding significant new analytic and intelligence capabilities from hiring skilled civilians, which enabled sworn staff to be redeployed to patrol duties.

Since the 1980s, a number of local and state police agencies have examined the opportunities that have been made possible by implementing a civilianization program. These agencies are Berkley Police Department (California), Chicago Police Department, Kansas City Police Department (Missouri), Los Angeles Police Department, Maryland State Police, and San Jose Police Department (California). The details of the agency, the year that the civilianization review was undertaken, and the number of sworn positions, which

Table 5.1   U.S. Police Agencies That Have Completed Civilianization Reviews

Police Agency	Year of Civilianization Review	Number of Positions Identified to Convert to Civilian	Number of Sworn/Civilian at Year of Review
Berkeley PD	2002	14	182/110
Chicago PD	2013	292	11,944/822
Kansas PD	1998	40	1,459/675
LAPD	2008	500	9,843/2,773
Maryland State	2004	80	1,571/774
San Francisco PD	2010	328	2,552/495
San Jose PD	2010	88	900/370

Source: Author.

were identified as being suitable for converting into civilian positions, are presented in Table 5.1.

In a memorandum to the California Berkeley City Council in 2004, Council Member Mim Hawley suggested that despite the complications of introducing a civilianization program there may be a number of advantages in civilianizing some sworn functions in the Berkeley Police Department (BPD) (Hawley, 2004). Councilor Hawley noted that during the time of budget cuts, the possible savings from introducing a civilianization program could be considerable. Replacing a patrol officer with a Community Service Officer (CSO), a civilian patrol person, could, for example, save more than 50% in personnel costs per position converted. It was suggested that CSOs could be either full-time or part-time nonsworn, uniformed employees who could handle minor calls for service and provide additional support to uniformed officers, such as at crash scenes or investigation sites. Other intangible benefits included an enhanced police presence in the community, the alleviation of staff shortages, and an increase in the number of women and minorities recruited (Hawley, 2004).

A number of police agencies in the United States have created CSO positions to respond to low priority public calls for assistance, attend nonviolent crimes, and undertake community patrols. The establishment of a CSO program may have an effect on an agency's budget depending on whether the program is over and above the existing staff numbers, or whether the CSOs are replacing sworn officer positions.

Civilianization in Canada

Canadian police agencies appear to have been more accepting of the idea of civilianization with the ratio of sworn police officers to civilians increasing from 4.6 to 1 in 1962 to 2.5 to 1 in 2007 (Curry, 2014), with a decrease of 2.90

to 1 in 2012 (Winnipeg Police Service, 2012). The number of police officers in Canada rose from 62,461 in 2006 to a peak of 69,505 in 2012 before declining slightly to 69,272 in 2013, while the number of civilians working for police departments grew from 23,911 to a high of 28,202 in 2012 but decreased to 27,872 in 2013 (Curry, 2014).

There were four factors that contributed to the introduction of civilianization in Canada. These were as follows:

1. The increasing cost of delivering police services and the need to reduce personnel and operating costs
2. An emphasis placed on improving the efficiency and the effectiveness of service delivery by police management
3. A need to increase the number of sworn officers available for frontline duties
4. An increase in the complexity of policing and the subsequent amount of time that sworn officers spent on paperwork and other duties that took them off the streets (Winnipeg Police Service, 2012)

The Winnipeg Police Service (WPS), when examining the proposed enlargement of its civilianization program, adopted a strategic approach to measuring the personnel composition of its agency. The WPS perspective was to ensure the optimal use of civilian staff by training people in their assigned role at the right cost to support the achievement of the objectives of the agency (Winnipeg Police Service, 2012). WPS also came to the conclusion that once the appropriate type of employee was determined for the position, then the agency would be able to determine the correct number of staff for the agency.

In 2012, the WPS employed 423 civilian full-time staff and 1443 sworn (Winnipeg Police Service, 2012). Owing to increasing operational costs, the WPS implemented a civilianization program as a means of delivering services in a cost-effective manner. Using the sworn officer to civilian staff ratio to measure an agency's civilianization levels, the WPS, when compared to other Canadian police agencies, lagged behind as the second least favorable of 19 jurisdictions with a ratio of 3.80:1 (Winnipeg Police Service, 2012). Toronto Police Service had the most favorable ratio of 2.05 (Winnipeg Police Service, 2012).

To implement a civilianization program, the WPS commenced an audit of all of the positions within the agency between January 1, 2007, and December 31, 2011. The review identified 27 positions that were performed by uniform staff that could potentially be performed by civilian staff and that employing civilians in these positions could result in an annual saving of $890,000 with sworn officers being redeployed to core police duties (Winnipeg Police Service, 2012).

In comparison to the WPS, the Vancouver Police Service (VPS) developed specific criteria for evaluating individual positions that could potentially be converted into a civilianized position. The evaluation criteria used to classify whether a position could be determined as civilian were based on the answers to three key questions:

1. Does the position require law enforcement powers (powers of arrest, use of force, statutory requirement, carrying a firearm)?
2. Are the skills, training, experience, or credibility of a sworn police officer required to fulfill the duties of the position?
3. Can the requirements of the position be fulfilled by a specially trained civilian? (Winnipeg Police Service, 2012)

Civilianization in the United Kingdom

Since the early 1980s, police forces in the United Kingdom have implemented significant civilianization change programs, and by 2006, between 35% and 40% of a force's payroll was for civilian staff (Loveday, 2007). Other researchers have also acknowledged this trend and have noted that

- In March 2009, 13 police forces across the country had more than 90% of their control rooms (communication centers) staffed by civilians with a national average of 85%.
- Seventy-two percent of the London Metropolitan Police were civilian.
- In March 2010, Surrey Police had a 55% civilization rate and the West Midlands police forces had a civilianization rate of 34% (adapted from Boyd et al., 2011).

The trend toward civilization has been encouraged in the United Kingdom by the introduction of the Police Community Support Officers (PCSOs) program and Mixed Economy Teams (METs). Patrol officers with limited police powers have been recruited and deployed to deliver Community Policing under this program. This program, however, has not yet been evaluated. METs are defined as a squad of police personnel that may include an officer or a detective and civilian personnel, who are deployed to police a specific community event or to investigate and make inquiries in relation to occurrences of crimes or offences. Evidence from police agencies showed that the introduction of METs, consisting of police officers and civilian investigators, led to a decrease in the average incident investigation time, falling from 50 to 16 days while the detection rate rose by 15%(Loveday, 2008). The introduction of the METs resulted in time being made available for detectives to deal with more serious offences. These results suggest that expanding the employment of civilian staff in operational roles offers cost savings and potential gains in service delivery (Loveday, 2015).

While civilization is one of the major approaches that agencies have implemented to reduce costs, other than anecdotal evidence, evaluations have not been conducted to investigate whether such a program actually reduces costs. Second, a number of researchers have identified that using civilianization as a comprehensive policing strategy raises a number of fundamental questions:

1. To what extent is it possible to substitute civilian employees without loss of service delivery efficiency and effectiveness?
2. Are civilian employees substitutes or complements to officers in organizational service delivery?
3. How elastic* is the demand for these factors in the production of police services?
4. Will a civilization program yield substantial reductions in unit costs of police services? (Gyapong & Gyimah-Brempong, 1988)

Outsourcing, Alliances, and Police Interagency Collaboration

Both outsourcing and collaboration are viable options to reduce police organizational costs and to increase service delivery efficiency and effectiveness. Collaboration with another police agency and outsourcing to an alternate service provider can free agencies from administrative tasks and make resources available, enabling core responsibilities to be accomplished.

Collaboration is often viewed as being more of a strategy than as being a part of a comprehensive organizational resource management method. However, the implementation of both collaboration and outsourcing in parallel could provide budget savings and improve service delivery efficiency and effectiveness.

The outsourcing of a process or output involves the contracting out of the completion of a process or the delivery of an output to a third-party individual or organization. The practice of outsourcing a specific process or the delivery of an output is a common procedure across government agencies and the private industry and is being implemented by a number of police agencies in the United States, the United Kingdom, Canada, Australia, and New Zealand.

Outsourcing has often been described as a process of modernizing an organization and usually comprises of three implementation stages:

---

* Elastic or elasticity is the measurement of how responsive an economic variable is to a change in another.

1. The identification of an easily replicated model of outsourcing
2. The determination of which tasks can be outsourced and whether the task to be outsourced could be outsourced in collaboration with another police agency
3. The ability to be able to strike a balance between local control over procurement and driving best practice from the center (adapted from Loveday & McClory 2007, p. 36)

Outsourcing may take place at a number of different levels within an organization or may include an entire aspect of an agency's outputs. An agency may, for example, contract its SWAT team requirement from a neighboring agency, or it may outsource all of its municipal policing needs from another police agency.

When outsourcing products or services, it is important to ensure that the terms of the contract are flexible. Acceptance of a contract for the supply of goods or services should only be in force for short, but renewable periods and must result in significant operational cost savings. Short-term, renewable contracts will enable an agency to alter the contract to suit at the completion of each contracted period.

The major problem with outsourcing is that while it may offer a reduction in overhead costs, the agency may become a captured consumer (Hirschman, 1970). If an agency is captured then the agency may be totally reliant on the services provided by the outsource contractor or supplier. The imbalance of power has the potential of growing over time in the supplier's favor (Hirschman, 1970) or may even create a monopoly situation in the supplier's favor.

The value of an outsourcing program to an agency is currently unknown. Evaluations of an agency's pre- and post-outsourcing costs have not been conducted, and therefore, it is not known whether outsourcing improves the efficiency of an agency's service delivery. Schafer (2012), however, concluded that it is irrelevant whether outsourcing reduces costs and claimed that what is important is that outsourcing has been adopted by police agencies and that it is just one option to provide services at a lower cost. What it means in the longer term for policing is unknown, but outsourcing signifies that police organizations, their leadership, how they undertake operations, and their traditions and culture are changing.

The collaborative approach is similar in many respects to outsourcing. However, collaboration, as with outsourcing, can take many forms depending on the mutual aims, goals, and objectives of the agencies involved. The multiple forms of collaboration have been described by Loveday and McClory (2007), as being a spectrum. An example of the spectrum of the forms that are made possible by establishing a model of collaboration between agencies is presented in Table 5.2.

The spectrum of collaboration depends upon two strategic drivers or catalysts: local or central. According to Loveday and McClory (2007), locally

Table 5.2 Spectrum of Police Agency Collaboration

Form of Collaboration		Description	Detail	Benefit
Locally driven	No collaboration			
	Mutual support	Limited in scope	Commitment not always tested	No guarantees
	Ad hoc collaboration	One-off venture	Set up to deliver specific benefits	May be subject to a memorandum of understanding
	Lead agency	One lead agency	For a specific task	
	Legally binding	Legal venture	Penalties for breaches	
	Strategic alliance	Can cover several areas	Bottom up, locally driven, long term	Provides platform for further ventures
	Federation	Creation of separate entity		Separate governance and funding
	Voluntary merger	Complete interoperability		
Centrally driven	Centrally coordinated	Central guidance	Incentives to participate	
	Direct sharing	Joint resources or assets		
	Central federation	Creation of separate entity	Centrally driven for greater good	
	Imposed merger	Complete interoperability		

Source: Adapted from Loveday, B., and McClory, J., *Footing the Bill: Reforming the Police Service*, Policy Exchange, London, U.K., 2007, p. 20.

driven collaborations are more likely to result in cost savings. Locally driven agency collaboration and the sharing of services can reduce an agency's operating costs and could, as noted by Kocher (2012), essentially replace the era of the traditional, individual police department for many communities. However, police managers need to examine the distinct advantages and disadvantages offered by each type of collaboration (Kocher, 2012). The advantages and disadvantages of each form of collaboration are presented in Table 5.3.

The implementation of a collaboration program can take either one of two forms. Collaboration can be either implemented in stages or introduced in a single phase. Generally, there are four stages to collaboration, and these have been listed as follows:

1. Mutual support between agencies—this stage carries no formal commitment or guarantee of support.
2. Ad hoc collaboration—this can be on a case-by-case basis, a one-off venture, or a semipermanent arrangement.
3. The creation of a lead agency—responsible for a specific service over a given geographical area.

Table 5.3   **Advantages and Disadvantages of Different Types of Collaboration**

Type of Collaboration	Advantages	Disadvantages
No collaboration Mutual support	Involves minimal risk and limited change, retains established governance.	Risk is randomly distributed; the status quo fails to maximize efficiencies.
Ad hoc collaboration	Can be established to meet a specific need; success can be measured.	New needs to be established, fragile when interests cease to be mutual.
Lead agency	Can be established to meet the responsibility of the lead agency, clear accountability.	Interests may become those of the bigger agency.
Legally binding	Tends to be more enduring in the long term.	Requires legal advice, costly and inflexible.
Strategic alliance	Provides a viable long-term solution.	May inhibit collaboration outside the alliance.
Voluntary federation	Provides a viable long-term solution.	Complex, requires active participation.
Voluntary merger	Achieves full interoperability.	Significant costs and risks.
Centrally coordinated	Able to share good practice and ideas.	No guarantee that forces and authorities will commit.
Directed and sharing Central federation Imposed merger	Action for the greater good.	Limited scope. Erodes accountability.

Source: Author.

4. A strategic alliance between agencies—this offers the best and widest range of benefits. A strategic alliance covers several areas of collaboration between forces, delivering more than an increased capacity for the delivery of services (Loveday & McClory, 2007).

Historically, in both the United States and the United Kingdom, the majority of collaboration agreements have focused on high-end* policing. Collaborative agreements, for example, have usually been made to assist contiguous agencies to respond to a terrorist or a civil disorder incident. However, the use and the scope of collaboration can easily be extended to include the joint procurement of resources or shared support or administrative services. Loveday and McClory (2007) advocated that collaboration, especially strategic alliances, offers immense benefits, such as providing purchasing power and providing the resources necessary for large-scale investigations. However, a major problem is that the majority of police managers do not have the experience necessary to manage large and complicated legal arrangements.

An alternative to collaboration and to outsourcing is public–private partnerships (PPPs). A PPP is still a form of outsourcing and has been defined as "a risk-sharing relationship between the public and private sectors based upon a shared aspiration to bring about a desired public policy outcome" (Loveday & McClory, 2007, p. 34). This arrangement enables large-scale projects to be undertaken, such as the construction of police stations and the delivery of public services by private-sector providers (Loveday & McClory, 2007).

PPP has the potential for reducing operational costs and for improving the efficiency of service delivery by making more officers available for patrol and investigative duties. The benefit is achieved from the outsourcing of administrative and policing or security support roles. A police agency could, for example, contract a private security company to deliver forensic laboratory services, monitor burglar alarms, or fulfill the role of static security guards at the scene of a serious incident. However, each situation is different, and each agency will need to identify which support functions can be outsourced that will result in cost savings.

Alliances and coupling are two forms of collaboration. According to Delone (2009), an alliance can increase an agency's service delivery effectiveness beyond that which a single agency can achieve. An improvement in service delivery is achieved by creating linkages and networks with other

---

* The term "high policing" was introduced into English language police studies by Canadian criminologist Jean-Paul Brodeur in a 1983 article entitled "High Policing and Low Policing: Remarks about the Policing of Political Activities" and refers to a form of intelligence-led policing that serves to protect the national government from internal threats, that is, any policing operations integrated into domestic intelligence gathering, national security, or international security operations for the purpose of protecting government.

law enforcement agencies and organizations with a vested interest (Delone, 2009). Coupling was defined by Delone (2009), as the "connections and inter-dependencies between different agencies" (p. 37). However, the problem with coupling is that the utilization of the concept has not been accepted, and as a result, it has not been used by police agencies (Maguire, 2003).

Mergers, Amalgamations, and Regionalization

There are two principal reasons why agencies consider merging or amalgamating. One reason is to reduce operating costs and the second is to increase sustainability. The fundamental proposition pertains to how police agencies are expected to maintain services at the same level that the community expects, with fewer resources and decreasing levels of funding. There is also the question of how smaller-sized agencies face the challenges of gangs, school violence, and lawsuits (Pennsylvania Governor's Center for Local Government Services, 2012). Police managers need to consider whether merging or amalgamating actually enhances the delivery of services to better serve the community, or whether the provision of services diminishes and becomes anonymous.

The organization of police agencies is often mismatched to the incidence of crime as police agencies are usually organized along geographical lines. However, criminal networks do not operate according to geographical boundaries, and, as a result, are able to take advantage of the opportunity to offend and exploit the disparate organization of police agencies.

There are two major points of contention regarding the regionalization of police agencies. The first is that, in a number of cases, the newly consolidated agency does not provide all of the benefits that were predicted in the original proposal to merge. The second is that the new agency can become centralized and isolated from the community. To clarify any confusion in the planning of any proposed merger in the United States, the New Jersey State Association of Chiefs of Police in 2007 commissioned a report titled "Police Department Regionalization, Consolidation, Merger and Shared Services: Important Considerations for Policy Makers." This document enables the various options to be examined when an agency is considering a regionalization, merging, or amalgamation program.

The New Jersey State Association of Chiefs of Police (2007) identified five elements that should be considered by police agencies during the planning of a proposed merger:

1. What are the core services that are needed by the community in order for it to function properly and effectively?
2. What level of service, for both core and ancillary functions, is needed by the community?

3. What are the specialized services that are actually needed by the community?
4. What functions, even if not entirely critical and necessary to the functioning of the community, should be provided in order to project a certain desired image to residents and visitors?
5. What are the costs involved with each option, and what is the community willing to pay for its police services?

The size that an agency should be, and how it should be structured is one of the most important questions for police administrators (Wood, 2007). However, any discussion relating to an agency's size can lead to an either/or dichotomy, which can suggest that policing should be organized either locally or regionally (Wood, 2007). This phenomenon is similar to that found in the United Kingdom, where the solution to new challenges in the criminal context appeared to be based on increasing the size of police agencies (Loveday, 2008), rather than refining the processes involved in delivering police services.

There is little evidence of any research having been conducted as to the optimal size of a police agency, nor has there been a costs/benefit analysis or any statistical analysis evidence presented in the support of mergers, or not supporting mergers (Loveday, 2008). Recommendations for merging or amalgamating local police agencies are usually based on three underlying and little-examined assertions:

1. Specialization and professionalization are necessary requisites for effective urban law enforcement.
2. Large-sized agencies are necessary for specialization and professionalization.
3. Large-scale police agencies are thought to be more efficient in that they are able to produce the same or higher levels of output at lower costs than small-sized departments (Ostrom, Parks, & Whitaker, 1973, p. 423).

These assertions form the basis for the proponents of police agency mergers to argue that small-sized departments cannot provide the level and type of service needed in complex, urban areas and that they cannot provide services at costs as low as large-sized departments (Ostrom et al., 1973). These claims are intertwined with the economic theory of organizational economies of scale. Smaller-sized police agencies "with lower per capita expenditure levels than larger departments are automatically assumed to be providing inferior services" (Ostrom et al., 1973, p. 423). However, police managers must be careful in assuming that improvements in service delivery effectiveness are made possible just by increasing the size of an agency.

The problem with policing is that it is extremely labor-intensive and increasing the size of an agency in itself may not improve the effectiveness and the efficiency of an agency or reduce costs. In research undertaken by Rutgers University in 2008, it was found that municipalities with between 25,000 and 250,000 were more efficient than smaller- and larger-sized municipalities, but the relationship did not hold for the provision of all police services (McLaughlin, Atherton, & Morrison, 2009). O'Byrne (2001), however, claimed that when agencies implement economies of scale in senior command, research and technology, significant savings may be made.

Early research, which examined economies to scale in policing, generated mixed results. Waltzer (1972), and Chapman, Hirsch, and Sonenblum (1975), for example, found that larger-sized and merged police agencies enjoyed increasing returns to scale, but Ehrlich (1973), Popp and Sebold (1972), and Votey and Philips (1972), using disaggregate police outputs, found decreasing returns to scale in all police outputs.

The findings of earlier research are mixed and have resulted in supporters and nonsupporters of police agency mergers. The problem with the mixed results of the research is compounded by the fact that while one group used disaggregate rather than aggregate information, both groups used the same research methodologies: the Cobb–Douglas function based on an agency producing a single output (Gyimah-Brempong, 1987). The weaknesses in this research is the use of the Cobb–Douglas function, which places restrictions on the production function of an agency, but police agencies produce many services using the same inputs and resources, and this was not accounted for in the analysis (Gyimah-Brempong, 1987).

Later research conducted by Darrough and Heineke (1978) was not able to provide any clarification on the topic. Using a multiproduct translog cost function and data from police agencies in medium-sized cities in the 1970s, Darrough and Heineke found that there were no increasing or decreasing returns to scale in the average police agency. This was despite Darrough and Heineke finding a wide variation in scale economies among the police agencies that were included in the research (cited in Gyimah-Brempong, 1987). Using the same cost function in the Darrough and Heineke research (1978), Gyimah-Brempong (1987) found that police agencies in large-sized cities were the major cause of scale diseconomies. Their findings along with earlier research on economies of scale in police agency size led Gyimah-Brempong (1987) to note that the results and the conclusions from previous studies did not support the argument made by the proponents of consolidation that consolidation improves the organizational scale of economy.

The balancing factor in the discussion of the optimal size of a police agency is that smaller-sized police agencies do not usually have the capacity or the access to the same level of resources as do larger-sized agencies. Noting this fact, Ostrom et al. (1973) claimed that deciding whether a police agency should merge or decentralize is not an either/or question, but agencies of varying sizes that have contiguous or overlapping jurisdictions may be able to make use of the advantages of both small- and large-sized organizations. This means that rather than agencies merging, extant agencies may deliver more efficient and effective police services in large urban areas by sharing services (Ostrom et al., 1973).

Later research supports the findings of Ostrom et al. (1973). In 1978, Ostrom, Parks, and Whitaker examined the provision of government services in 80 metropolitan areas and found extensive interdepartmental communication and coordination of services across a number of units and divisions within police agencies (Ostrom et al., 1978). The researchers argued against police agencies merging and stressed that not all parts of a large organization are effective. They also claimed that the inclination to merge police agencies into one regional agency is based more on conventional wisdom rather than on empirical evidence as to the benefits of such a structure (Lithopoulos & Rigakos, 2005, p. 342).

Whether or not an agency should consider merging with another agency underscores the question—what is the optimal size of an agency? According to McLaughlin et al. (2009), considerable savings can be achieved by rightsizing an agency or its individual services. In the McLaughlin et al. (2009) context, rightsizing is defined as the capability of changing an agency's geographical boundary and creating cost sharing from the establishment of regional forces or intermunicipal agreements. Whether rightsizing and amalgamations reduce costs in the long term is unknown.

According to Loveday (2006a), neither rightsizing nor amalgamations reduce costs. It is not currently possible to show whether the size of a force affects its cost efficiency, spending or performance to any significant degree. There is no clear evidence that an individual police agency's performance (measured by the reduction in the level of crime, or by the public's confidence in the agency) is related to its size, or to the number of police officers, as some smaller-sized agencies perform well, and some large-sized agencies do not perform so well ([Harrad, 2006, p. 26] cited in Loveday, 2006a). If Harrad (2006) is correct, the only method to reduce organizational costs is to reduce both officer and staff numbers.

Regionalization in the United Kingdom

In the United Kingdom, the idea of merging police agencies to improve efficiency is not new (Simper & Weyman-Jones, 2008). In 2005, the UK Home Office devised a plan to regionalize or amalgamate the 43 police forces of England and Wales into 13 police forces. In 2006, the plan was withdrawn by the Home Office as research revealed that the proposed regionalization program may have centralized decision-making, thereby weakening the ability of the police to provide a community-centric service.

Loveday (1995b) argued that at the time of writing, the structure of the English and the Welsh police forces was a product of the 1960s' amalgamations and was based on false management perceptions and not on the needs of the community. Loveday also maintained that amalgamating police forces did not necessarily translate into an improved provision of service or in a more efficient and effective police force.

In 2007, Simper and Weyman-Jones found that there was a range of between 2% and 10% improvement in the technical efficiency of merged police agencies in the United Kingdom (Simper & Weyman-Jones, 2008). However, the researchers stressed that this improvement was only analyzed over the short term and that further long-term improvements may be needed (Simper & Weyman-Jones, 2008).

Simper and Weyman-Jones (1978) claimed that the improvements in technical efficiency in merged police agencies in the United Kingdom arose from the significant variability in the provision of police services as a form of output. This phenomenon occurs because when police agencies merge, the service provided by the better agency becomes a potential target for other member agencies (Simper & Weyman-Jones, 2008). This means that when comparing an agency that has merged with an agency that has not merged, both with similar-sized budgets, resolution rates, and number of crimes reported, the merged agency is able to offer a wider range of services than an agency that has not merged (Simper & Weyman-Jones, 2008).

Simper and Weyman-Jones (1978) also noted that the results of their research not only identified the relative efficiency of a police agency, but that there were also "possible efficiency savings associated with staff resources [of] between 10 and 70 percent after agencies merged" (p. 21). However, the researchers stressed that efficiency gains were independent of the size of the merged agency and that agency size itself does not provide any improvement in efficiency (Simper & Weyman-Jones, 2008).

To date, conflicting research results have been a major problem when determining whether regionalization, amalgamation, or merger is the appropriate strategy for an individual agency. After several decades of research into the amalgamation of police agencies, there has yet to be any systematic, empirical testing of, or comprehensive examinations of police amalgamations (Lithopoulos & Rigakos, 2005). Furthermore, parameters for undertaking an evaluation are distinctively missing from current literature. Identifying assessment parameters would enable an extensive and comprehensive evaluation of any efficiency and effectiveness improvements that may be gained from the introduction of a regionalization program to be made (Lithopoulos & Rigakos, 2005).

Use of Technology

It is difficult to discuss any improvement in the efficiency and effectiveness of policing without recognizing the significant impact that technology has had on practically every facet of policing (Murphy, 2002). In a 2001 survey of Canadian police agencies, more than 83% of respondents stated that their police service had "invested in new communication and information technology in the last five years" (Murphy, 2002, p. 27). However, despite the cost of designing and implementing technology, there has been very little evaluative research of the effect that technology has had on policing and how the use of technology has affected the level of service delivered.

The increasing use of, and the reliance on, technology reflects a strong police and public belief in its capability and its potential to improve the effectiveness and the efficiency of police service delivery. It is believed that the introduction of, and the use of, new technology will improve police crime control efforts and decrease the level of crime.

However, Koper, Lum, and Willis (2014), as a result of their study of three larger-sized U.S. agencies, warned of overreliance on technology. Koper et al. (2014) claimed that the introduction of new technology by a police agency may generate organizational and service demands and create unanticipated complications that could have the potential to undermine any possible gains made in the efficiency and the effectiveness of service delivery. Owing to the absence of research into the link between the introduction of technology and its effect on service delivery, it is unknown as to whether technology improves effectiveness, and if it does, how it does. Nor is it known as to what other effect it has on an agency. The connection between new technology and the different components of a police organization, such as its structure and its service delivery processes, needs to be known (Koper et al., 2014).

Research into technology and the impact that its introduction can have on police organizations are undervalued aspects in understanding the role of policing. The implementation of any new technology alters the processes used and the management of any existing organizational structure. As agencies reorganize or consider the introduction of methods to reduce operating and administrative costs, an understanding of how an agency functions as a system is essential. Police executives, for example, need to know how the proposed implementation of technology affects the hierarchical structure of an agency. As a result of the implementation of technology, in a 2001 Canadian survey, 55% of the respondents identified that "their police service had eliminated some senior ranks and 57 percent said they had decentralized some management functions" (Murphy, 2002, p. 28). Such an approach to reorganizing an agency's management structure will impact the planning and the implementation of a proposed technology replacement program.

Conclusion

There are a large number of areas that police can examine to improve the efficiency and the effectiveness of its service. Examining the structures of police agencies is only one area that may result in an improvement of service delivery. Organizational processes, management methods, the sharing of services, the introduction of new technology, and contracting for services and outsourcing are other areas that can improve an agency's efficiency and service effectiveness.

However, there are two problems when evaluating which strategy or combination of strategies could improve the efficiency or effectiveness of a police agency. Police agencies are not simple or uncomplicated, and as Fijnaut (1999) explained, all agencies are structured in a multipart mode and provide multifaceted services. This means that police should take a high-level perspective when examining potential improvement strategies, as it is unknown how the implementation of a specific strategy will affect other parts of an organization. The second problem is that there has been very little research and evaluation of the strategies used to improve the delivery of service. The lack of research means that it is not known what the impact is of introducing service delivery improvements on police agencies, and this creates a gap in our understanding and knowledge of police organizational theory.

Strategies Employed to Improve Service Delivery in Australia, Canada, England and Wales, New Zealand, and the United States

II

Strategies Employed to Improve Service Delivery in Australia

6

Introduction

The governance of policing in Australia takes place at the state and federal levels. Australia has six state police forces (New South Wales [NSW], Queensland, South Australia, Tasmania, Victoria, and Western Australia), two territory police forces (Northern Territory and Australian Capital Territory), and one federal police force (Australian Federal Police). All of the forces deal with a full range of policing duties from traffic enforcement and Community Policing to major investigations. According to Fleming and Lafferty (2000), prior to the 1980s, Australian police forces were "structured on authoritarian, para-military lines, [and were] regulated through strict organizational rules and legislation" (p. 155). Today, however, although Australian police forces are still organized along paramilitary lines, as are the majority of police forces in western democratic countries, they are among the most adaptive and innovative of all police forces.

The eight Australian forces range in size, jurisdictional area, and population served. Details of each of the eight forces are presented in Table 6.1. Both the Queensland Police and the Western Australia Police have extremely large jurisdictional areas. Queensland is approximately the same size as Alaska, the largest state in the United States, while Western Australia is just over twice the size of Alaska. Western Australia is the world's largest nonfederated jurisdictional area. Three other states, NSW, Northern Territory, and South Australia, are all larger in size than Texas.

This chapter examines the changes and the strategies that have been implemented by Australian police forces and the impact that these changes and strategies have had on Australian policing in recent times. The case study of the New South Wales Police Force (NSWPF) is based on the work of Carrington, Puthucheary, and Rose (1997), and the case study of the Queensland Police Service is based on the research of Fleming and Lafferty (2000) and Hoque, Arends, and Alexander (2004). While there have been differences in the changes borne by the Australian police forces, it appears that the universal principles of public sector organizational change have had an influence on all of the changes made.

Table 6.1   Details of the Eight Australian Police Forces

State Police Force	Number of Sworn Employees	Number of Civilian Employees	Year Formed	Area of Jurisdiction (Miles²)	Population
New South Wales	16,467	3862	1862	312,742	7,303,700
Northern Territory	1,302	297	1911	520,901	229,700
Queensland	11,500	515	1864	667,956	4,537,700
South Australia	5,000	1016	1838	402,903	1,650,600
Tasmania	1,231	404	1899	26,572	503,292
Victoria	14,836	2590	1853	91,749	5,603,100
Western Australia	7,526	1220	1834	1,021,477	2,118,500
Australian Federal Police[a]	4,271	2582	1978	987	373,100

Source: Author.

[a] Includes Australian Capital Territories.

Changes to the Australian Public Service and Police

Australian government agencies and police forces have, since the late 1980s, undergone extensive organizational and service delivery reform, which has resulted in an administrative transformation of policing. The changes came about because the government wanted to cut its operating costs, improve the performance of government agencies, and advance its social outcomes. The government subsequently placed pressure on the Australian Public Service (APS) to improve their management of resources and their service delivery. Agency budgets were capped and cash accounting was replaced with accrual accounting (Armstrong, 1998). The government believed that the internal culture of government departments needed to change and that their efficiency and their performance needed to improve (Fleming & Lafferty, 2000). The government wanted government agencies, including the police to be "more effective within existing resource levels" (Mazerolle, McBroom, & Romboutes, 2011, p. 128).

The Australian Government determined that a "private sector solution to the public sector problem" (Dixon, Kouzmin, & Korac-Kakabadse, 1998, p. 1) was needed and that the public sector would adopt commercial practices. Business principles used in the private sector were introduced to government agencies that enabled them to develop new modes of operation and retain and consolidate the positive aspects of the public sector (Brown, Ryan, & Parker, 2000, p. 207). The major vehicle used to implement business principles in the public sector was New Public Management (NPM). NPM was believed to yield greater economy and efficiency and would raise the standards of the public service.

The introduction of NPM had profound consequences for the management of the Australian police forces. Police forces underwent major restructuring and adopted a corporate culture. Organizational structures were flattened and regionalization and civilianization programs were introduced (Fleming & Scott, 2008; Palmer & Cherney, 2001). Various managerial programs were also introduced, such as strategic planning, performance management, the devolvement and decentralization of managerial responsibility for budgets and business planning to middle-level managers, process reengineering, and, to encourage local accountability, performance-based employment contracts for senior management and executives (Fleming & Scott, 2008; Palmer, 1994; Palmer & Cherney, 2001).

The theory behind the changes was that by using the resources derived from the commercialization of the public sector, both management and service delivery effectiveness would improve. In the Australian context, commercialization was defined as a "process where markets are established for selected public sector goods and services in order to increase competitive pressures on suppliers" (Australian MAB-MIAC, 1992, p. 1). According to Brown et al. (2000), commercialization in this sense was "concerned both with delivering services on a commercial basis to increase efficiency through competitive mechanisms and reorienting budgetary processes and funding regimes to a more commercial focus to achieve cost savings" (p. 207).

Wanna, O'Fairchealliagh, and Weller (1992) claimed that it was debatable whether commercialization was the appropriate philosophy to use when delivering government services. They believed that in commercializing government agencies, commodified and merchandized services and resources result, which occurs when a market price is created for the goods and services provided. This means that a price should be identified for all government goods and services and should include the element, public interest (Brown et al., 2000). However, according to two researchers (Australian MAB-MIAC, 1992; Mellors, 1993), the notions of a public good and public interest remain problematic when adopting market solutions to service provision.* The problem arises because a public good is a service made available to the public, but it may not be in the public's interest for a public agency to provide it.

The purpose of introducing a strategy of commercialization was to create a more efficient and effective public service by adopting private-sector management techniques (Braddon & Foster, 1996). However, debate arose in relation to the ethics of introducing a commercial philosophy into the public service, and the robustness of the accountability structures in the proposed commercial approach was questioned. Furthermore, according to Johnson (1995) and Moss (1997), there was a clear weakness in the proposal if the applicability of commercial principles in the areas of service delivery

---

* Public good—a commodity or service that is provided without profit to all members of a society, either by the government or by a private individual or organization. Public interest—the welfare or well-being of the public.

provision was not contestable. Wanna et al. (1992) noted that any commercialization of public-sector operations could create problems with individual and organizational accountability when management needed to focus on resource allocation and making policy decisions to meet the goals of the government and the public.

Another element that influenced the need for change in the Australian public service in the early 1990s was globalization (Dixon et al., 1998). According to Vickers and Kouzmin (2001), globalization had a profound effect on how Australian public-service agencies were structured, organized, and managed.

The first state to respond to the demands made by globalization was Victoria, which introduced reforms across the entire public sector (Armstrong, 1998). The comprehensive reforms that were introduced in Victoria were in response to the weak condition of the state's finances and included cost-cutting measures, transparency in the allocation of resources, performance indicators, "activity or formula based funding and accrual accounting" (Armstrong, 1998, p. 16). The reforms in Victoria also included the extensive restructuring of agencies, the decentralization of authority, and the flattening of organizational structures. This was to make government departments more flexible, give managers greater autonomy to manage, and make staff members at all levels more accountable for their performance (Armstrong, 1998).

The reforms were supported by the introduction of performance management frameworks, which measured the productivity of the organizations and their personnel. The performance regime for measuring the productivity of an organization comprised "planning for performance, setting performance criteria, reviewing actual performance against plans, rewarding performance and using the information provided in this process to improve competencies" (Armstrong, 1998, p. 20). The performance regime measured the productivity of personnel through the use of performance targets, indicators, and output objectives (Armstrong, 1998).

Victoria, in 1982, was the first state to use performance management for planning, identifying performance measures, and reviewing actual performance against that which was planned (Armstrong, 1998). As part of the Victoria State Government agencies reform program, the Victoria Police eliminated two ranks and regionalized a number of geographical areas (Palmer & Cherney, 2001). The changes were more of a refinement to existing programs and practices, even though much of the change continued in the direction of improving the quality of response to calls for assistance and in other elements of Community Policing (Palmer & Cherney, 2001).

The regionalization program of the Victoria Police devolved responsibility, authority, and control of resources to Area Commanders, reduced geographical command overlap, improved service delivery efficiency, and strengthened accountability. According to Fleming and Lafferty (2000), the Victoria Police replaced strong centralized control and coordination with "local accountability, autonomy, delegation and discretion" (p. 156).

According to Armstrong (1998), the reforms of the Victoria State Government produced greater economy, efficiency, and improved standards of service. Over a four-year period, the state reduced the number of departments to eight and the number of employees by 61,000 people (24%) (Armstrong, 1998). These reforms returned the state budget to surplus and reduced the state debt by one-third (Armstrong,1998).

The first management practices imposed on the police in Australia during this period were strategic planning, performance management, and performance-based employment contracts for senior executives (Palmer, 1994). The responsibility for these new practices, as well as budgeting, was devolved to unit and area managers, and the emphasis changed from the management of police to the achievement of financial targets and operational outcomes.

Following the State of Victoria's lead, both the Queensland Police Service and the NSWPFs introduced elements of NPM. Both forces implemented "flatter managerial structures, decentralised decision-making and doing more with less" (Fleming & Lafferty, 2000, pp. 164–165). The reforms were not only undertaken for financial reasons but were also conducted as a result of the recommendations made by the Commissions of Inquiry (CoI). The reforms proposed by the CoI were introduced in response to the allegations that corruption was endemic in both forces.

Both the Queensland and NSW Police implemented processes that "devolved responsibility, authority and control" to unit and area managers, which replaced extensive organizational centralization (Fleming & Lafferty, 2000, p. 156). These new management processes were designed "to reduce overlap and duplication, improve efficiency and strengthen accountability" (Fleming & Lafferty, 2000, p. 156).

Vickers and Kouzmin (2001) claimed that a major problem with the implementation of these reforms was that they were based on experiences in the manufacturing sector and that the literature had been extrapolated inappropriately and applied to police forces where they were "uncritically embraced by Australian police organizations as the ultimate solution to all managerial problems" (p. 7). McKenna (1996) claimed that the reform strategies were designed to include management practices and procedures "from businesses to public administration to turn government and its associated bureaucracy (in this case, policing) into a business" (p. 210).

There have been significant changes made to police agencies and how policing is delivered in Australia since the police reforms were introduced in the late 1980s, with the most fundamental change having taken place in Victoria, where the community has benefited from the improvement in police response (Palmer & Cherney, 2001).

New South Wales Police Force Case Study

In the early 1990s, the NSW Government implemented a financial framework that was designed to encourage government agencies to become more efficient and effective. To measure the improvement in the service delivery of the agencies, the NSW Treasury used the statistical method data envelopment analysis* (DEA), which will be discussed later. The introduction of the financial framework and the evaluation process reflected the NSW Government's need to improve the financial condition of the state and to continue the program of financial reform, which was being implemented by both the Commonwealth and the state governments. The reforms were mainly contractual and based on an economic approach where the state government entered into an agreement with the NSWPF to purchase the services that would assist in achieving government policy objectives instead of basing the funding of police services on historical budgets or expenditure patterns.

It was envisaged that the implementation of a contractual arrangement would lead to the identification of processes, which would enable the purchaser and the provider roles of the government to be separated. According to Carrington et al. (1997) and Boston (1991), the separation of a government's purchase and provider roles allows a government to make more objective decisions and enables them to identify the most efficient and effective methods for achieving desired economic and social outcomes.

The design and the introduction of a performance measurement system complemented the contractual process and provided an incentive for the NSWPF to deliver a service that was efficient and effective.

Performance indicators provide information that makes police agencies more accountable to governments and can be used as a form of competition, acting as an internal management tool to examine the reasons for poor individual or group performance.

The following three objectives were developed to assess the performance of the NSWPF:

1. To protect, help, and reassure the community—this included a number of effectiveness indicators, such as the number of people admitted to hospital and the number of fatal road crashes, the percentage of vehicles stolen and recovered, and the number of complaints about police actions. There were also a number of efficiency indicators, such as the average running cost of police vehicles per kilometer.

---

* Data envelopment analysis (DEA) is a nonparametric method in operations research and economics for the estimation of production. It is used to empirically measure productive efficiency of decision making units.

2. To prevent crime.
3. To enforce the law.

The assessment of the NSWPF primarily focused on the efficiency of police services and calculated efficiency scores for each patrol using the DEA method. The DEA method provided a single measure of efficiency for each patrol. An efficiency score was awarded to each patrol, which was obtained by comparing the performance of a patrol to that of the best patrols. The efficiency score reflected the performance of a patrol in producing a particular service using an allocated level of inputs.

The results of the DEA suggested that the NSWPF police patrols could, on average, produce the same level of service output using 13.5% less inputs if the NSWPF were to use its inputs more efficiently. The analysis also suggested that if the NSWPF were able to reorganize how patrols were deployed, it would be possible to make a 6% savings in the amount of inputs used. The results also indicated that any difference in the patrol operating environment, that is, the social demographics of a patrol area, did not have a significant influence on the efficiency of the police patrols.

Carrington et al. (1977) cautioned that the results of the analysis should be interpreted with care as the results were only indicative of the technical efficiency of the NSWPF patrols. Carrington et al. were also unsure as to how the quality of a police patrol influenced the quantity of police patrol outputs and signaled that the level of efficiency of the patrols is not a major source of input reduction. This means that for the NSWPF to increase the efficiency of its patrols, the structure of its organization and patrol divisions, and the size of each area to be patrolled, should be examined.

Queensland Police Service Case Study

The Queensland State Government established a Commission of Inquiry (CoI), in 1987, which was chaired by Tony Fitzgerald, QC, following media allegations of criminal activity within Queensland's 6000-strong Police Service (QPS). Upon its completion, the CoI made a number of recommendations in relation to the future of the QPS. The principal recommendation comprised a program of reforms based on contemporary theories of public management. This program included not only police organizational aspects, such as supervision and discipline, but also included aspects of NPM, such as management style and personnel practices.

Since the implementation of the recommendations that were made in the 1988 CoI Report, the QPS has adopted all aspects of NPM. The early reforms, together with the recommendations made by the CoI as a response to policing problems in other Australian states, have been the main catalyst for the strategic change in the QPS. Although the state did not accept the philosophy of public sector reform to the same extent as other Australian states, Hoque et al. (2004) claimed that the continual improvement of the QPS and its organizational strategy provided the foundation for defining the vision and the direction of its operations.

The vision and mission statements that define the purpose of the QPS were presented in its strategic plan. The plan determined that the direction of its service would enhance community safety and security. Guiding principles were also used to specify two high-level outcome objectives: enhance community safety and increase community confidence and satisfaction with police (Queensland Police Service, 2011). The plan was supported by the introduction of accrual accounting and a budgeting process.

The management and the measurement of the QPS outcomes, together with the outcomes to be achieved by other justice sector agencies, made up part of the state's social outcomes, which the state had funded to achieve the overall social outcomes of the federal government. As part of this process, the QPS identified outcome performance indicators that were congruent with the strategic priorities of the state government. The outcome statements were discussed with, and agreed to, by the state and provided the main catalyst for prioritizing the services and products (outputs), which had been funded through the budgeting process. Each outcome had specific performance targets that were consistent with the Queensland State Government's social priorities and were defined in terms of quality, quantity, timeliness, cost, and location. The outputs of the QPS have changed since the 1990s to meet the outcomes specified by each subsequent government. Table 6.2 presents a comparison of the QPS 1999–2000 outputs with the 2011–2012 outputs.

Table 6.2   Comparison of Queensland Police Service Outputs for 1999–2000 and 2011–2012

1999–2000	2011–2012
General duty—proactive, problem-oriented policing	Service: Professional standards and ethical practice
General duty—crime detection, investigation, and prosecution	Service: Personal safety/property security
Preservation of public safety	Service: Traffic policing
Combating major and organized crime	Service: Public order and safety
Traffic policing, speed management, and camera operations	Service delivery support
Ethical standards and public accountability	

Sources: Adapted from Queensland Police Service, *Annual report 1999–2000,* Brisbane, Queensland, Australia, 2000; Queensland Police Service, *Annual report 2011–2012,* Brisbane, Queensland, Australia, 2012.

A service delivery performance framework provided an evaluation process, which was based on QPS outputs that contributed to government outcomes rather than on QPS programs. According to Hoque et al. (2004), this structure shifted the focus from financial compliance to the achievement of clearly defined targets and goals. As a result, the purchaser/provider model of NPM and the performance measurement framework provided a better system for evaluating the organization and augmenting accountability.

The performance measurement structure enabled the QPS to self-monitor its performance in terms of the quantity of specific services and the quality and the effectiveness of the services delivered. This process has meant that the QPS is now able to concentrate on managing its resources to achieve the social outcomes of the Queensland State Government. This was an evolutionary process and meant that the operational aspects of delivering a service would be aligned to organizational outputs from the setting of performance indicators.

As a result of the NPM reforms, the QPS works with the community, has become more customer focused, and attends to the needs of the community more effectively and efficiently.

Conclusion

The Australian police forces have been able to improve their responsiveness and service delivery through the introduction of NPM and organizational reform. The major strength of NPM, in the Australian context, is that it has been capable of incorporating social needs and political influences within the services delivered by police. Brown et al. (2000) reinforced that there had been an improvement in the efficiency and the effectiveness of the service delivered by the police as a result of implementing NPM. Australian police agencies are now focusing on delivering outputs and use a reporting structure that incorporates organizational inputs and outputs and measurable objectives and targets.

Although there were initial concerns regarding the impact that introducing aspects of a commercial approach would have on police organizations, time has shown that adapting a commercial approach to fit a specific environment may improve an organization's service delivery (Brown et al., 2000). Such an approach to improving service delivery can also lead to organizational change and gains in productivity (Brown et al., 2000).

While it was initially believed that NPM may not have been able to fit comfortably with the core activities of police organizations (Vickers & Kouzmin, 2001), that it had a narrow focus of cost reduction and required a significant level of organizational change, its introduction has enhanced the management of resources, the capacity of the police, and the relationship of the police with the community (Brown et al., 2000).

Strategies Employed to Improve Service Delivery in Canada

7

Introduction

The reasons for the reform of the police and government agencies in Canada were the same as the reasons why police and government agencies were reformed in other western nations. State governments in Canada needed to reduce the amount of government spending as they wanted to keep operating within their existing levels of public funding and did not want to increase state taxes. They also attempted to limit the role that the federal government had in the governance of the states.

In the 1990s, state governments implemented policies to justify the reduction in the size and funding of government agencies and the minimizing of their role (Murphy, 2002). The strategies that the state governments used to reduce the cost of government services and to limit the growth of the public service were similar to the strategies that were adopted by many other governments around the world. The strategies that were employed included "private-sector managerial and organizational values and strategies," "greater fiscal accountability, cost efficiency and value for money" (Murphy, 2002, p. 6).

The introduction of strategies to reduce costs and the introduction of an accountability framework that would increase the level of active police governance had a profound impact on the way that police agencies would be managed. Active police governance has been described by Murphy (2002, p. 6) as "greater fiscal and operational accountability, performance expectations, new knowledge and information requirements, business-based planning models, and joint municipal budgeting."

Increasing operating costs, decreasing levels of funding, and political pressure to be more accountable to the public and the government (Murphy, 2002) also changed the way that police agencies in Canada would operate. Agencies had experienced organizational growth and service expansion since the 1980s, but owing to the changes required by state governments, police managers found themselves "confronted with inexorable political demands to find ways to cut costs, increase efficiency, improve productivity and demonstrate what is called value for money" (Murphy, 2002, p. 4). In response to the drive for more efficient delivery of police services, police agencies in Canada implemented a number of change programs such as regionalization and new public management (NPM) and applied private-sector management approaches, strategy development, and business-based planning (Murphy, 2002).

Canadian Police

Policing in Canada is structured similar to that in the United States. Canadian policing is decentralized and comprises 176 agencies across three levels: federal, provincial, and municipal. The number of agencies does not include the 32 First Nation (or tribal in the U.S. context) police agencies.

In 2011, there were more than 69,000 public police officers in Canada that provided service across the federal, provincial, and municipal levels. This number does not include the number of First Nation police officers. Constitutionally, policing is assigned to each province, and most urban areas have been given the authority by the provinces to maintain their own police force. All but three provinces, Newfoundland, Ontario, and Quebec, have contracted out their provincial law enforcement responsibilities to the Royal Canadian Mounted Police (RCMP). The RCMP serves as the local police in a number of smaller municipalities within the seven provinces that it has been contracted to deliver policing services.

The provinces of Newfoundland, Ontario, and Quebec maintain their own provincial police agencies. Within these provinces, smaller-sized municipalities contract police services from the provincial policing authority, while larger-sized municipalities usually maintain their own police agencies.

Although the national structure of Canadian policing is similar to that in the United States, in that it is decentralized and spread across a number of levels, Canada only has a total of 208 police agencies in comparison to the more than 18,000 police agencies in the United States. Table 7.1 presents a summary of the number of public police agencies by province.

Rationalization of Police Agencies and Police Services

Since the early twentieth century, policing in Canada, similar to policing in New Zealand, Australia, and the United Kingdom, has been in a state of transition. State governments in Canada, as in other countries, called into question the effectiveness of the provision of local police services (Cooper & Koop, 2003). Critics claimed that the provinces could provide cheaper local policing services than the Canadian Federal Government or the RCMP and that a provincial structure could provide a "better police service because the provincial government is more responsive to local needs, local culture and local context than the federal government" (Cooper & Koop, 2003, p. 6).

Table 7.1   Number of Canadian Police Agencies by Province

Province	Municipal	First Nation
Federal	9	0
Alberta	10	4
British Colombia	15	1
Manitoba	8	2
New Brunswick	11	4
Newfoundland	1	0
Nova Scotia	13	0
Ontario	55	11
Prince Edward Island	5	0
Quebec	34	9
Saskatchewan	15	1
Total	176	32

Source: Author.

State governments, examining the service delivered by local police services, determined that rationalizing the number of local police agencies would result in considerable savings, by reducing administrative duplication, and the delivery of a more efficient and effective service would result.

Another method used to restrain the cost of providing policing services was the introduction of legislation that set standards for policing (Murphy, 2002). Murphy (2002) claimed that the Canadian provincial governments used the enactment of legislation as a means of controlling policing standards and influencing the direction of policy for the delivery of policing services. As a result of the compliance costs of meeting the standards, small- and medium-sized police agencies found that they needed to amalgamate if they were to meet legislative requirements (Murphy, 2002). This meant that standards that endorsed centralization determined the approach that local police would adopt and caused conflict in the prioritization of service delivery elements (Murphy, 2002).

Police executives responded to the centralized, standardization approach that was imposed on their agencies by changing from the traditional delivery of broad policing services to the provision of a more realistic, but limited, prioritized core service (Murphy, 2002). The most common response by agencies to the changes imposed by government was to simply do less, while a number of agencies eliminated or restricted the delivery of some services (Murphy, 2002). In a survey undertaken by Murphy (2002), 65% of the survey respondents indicated that they had reduced or eliminated a variety of core policing services. To reduce agency costs, survey participants indicated that provincial governments had considered charging citizens or users for police services (Murphy). Murphy's (2002) survey findings implied that more than

70% of the respondents charged a user fee for a range of police services that had previously been supplied free of charge.

Regionalization of Canadian Police Agencies

Regionalization programs have been implemented by provincial, city, and town governments across Canada in an attempt to improve police service delivery and reduce operating costs. The trend has been to construct larger, regional police agencies by merging and amalgamating smaller-sized agencies. Larger-sized police agencies have been viewed as being better than smaller-sized agencies because of the advantages of an economy of scale.

Ontario Province has undertaken the largest number of police agency mergers (Martin, 1997). The largest merger took place in 1957, where 13 police agencies formed one metropolitan department in Toronto (Oppal, 1994). Between 1962 and 1977, 150 police departments merged to form a further 10 regional police agencies (Seagrave, 1997). In 1978, Ontario Province "had ten regional police forces serving more than 50 per cent of the population and 118 municipal forces serving" the balance of the population (Lithopoulos & Rigakos, 2005, p. 340). Amalgamations of agencies in other Canadian provinces followed. In the early 1970s, 29 police agencies were amalgamated to form the Service de Police de la Communauté Urbaine de Montréal, which became responsible for policing 28 municipalities within its geographical jurisdiction (Wood, 2007).

The introduction of regionalization programs in the Ontario Province was based on the recommendations of a 1978 report, which was written by the Ontario Police Commission. The Ontario Police Commission reviewed and compared eight regional and eight municipal police forces in Ontario to evaluate the effectiveness of their service delivery (Lithopoulos & Rigakos, 2005). However, the results are debatable academically, because of the small size of the sample used. "The [Commission's] report contended that regional policing was the most economically and operationally viable form of policing and that regional policing was best suited to deal with law enforcement challenges of the future" (Lithopoulos & Rigakos, 2005, p. 340).

As a result of the number of regionalization programs developed and implemented in the Ontario Province, the state government identified six viewpoints:

1. Regionalizing police services does not result in a loss of community control over police services.
2. The primary opposition to regionalizing police services has come from the political level rather than from the police or the community.

3. Regionalization has the potential to significantly improve the deployment of patrol and investigative resources.
4. There is no movement toward decentralizing police services and returning to preregional policing arrangements.
5. Concerns among municipalities were that there would be a decrease in service levels and a reduced capacity for input into policing, but these concerns have not been realized.
6. Regionalization is supported by municipal mayors and community residents, and there is no indication that either stakeholder group would wish to return to preregionalization arrangements for the delivery of policing services (Vancouver Police Department, 2008).

Lithopoulos and Rigakos (2005) claimed that regionalization programs are favored by larger-sized police agencies and local governments for expansionist reasons. However, concerns about regionalization voiced by smaller-sized jurisdictions appear to researchers as smaller jurisdictions wanting to retain the status quo (den Heyer, 2013a). The concerns of smaller-sized jurisdictions usually pertain to

- Loss of local police control
- Loss of local police agency identity
- Impediments to maintaining the aspects of Community Policing
- Loss of jobs and a range of services
- Excessive establishment costs (Lithopoulos & Rigakos, 2005)

A report completed by Fairweather (1978) did not support the concerns held by smaller-sized jurisdictions. According to Fairweather (1978), there were three arguments used against the regionalization of police agencies: that the new agency's operating costs are higher than the separate agencies, that there is no genuine need for regionalized agencies, and that regionalization has a negative effect on the police–community relationship. The report claimed that there was no difference in patrol coverage or clearance rates in regional or nonregionalized agencies. However, operating costs for regionalized agencies, in aggregate, were 16.7% less than those in nonregionalized agencies (Fairweather, 1978).

In a later study, which examined policing in British Columbia, the majority of respondents favored regionalizing police services based on the view that policing "could be more effective and cost efficient if resources were consolidated and re-organized" (Lithopoulos & Rigakos, 2005, p. 340). However, the study did not include any empirical evidence that supported the view that the regionalization of policing was a more efficient or effective model.

Case Studies of the Regionalization of the Canadian Police

This section presents brief summaries of five Canadian provinces and municipalities that are contemplating regionalization or have implemented extensive police agency regionalization programs.

British Columbia Province

There has been extensive debate relating to the amalgamation and regionalization of police services in British Columbia (British Columbia Chamber of Commerce, 2011). The debate has centered on a number of major issues. The first was the large number of police agencies operating across the province and that each agency was managing investigations differently (British Columbia Chamber of Commerce, 2011). The second issue was that some officers in the smaller-sized agencies lacked adequate training in investigation and intelligence methods (British Columbia Chamber of Commerce, 2011). The third issue to be raised was the increasing cost of delivering police services across the province (British Columbia Chamber of Commerce, 2011).

Supporters of regionalization held the view that amalgamation would solve some of these problems. It was believed that the amalgamation of police agencies in British Columbia would "provide uniformity of enforcement, specialization, better coordination of resources, on-going, in-service training, fewer infrastructures, improved efficiency and the avoidance of duplication" (British Columbia Chamber of Commerce, 2011). However, a number of local mayors were concerned that the regionalization of police services would have an effect on their municipalities. Mayors were particularly concerned about losing local control and that there would be a decline in the provision of police services (Wood, 2007). The mayors were also aware that a major problem in regionalizing police agencies across British Columbia was that the RCMP provided policing services in the rural areas. The RCMP was contracted to provide police services across the province, and regionalizing local police agencies would provide more benefits than if local police agencies were to merge with RCMP detachments.

The British Columbia Provincial Government examined four derivatives of regionalization or regionalization programs of a limited extent:

1. Informal agreements—informal cooperation between two or more police agencies
2. Tiered amalgamation or regionalization—informal agreements that become formalized over time
3. Formal arrangements—the establishment of shared common police systems, for example, centralized 911 or communications systems

4. Rationalization—provides a framework in which informal agreements and a tiered structure of policing become formalized further (Wood, 2007)

Greater Vancouver Region

The topic of police regionalization was first raised in 1924 in a newspaper in Vancouver and has been the subject of debate throughout the Province of British Columbia ever since (Vancouver Police Department, 2008). The debate reached a peak between 1978 and 1994 when eight separate regionalization studies were conducted on police services in British Columbia during this period (Vancouver Police Department, 2008).

In recent years, a number of regionalization programs have been implemented, primarily in the health and transit services (Vancouver Police Department, 2008). Despite the extensive regionalization of police agencies and services in the eastern provinces, to date, there has been no informed public debate as to the various options available for organizing the police agencies in the Greater Vancouver Region (GVR) (Vancouver Police Department, 2008). This has meant that "alternative models of police ser vice delivery that hold considerable promise in increasing the effectiveness and efficiency of the police in the GVR have not been explored" (Vancouver Police Department, 2008, p. 1).

More recently, the GVR recognized that the delivery of police services could be improved across the province and that regionalization could be one option that could be used to achieve this. In addition to regionalization, to improve policing in the province, police agencies needed to demonstrate that their resources were being utilized as effectively and efficiently as possible and that the police were maximizing their organizational, community, regional, and provincial policing capacities (Vancouver Police Department, 2008).

There have been a number of studies that have examined policing in the GVR. The majority of these studies have questioned "whether the current arrangements for the delivery of policing services are cost effective, provide for the effective and efficient deployment of resources, and whether these arrangements actually hinder effective crime prevention and crime response" (Vancouver Police Department, 2008, p. 4). In 1992, the Commission on Policing in British Columbia (Oppal, 1994) noted that the GVR police structure impacted the equity and the consistency of the delivery of policing and investigative services (Vancouver Police Department, 2008).

The GVR is examining various options as to how to improve policing services. In parallel to improving the delivery of services, there are two significant influences impacting criminal offending, which provide the reasons for questioning the rationale for maintaining municipal boundaries as the basis for deploying policing services (Vancouver Police Department, 2008). The first influence, which was identified by the Vancouver Police Department from an analysis of the incidents of crime in the GVR, is that offenders do not offend only in one police jurisdiction but move across municipal boundaries committing crimes in a number of different police jurisdictions (Vancouver Police Department, 2008). The second significant influence relates to the increase in drug- and gang-related violence in the GVR and the challenges that are faced in the handling of the investigation of these top-end offences by disparate, smaller-sized police agencies.

These influences are forcing the GVR to examine how the capabilities and the capacities of police agencies can be improved. The option most frequently referred to is the establishment of a GVR police service (Vancouver Police Department, 2008). The creation of a GVR police service would provide a platform to reduce the duplication of services and administrative overheads and standardize policies and practice. The structure that is currently in place has a number of hidden costs, such as the competition among police agencies for new recruits (Vancouver Police Department, 2008, p. 3).

The proposal for establishing a regional GVR police agency has received strong support. The Vancouver Police Department lists the reasons for the support as follows:

1. A regional police agency would create a regional focus on crime and "provide an enhanced capacity to address crime 'hot spots' across the region."
2. A regional police agency would result in an improved level of communication, standardize policies and practices across a region, improve the ability to rationalize and monitor resource utilization, improve investigative and patrol capacities, reduce duplication of services, and end the competition between police services for recruits, in-service police personnel, and civilians with specialized skills.
3. A regional police agency would benefit the community financially and would provide career development for police officers.
4. Regionalization would enhance police–community relations.
5. At a practical level, regionalization has been identified as being able to provide
   a. Better equipment
   b. More staffing
   c. The ability to deploy and support specialty squads and maintain an interface between specialty squads and the service as a whole (something that is not generally possible with integrated, provincial level units)
   d. The ability to back fill positions

e. The ability to move people and expertise across the region in a seamless manner

f. The ability to supplement staffing levels in one district from another, should levels fall below the mandated staffing minimums (Vancouver Police Department, 2008)

There have also been a number of arguments opposing the establishment of a regional GVR police agency. The reasons for the opposition are as follows:

1. The initial costs of the new agency. Costs could include the cost of changing the uniform of officers, changing the color of the vehicles, and the cancellation of contracts or leases on buildings.
2. Decline in service levels.
3. Personnel issues, such as staff redundancies, the relocation of staff, and the qualifications needed for specific positions.
4. Domination by the largest police agency.
5. How effective the service delivered by the new agency will be.
6. The loss of control by local politicians (Vancouver Police Department, 2008).

However, before a regionalization program can be developed and implemented, the problems with the current GVR police structure would need to be addressed. The Vancouver Police Department has acknowledged the following problems with the current GVR police structure:

1. That the RCMP is contracted to deliver services in some, but not all of the municipalities
2. The capability of police agencies to develop and coordinate comprehensive crime prevention and crime reduction strategies
3. The capability of police agencies to develop and coordinate the effective use of Problem-Oriented Policing, intelligence-led policing, and initiatives to address crime hot spots, chronic offenders, and transnational crimes such as human trafficking
4. Challenges for police agencies in case investigation, information and intelligence sharing, and the continuity of collaborative investigations
5. The provision of unequal policing services to taxpayers
6. The coordination of regional deployment in the event of a major incident or natural disaster (Vancouver Police Department, 2008)

A major problem for GVR policy and decision-makers is the absence of any empirical analysis and documentation that either supports or refutes the benefits of establishing a regional police agency. According to the Vancouver

Police Department (2008), "to date, there have been no systemic evaluations of the impact of regionalization on costs, [or] the effectiveness and efficiency of service delivery" (p. 5). Furthermore, "nor have controlled before and after studies been conducted that would facilitate a comparison of costs and policing outcomes prior to, and following regionalization been conducted" (Vancouver Police Department, 2008, p. 5).

Ontario Province

Following its successful election in 1995, the Ontario Conservative Government commenced an extensive municipal reform program (Kushner & Siegel, 2005b). The program was based on achieving two goals: increasing the efficiency of its service delivery and providing "high-quality services at the lowest possible cost" (Kushner & Siegel, 2005b, pp. 73–74). The amalgamation or regionalization of municipalities and police agencies was proposed and was to form a part of the reform program. However, the proposed program created considerable debate, with much of the debate focusing on whether the proposed regionalization program would be more cost-effective than the existing structure. The discussion was based on a number of historical regionalization studies, but the studies had generally focused on the change in the level of expenditure without considering the change in the quantity or the quality of services delivered (Kushner & Siegel, 2005b). This posed a problem when analyzing the effectiveness of previous regionalization programs.

In 2004, Kushner and Siegel (2005a) analyzed the effectiveness of regionalization by comparing the 1999 expenditures of three regionalized municipalities with their 1996 expenditures as constituent municipalities. The review focused on the "two years prior to and two or three years after the amalgamation in order to eliminate one-time effects of the amalgamation and to examine more normal years" (Kushner & Siegel, 2005a, pp. 252–253).

The research found that the predicted economies to scale and the savings that were to be made from regionalization did not occur, and instead, there were large cost increases (Kushner & Siegel, 2005a). The researchers also signaled that the relative size of the municipalities that formed the amalgamation could "impact on the efficiencies generated by the amalgamation" (Kushner & Siegel, 2005a, p. 266). Kushner and Siegel (2005b) summarized the findings of their examination of the three regionalization projects as, that from the public's perception of the quality of service, not much had happened. There were clearly pockets of dissatisfaction, but most residents did not see a "significant change in the quality of services" (p. 93).

The philosophical problem with amalgamations is that they are viewed as being either black or white without any middle road (Kushner & Siegel, 2005a). Supporters view all amalgamations as beneficial and opponents view all amalgamations as not being cost-effective (Kushner & Siegel, 2005a). However, a more balanced perspective "would suggest that all amalgamations are not the same; different amalgamations are likely to produce different results" (Kushner & Siegel, 2005a, p. 266). Kushner and Siegel (2005a) also maintained that amalgamations of small communities "can generate savings, but, in other cases, there are no savings" (p. 266). The weakness with this finding is that Kushner and Siegel do not define the size of small communities, nor do they identify the aggregate size of an amalgamation when the savings start to decrease.

Halifax City

On April 1, 1996, Halifax amalgamated with the contiguous local governments of Dartmouth and Bedford and formed the Halifax Regional Police Department. During the amalgamation, the three departments integrated to deliver police services to the municipalities (McDavid, 2008).

The Halifax amalgamation was expected to improve service levels and make cost savings (McDavid, 2008). However, claims were made that the level of service did not improve and nor were any savings made. Bish (2001) asserted that the expected benefits of the amalgamation did not materialize, and any "predictions of cost-savings, improved services, and improved governance have not been corroborated by the research" (McDavid, 2008, p. 541). In fact, McDavid (2008) concluded that "research on the impacts of amalgamating police departments tends to support the conclusion that costs increase, and, where they do not, service levels are reduced as the numbers of sworn officers are reduced" (p. 542).

Proponents of the Halifax amalgamation disputed the results of the research and argued that merging the three police services would produce economies of scale. However, research on the economies of scale conducted by McDavid (2008) tended to support the finding that as the size of police departments increases, their "unit costs [also] tend to increase" (p. 542). This means that there are negative or diseconomies of scale in police agency amalgamations. Koepsell and Girard (1979) supported this view. In their research of 34 U.S. police agencies that took part in amalgamation projects, they concluded:

> that consolidation rarely reduces the cost of police service in terms of actual dollars. Consolidation may provide for more law enforcement service per dollar than could have been provided under the individual police services but the actual dollar cost of policing in these amalgamated areas is higher than that of the independent police agencies prior to amalgamation.
>
> **Cited in McDavid (2008, p. 542)**

The lack of research into police agency amalgamations is problematic. The absence of multiple-year before and after research has meant that the establishment costs and the economies of scale cannot be analyzed. McDavid (2008), for example, argued that "there does not appear to be any substantial economies in the production of police services overall," but then stated that there "may be scale economies in the production of support services" (p. 544). These comments are contradictory and neither statement can be proven to be either correct or incorrect, which allows the debate to continue. An analysis of the costs and the benefits of the establishment of the Halifax Regional Police Department also appear to be contradictory. According to McDavid (2008), the "amalgamation in the Halifax region is associated with higher costs (in real-dollar terms), lower numbers of sworn officers, lower service levels, no real change in crime rates, and higher workloads for sworn officers" (p. 562). However, in the Interim Report of the Municipal Reform Commissioner Halifax County, savings were identified as $800,000 per year postamalgamation (McDavid, 2008).

Conclusion

The policing environment is undergoing change, and policing in Canada is no exception. The delivery of police services was affected not only by the 2007 worldwide fiscal crisis but also by the subsequent decreases in government funding and the philosophy of limiting the size of government agencies.

The major approaches adopted by Canadian police agencies in response to the changes in the environment have been the implementation of market or private-sector service values and the merging of agencies to improve service delivery efficiency and effectiveness (Murphy, 2002). The merging of agencies to improve service delivery has created debate within local government and police agencies. While a number of provinces are more positive about establishing regionalization programs than others, Canada has merged more police agencies than any other western country.

Strategies Employed to Improve Service Delivery in England and Wales

8

Introduction

While academics have written extensively about policing in the United States, policing in the England and Wales has also been of extensive research interest. The large amount of research conducted makes it difficult to establish whether the police forces in the United Kingdom have implemented more change management projects than those in New Zealand, Canada, the United States, and Australia. Since the mid-1980s, police forces in England and Wales have undergone significant change and have implemented a number of different management process and performance measurement frameworks, all in the name of increasing police service delivery efficiency and effectiveness.

The interest taken in whether the British police were performing effectively was a result of the perception that they accounted for an increasing share of public expenditure while the level of recorded crime was increasing (Cope, Leishman, & Starie 1997). The first document that discussed improving police service delivery in the United Kingdom was the 1983 Home Office Circular 114/83 Efficiency, Effectiveness and Economy. O'Byrne (2001) claimed that the document was probably one of the best guides produced by the Home Office and that it explained in detail how the English police forces were to achieve the three Es: efficiency, effectiveness, and economy. At about the same time that the report was written, Her Majesty's Inspectorate of the Constabulary was advocating the notion of policing by objectives (O'Byrne, 2001). This led to the government initiating a number of police reforms, primarily based upon the principles of new public management (NPM). The following four elements also contributed to the decision that was made to reform the police:

1. Inquiry into police responsibilities and rewards (known as the Sheehy Inquiry)
2. The development of the White Paper on Police Reform (completed by the Home Office in 1993)
3. The introduction of the Police and Magistrates' Courts Act 1994
4. The Home Office Review of Police Core and Ancillary Tasks (known as the Posen Inquiry) (Cope et al., 1997)

However, the reform plans of the government were only partially implemented in the 1990s, as a number of programs and initiatives were dropped or weakened because of resistance by police and parliament (Leishman, Cope, & Starie, 1995).

In June 1993, proposals for a future structure for the police forces in England and Wales were released in a report entitled "Police Reform: A Police Service for the Twenty-First Century" (Loveday, 1995a). The report stated that the reason for the number of police forces was the result of historical accident and the arbitrary merging of police forces over the past 100 years. The government doubted whether the 43 police forces in England and Wales were an effective use of resources and argued that the functions carried out by specialist squads and headquarters staff were duplicated (Loveday, 1995a). The implementation of the recommendations documented in the report was delayed owing to a barrage of protest (Loveday, 1995a), from both the police and the public.

During the period 1993–2012, the government, the Home Office, and Her Majesty's Inspectorate of Constabulary released a large number of reports that were related to improving the delivery of police services. Two of the Her Majesty's Inspectorate of Constabulary reports attempted to create the conditions for a more rationalized approach to delivering effective and efficient police services (Rogers & Gravelle, 2012). The first of these reports, "Closing the Gaps," was released in 2005. This report documented a review of the structure of the police in England and Wales to determine its fitness for purpose. The second report, called the Comprehensive Spending Review, was released in early 2011 and discussed the preparedness of the forces and the authorities across England and Wales to make cost savings over the following four years (Her Majesty's Inspectorate of Constabulary, 2011).

The number of reports released during the 1993–2012 period was unprecedented (Rogers & Gravelle, 2012), and while British policing had been shaped by earlier cycles of reform (Reiner, 2010; Savage, 2007), the government appeared to want to implement more fundamental changes to policing. The number of government reports documented signaled that there was a need for radical reform, system redesign, and organizational transformation (Her Majesty's Inspectorate of Constabulary, 2010; Home Office, 2010). The release of the large number of reports, together with a reduction in government spending and the introduction of austerity measures, contributed to the most significant transformational change that the British police had experienced since the creation of the force (Orde, 2012).

Brief History of Police Reform in England and Wales

Policing in the United Kingdom, until the early 1960s, was structured and funded locally and focused principally on local crime and disorder

(Association of Chief Police Officers, 2008). During this period, it was believed that there was a relationship between the size and the efficiency of a police force and that local forces were more efficient than larger, regional forces. As a result of this belief, forces were more inclined to collaborate rather than to contemplate the possibility of amalgamating. The failure of the police to respond to changes and to the increasing liberalization of society resulted in the government establishing a Royal Commission in 1962. The Royal Commission recommended that local city and borough police forces merge, as it was thought that this would improve efficiency and effectiveness (Association of Police Officers, 2008). It was also thought that a force of 500 officers would be the most efficient size (O'Byrne, 2001).

By 1974, in response to the Royal Commission recommendations, a number of local police forces merged, which resulted in the formation of 43 forces throughout England and Wales. At the same time, some local governments were reorganized into a number of large metropolitan authorities (O'Byrne, 2001). However, in 1979, in response to the increasing cost of delivering police services, an increase in the fear of crime and rising crime rates, the newly elected Conservative Government concluded that there was a need for further police reform (Drake & Simper, 2000).

In the late 1980s, a review of the British police service was undertaken by Sir Patrick Sheehy because the government thought that the police service had not fully implemented a number of earlier government modernization programs, which had been designed to increase efficiency. The review recommended that the police change from a public to a business-oriented organization and that organizational efficiency targets should be discussed and agreed upon by local police authorities (Drake & Simper, 2000).

Efficiency became the primary focus over the following years. Efficiency had initially been perceived as reacting as quickly as possible to an incident and by establishing centralized communications rooms and computer systems (Association of Chief Police Officers, 2008). How police forces were structured or organized was not deemed to be a factor in their level of efficiency. However, the drive for efficient service delivery intensified during the early 1990s with an increase in focus on modernizing organizational systems and procedures, which included NPM and Policing by Objectives (Association of Chief Police Officers, 2008). These changes, according to Sullivan (1998), led to the "managerialism" of policing of which Drake and Simper (2000) described as being the adoption of private-sector values.

Structure and Size of the Police Service in England and Wales

Prior to April 1, 2013, the police service in the United Kingdom comprised 51 separate forces that were geographically spread across England, Wales, and Scotland. On April 1, 2013, Scotland's eight local police forces merged to become one national police service, reducing the number of forces throughout the United Kingdom to 43. O'Byrne (2001) claimed that the structure of the UK police service was an accident of history and was "not underpinned by any logic in terms of size, complexity, or political congruence" (p. 146).

Five types of forces make up the UK police service:

1. Forces that are based on large conurbations or groups of conurbations, for example, Greater Manchester and West Midlands
2. Forces that incorporate more than two counties, for example, Thames Valley and West Mercia
3. Joint authorities of two counties, for example, East and West Sussex and Devon and Cornwall
4. Larger-sized forces based on a single county, for example, Kent, Hampshire, and Essex
5. Smaller-sized forces based on a single county, for example, Warwickshire, Northamptonshire, and Derbyshire (O'Byrne, 2001)

The government commissioned an investigation into the delivery of police services that was undertaken by the Home Office and resulted in the publication of the Green and White Papers. The papers questioned the need for the high number of police forces and whether the structure was appropriate to meet current and future policing needs (Home Office, 2004). The paper also noted that the performance and the efficiency of a police agency did not have any relation to its size (Godfrey, 2007). As a result of the reference made by the paper, Her Majesty's Inspectorate of Constabulary sought to demonstrate that only forces with more than 4000 officers could meet the performance and efficiency standards set by the Home Office and would be able to deliver the full range of police services (Godfrey, 2007). Research undertaken by Loughborough University supported the proposed minimum figure for an efficient police force, but their research indicated that the optimum size was between 1500 and 4500 officers (O'Byrne, 2001). However, this research was not helpful in determining the optimum size that a police force should be because the range was too wide and the figures were derived from the analysis of one variable: crime clear-up rates (O'Byrne, 2001).

In the late 1990s, Her Majesty's Inspectorate of Constabulary suggested that the optimal size for a police force should be 3500. However, O'Byrne (2001) argued that the costs used in the analysis were crude, were not comparable across the forces, and were not particularly good indictors of an agency's overall efficiency or cost-effectiveness. Loveday (2006c) claimed that basing the size of a force on establishment figures fails to take into account the functional needs of an organization or the community involved.

The 1998 report of Her Majesty's Inspectorate of Constabulary, which determined the minimum number of officers needed for force efficiency and effectiveness, produced extensive criticism. The figure used was, however, arbitrary and was not based on an analysis, or on any research, nor did it take into account actual local policing issues and risks (Godfrey, 2007). It was also alleged that the figure "had been settled on in order to justify a wholesale reorganization" as only 7 of the 43 forces in England and Wales had more than this number of officers (Godfrey, 2007, pp. 57–58).

The recommendations made in the White Paper were not implemented owing to the criticism received and because the government was not able to convince the public of the benefits of merging police forces. The public was also confused with the term "abstraction" (Godfrey, 2007, p. 64). Abstraction is a term that is defined as when officers are taken away from their local patrol area to assist with major incidents or investigations. The term was used by supporters of the government's merger proposals to argue that abstractions would not take place if police forces merged, as the forces would be larger and staff would be more efficiently deployed (Godfrey, 2007).

The government also realized that the debate regarding the structure of the police forces did not only relate to technical issues but went to the heart of the relationship between the police and the community (Godfrey, 2007). It also became apparent to the government that any restructuring of local government agencies needed to be integrated and involves not only the police but all local agencies (Godfrey, 2007).

Although the optimal size of a force disappeared from the debate regarding the improvement of police effectiveness, the topic of force mergers did not. The problem with debating the effectiveness of police structures is that there is no research to support either side of the argument, nor is there an ideal organizational model that satisfies the factors of organizational size and complexity or that corresponds with the existing political framework. O'Byrne (2001) determined that it was impossible to increase the effectiveness of the police service if it remained as 43 separate police forces and that larger-sized forces would ensure a varied and rewarding career for officers, with direct entry at senior officer level, and that it would have the capability to deal with a diversified workforce.

The merging of police forces, particularly at the regional level, appeared to be a logical choice to Lewis (1976), who favored the establishment of a regionalized structure with a national force accountable to the Home Office and to the government. Lewis (1976) also maintained that the establishment of a national police force would not remove police from the community because officers work from a local station. However, Loveday (2006c) noted that previous research indicated that as police forces become larger, the distance between the police and the community grows wider.

To quieten the debate regarding the optimal size of a police force and mergers, in the mid-1990s, the government developed the concept of a primary operational police unit, which was referred to as a Basic Command Unit (BCU). Each BCU comprised between 150 and 200 officers (O'Byrne, 2001) and was a two-tiered system designed to replace police divisions and subdivisions. BCUs were to be the future building blocks of police forces (Loveday, 2006c) and were to be self-sufficient and capable of providing administrative and operational support and conducting specialist investigations (O'Byrne, 2001). BCUs were designed to provide a basis for amalgamating local forces and would thereby result in a reduction in the number of forces. After a large number of the BCUs were established across the country, the question of the optimal size of a BCU was raised, as a number of BCUs had been established, which comprised more than 400 officers and at least one force had a BCU with more than 1000 officers (O'Byrne, 2001).

Larger-sized BCUs were viewed as being unsustainable over time, owing to external political demands and from the need to expand the internal span of control to manage the large numbers of officers (Loveday, 2006c). Even if BCUs were larger in size and required a tailored management structure, Loveday (2006c) claimed that they provided the best platform for improving both community involvement in policing and improving the delivery of services, especially community safety strategies.

What was significant at that time was how quickly police managers disagreed as to the ideal number of officers in a BCU (O'Byrne, 2001). This created an anomaly in local command structures and created a challenge for senior BCU officers to engage with the community (Loveday, 2006c). The growth in the size of the BCUs extended the management hierarchy and created problems for the Central Force Headquarters to delegate to a BCU commander (Loveday, 2007).

A limiting factor in the understanding of the performance of BCUs is due to the measures that were developed by the Home Office to assess their performance. These measures were used to standardize BCU processes around the country and did not take account of local operational priorities (Loveday, 2006c), and as a result, made it difficult to measure their performance.

Efficiency and Effectiveness of Police Service

Since the early 1980s, the efficient and effective delivery of police services has been an important component in the reform of English and Welsh forces. The first official document that discussed improving police service delivery was the 1983 Home Office Circular 114/83 Efficiency, Effectiveness and Economy. The release of the Home Office Circular coincided with the changes in the management of government departments, which was introduced by the Thatcher Government in the early 1980s. This period of change in police management culminated in the release of the Sheehy Report in 1993.

The Sheehy Report was primarily a review of police responsibilities and human resource management and made recommendations as to how the police services could be improved and how service delivery could be made more effective. The report recommended that police management take a more business-oriented approach and that performance measures should be developed with an input from the community (known as key performance indicators [KPIs]) (Drake & Simper, 2004). The report also created the environment for increasing the civilianization of the police service (Drake & Simper, 2004).

The implementation of the 1990s' civilianization program was designed to lead to an improvement in the efficiency and the effectiveness of police service (Drake & Simper, 2004). The civilianization program resulted from the 1998 release of a Her Majesty's Inspectorate of Constabulary report called "What Price Policing? A Study of Efficiency and Value for Money in the Police Service." The report reviewed the employment of civilian staff across the service in 1995 and found that civilian staff represented approximately 30% of the total number of staff employed (Her Majesty's Inspectorate of Constabulary, 1998). The report argued that the differentiation of officer and civilian roles was a redundant concept and deemed that it would be more appropriate to shift the focus from trying to establish the cost of policing to the actual cost of delivering a service (Her Majesty's Inspectorate of Constabulary, 1998).

According to Her Majesty's Inspectorate of Constabulary (2004), a major problem with the civilianization of police was that the forces had not made any attempt to monitor the impact of the strategy. There had been little, if any monitoring of the release of officers to operational duties once they had been replaced by a civilian member (Her Majesty's Inspectorate of Constabulary, 2004). Police were unable to present the benefits of civilianizing roles and, according to Loveday (2006c), would not be able to stop individual roles or positions from reverting back to being nonoperational. The failure of the police to monitor the increase in the number of civilian positions was significant, and the report emphasized that the police did not know whether civilianization increased the number of officers available for patrol or whether it improved the efficiency or effectiveness of service delivery (Her Majesty's Inspectorate of Constabulary, 2004).

The 1998 Her Majesty's Inspectorate of Constabulary report encompassed a second evaluation element: the policy of efficiency and value for money (VFM). The concept of VFM was defined as "getting the most from (often limited) resources—from each pound spent—closely interwoven, therefore with the concepts of economy, efficiency and effectiveness" (Her Majesty's Inspectorate of Constabulary, 1998, p. 6). The proposal for VFM was based on a thematic inspection of police forces and included the following objectives:

- Revisit the 1995 thematic inspection *Obtaining Value for Money in the Police Service* and assess the response of forces.
- Identify VFM best practice.
- Review procurement practices.
- Examine the methods used to cost police activity and develop costed policing plans.
- Provide assistance to forces to construct a VFM infrastructure that demonstrates and delivers future benefits (Her Majesty's Inspectorate of Constabulary, 1998).

The police had benefited from a significant increase in funding, but most of the increase had been absorbed by personnel costs. Staffing levels had increased by approximately 10% over the past 10 years (Her Majesty's Inspectorate of Constabulary, 1998). Demand for police services had, however, increased by 2%, and 999 calls had increased by 38% between 1993 and 1996 (Her Majesty's Inspectorate of Constabulary, 1998).

Two recommendations that were made in the report, that when implemented, would improve the efficiency of police. The first was to purchase products and services regionally or nationally in an effort to reduce costs. Attempts had been made previously to reduce purchasing costs but further collaboration was needed (Her Majesty's Inspectorate of Constabulary, 1998). The second recommendation that was made in the report was for the police to demonstrate VFM. To be able to demonstrate VFM, forces needed to be able to provide "clear links between inputs and associated outputs and outcomes" (Her Majesty's Inspectorate of Constabulary, 1998, p. 3). However, this was difficult owing to the complexity and the wide range of police services provided and the lack of availability of managerial and financial information (Her Majesty's Inspectorate of Constabulary, 1998).

Determining VFM is difficult, as VFM means different things to different people, and because its meaning has not been defined, it has been associated with the concepts of economy, efficiency, and effectiveness. The philosophy of VFM drove the debate of police reform in late 1990s and is now being used in the current discussions on austerity policing (Rogers & Gravelle, 2012).

Difficulty of Merging Police Services

One of the major problems with merging or amalgamating police forces is deciding upon the criteria on which a merger should be made (Loveday, 2006c). Merging police forces in the United Kingdom has usually been based on a number of officers, which Loveday (2006c) claims are "below which forces are not felt to be sustainable" (p. 331). O'Byrne (2001) argued that the officer staffing level is difficult to substantiate in real terms and is usually based on individual judgment.

As discussed earlier, the UK Government released two papers, one in 2003 and the second in 2004, which commented on the high number of police forces in existence and questioned whether the national structure that was in place was appropriate. In 2006 however, the government changed its policy of regional police mergers to one of collaboration between forces (Loveday, 2007). At the same time, the Home Office introduced a new strategy called Workforce Modernization, which recommended changes be made as to how officers are employed and to their working conditions (Home Office, 2006).

According to Loveday (2007), the change in government policy was appropriate because the creation of the 12 regional forces would have created the appearance of reform, rather than an actual reform being undertaken. Loveday (2006b) claimed that while there was a need for police service reform, effective delivery of police services could be achieved without moving to the regionalization of forces. The reform referred to, however, related specifically "to the internal management structure [and personnel practices] within the police service" (Loveday, 2007, p. 5). Further research was needed to examine the management structures and the delegation of budgets determine the ideal size of a BCU and an effective span of control, which would lead to an improvement in police service delivery (Loveday, 2007).

The reversal by the government on the policy of police force mergers was supported by public opinion polls. Opinion polls conducted in 2006 determined that the majority of the public were opposed to the merging of police forces. The results of the opinion polls revealed that the opposition grew when members of the public found that their local police were to be included in a proposed merger (Loveday, 2006b).

Five Reports That Have Examined Police Effectiveness

This section discusses five reports that have examined specific aspects of police service delivery. The reports have been recognized as providing the foundation for the future structure and direction of policing in the United Kingdom. Four of the reports were completed by government agencies, the Home Office and Her Majesty's Inspectorate of Constabulary, and one was completed by a not-for-profit research agency.

Her Majesty's Inspectorate of Constabulary (2004) Modernizing the Police Service: A Thematic Inspection of Workforce Modernization—The Role, Management, and Development of Police Staff in the Police Service of England and Wales

The Workforce Modernization program was introduced across the government service to improve efficiency and the overall capability (Loveday, 2008). Her Majesty's Inspectorate of Constabulary (2004) claimed that the 43 force configuration did not provide VFM and offered little to assist in reducing crime in urban or rural areas. This claim was based on the fear of crime that was held by the public and the difficulty that forces had in delivering visible policing in communities (Loveday, 2008).

The report claimed that one of the reasons why forces had difficulty in providing a visible uniformed police presence was owing to the increase in the number of hierarchical ranks and the number of support positions (Loveday, 2008). The increase in hierarchical ranks and the number of support positions led to an increase in the number of officers undertaking administrative rather than enforcement roles. These problems were exacerbated by a lack of effective management at the BCU level and the methods used by many of the police forces for deploying police staff (Loveday, 2008). External issues also compounded the problem. The introduction of government legislation led to an increase in the demand for policing services, which resulted in an increase in police bureaucracy (Loveday, 2008).

The report concluded with 28 detailed recommendations, which would ensure that the police would adopt a strategic and planned approach to establishing the optimum mix of staff and skills, which would be required to deliver policing into the future (Her Majesty's Inspectorate of Constabulary, 2004).

Her Majesty's Inspectorate of Constabulary (2005) Closing the Gap: A Review of the "Fitness for Purpose" of the Current Structure of Policing in England and Wales

This report presented an analysis of the key issues pertaining to the capability and capacity of police protective services, the economics of policing, and the risk of organized crime. The report concluded that while the BCU arrangements and neighborhood policing provided a solid local platform for the future, the "30 year old, 43 force structure of widely different sizes, and capabilities does not" (p. 1). While the report did not focus solely on organizational structure, it did include an evaluation of possible options that would secure budget savings.

In order to evaluate the environment that the police were operating in and the capability of the police service, the report sought to answer two fundamental questions:

1. Does the current structure of policing support the efficient and affordable provision of protective services and support services?
2. Are there indications of how changes in that structure could provide a more efficient basis for service provision? (p. 44)

The report was premised on a future policing environment that would be characterized by

- Widespread, enterprising, organized criminality, proliferating international terrorism and domestic extremism
- A premium on intelligence, expertise, and smart use of capacity
- The public's concern of risk and an intrusive media
- Increasing volumes of crime
- Focus on police performance
- Complex, volatile threats to individuals, neighborhoods, and businesses

Owing to the proliferation of violent and complex crime, the police needed to develop their capacity and examine the management structures and the organizational configurations that were in place at the BCU level. Realigning their structures and the organizational configuration would place demands on leadership, oversight, and support.

The report found that larger-sized forces were more "likely to have much greater capability and resilience whilst smaller forces, in many cases, found it hard to provide the services to an acceptable standard" (p. 2). Police forces with more than 4000 officers, or 6000 staff, met the thematic audit measures and demonstrated better reactive capability than smaller-sized forces.

The report acknowledged that while there had not been any force mergers since 1974, a number of challenges and threats facing the police were on the increase and that the 43 force structure, which was in place at that time, was deemed to be "no longer fit for purpose" (p. 11). It was also determined that the situation was likely to deteriorate and that the costs and the level of professional sophistication needed to provide adequate standards of protective services would become harder for smaller-sized forces to deliver.

The report claimed that force mergers could provide a range of efficiencies and could save £70 million annually. It also noted that "in creating a structure that is fit for purpose the overall goal should be the creation of organizations that are large enough to provide a full suite of sustainable services, yet still small enough to be able to relate to local communities" (p. 8). The report outlined the main design considerations when combining forces as follows:

- Size—the minimum size of a force should be over 4000 police officers and should be designed for resilience and spare capacity.
- Mix of capability—any structural change should take into account the capability of the forces that could be amalgamated.
- Criminal markets—there is a need to understand the underlying criminal markets and context in which any new entity is to operate.
- Geography—pragmatism is needed in relation to the scale and demography in any proposal for change.
- Risk—reduce any risk by considering the current capability and the proposed consolidation to generate new organizational service delivery benefits.
- Coterminosity—consider established political and partners' boundaries.
- Identity—keeping the focus of local public perception in mind, the historical and natural boundaries should be maximized (p. 8).

Any proposed service arrangement must take account of the following:

1. Configuration—the combination of structural, processes, and relationship developments that enable affordable protective services to flourish without undermining the existing strengths of local policing and local forces
2. Structure
3. Processes
   a. Enhancement of the collection, analysis, and use of intelligence to enable better focus of resources on countering terrorism, serious, and organized crime
   b. Development of a performance framework that acknowledges the importance of readiness to protect the public as well as control crime
   c. A comparative approach to efficiency that actively measures the allocation and impact of police resources and promotes workforce modernization
4. Relationships (p. 9)

The report recommended four structural options that would improve the protective services and the provision of VFM:

1. Collaboration
2. Strategic forces structure

3. Federal structure
4. Lead force/lead regional force (pp. 9–11)

The report acknowledged that the first two options may not provide an enduring solution as both "options would need appropriate accountability mechanisms at the local and strategic level" (p. 11). While the lead force/lead regional force option could be initiated more rapidly, it did "not deal well with the fundamental issues identified in this review" (p. 11).

The assessment by Her Majesty's Inspectorate of Constabulary was that there was "nothing incompatible between a move towards a more strategic organization" and an organization delivering Community Policing (p. 12). However, in order to reduce the risk of not being able to deliver neighborhood policing, the report recommended that any restructuring proposed should be completed within two years (p. 12).

The change in the policing environment placed pressure on the BCU structure, which decreased from 320 units in the mid-1990s to approximately 230 units by 2004 (p. 19). In 1994, the continual restructuring of BCUs had a flow-on effect, which caused flaws to develop in the ability of the structure of the national police force to cope with the increasing occurrence of transnational crime (p. 19).

In order to understand policing, a clear definition of the purpose of police should be known. One of the major gaps in our understanding of policing is that there is no definition of the purpose of policing at the local level. The report identified three levels of responsibility, which could form a part of a definition for a national level of policing:

1. The development of local and neighborhood policing
2. The provision of protective services to national standards
3. The organization of affordable support and strategic development (p. 58)

At the strategic level, a structure that is fit for purpose comprises "forces large enough to provide a full suite of sustainable services, yet still small enough to be able to relate to local communities" (p. 59). Any extensive reorganization would incur "up-front costs in terms of both money, potential diversion of resources, and disruption" (p. 77). While such costs can be reduced, they cannot be avoided completely, which means that any proposed "change needs to be thoroughly planned and well-coordinated" (p. 77).

Her Majesty's Inspectorate of Constabulary (2010) Valuing the Police: Policing in an Age of Austerity

This report considered the roles of both the police and the police authorities in the context of the 2010 economic environment and forecasted economic climates, both nationally and internationally. The report adopted the approach of doing more for less while assessing the police service in their achievement of the three Es: effectiveness, efficiency, and economy viability (Gravelle & Rogers, 2011). At the time that the report was released, the police service was already implementing budget reductions of between 16% and 20%, which was accompanied by significant structural reform (Gravelle & Rogers). The reduction in funding and the reform initiatives set the scene for the police to provide a better service for less expense (Gravelle & Rogers).

The report was written in response to the police service receiving "unprecedented increases in funding" throughout the previous 10 years, and as a result of the downturn, many police forces faced difficulties as the cuts in public spending were implemented (Gravelle & Rogers, 2011). The annual amount spent on policing in 2008–2009 totaled £13.7 billion, a 47% increase on the previous year (Gravelle & Rogers, 2011). Various statements made by the government considered the future of policing as being one focused on years of financial austerity owing to the economic downturn (Her Majesty's Inspectorate of Constabulary, 2010).

The problem with introducing funding cuts was how to maintain and deliver the same level of police services. Both the police and the government realized that "economic pressures [would] have an impact on the delivery of policing at the local, national and international levels in many and diverse ways" (Gravelle & Rogers, 2011, p. 225). It was expected that the demand for police services would increase and the global downturn would only exacerbate the problem.

Her Majesty's Inspectorate of Constabulary (2011) Adapting to Austerity

In October 2010, the government predicted that the central police funding budget for all 43 forces would be cut by 20% in real terms by 2014/2015 (p. 3). A review undertaken by Her Majesty's Inspectorate of Constabulary in early 2010 found that "all forces either had already identified how they intended to make (or exceed) the required savings, or were developing plans to do so" (p. 3).

Forces had adapted to the austerity by implementing 11 different strategies to improve efficiency (p. 7). The strategies were a mixture of approaches, of which some would require a fundamental reorganization of a force, while other approaches were not as deep-seated and could be implemented within a reasonable time frame. National and local programs designed to improve processes and achieve economies of scale were also included (p. 7). The 11 strategies have been listed as follows, with the number of forces that have implemented the strategy recorded in parentheses:

1. Neighborhood remodeling (19)
2. Shared service centers (23)

3. Outsourcing (24)
4. New BCU/policing model (28)
5. Collaboration (29)
6. Reallocation of workforce between functions (31)
7. Response remodeling (34)
8. Middle office remodeling (37)
9. Shift pattern review (38)
10. Back-office remodeling (39)
11. Demand analysis (43)

The report also found that a number of forces were benefiting from the regional initiatives, such as

- Streamlined command structures
- Collaboration between forces
- Standardized information systems
- Outsourcing and the sharing of procurement (p. 32)

Policy Exchange (2011) Cost of Cops: Manpower and Deployment in Policing

The Cost of Cops report claimed that while police forces were facing large, challenging but manageable budget reductions for the years leading up to 2015, the reductions could be controlled if the appropriate decisions were implemented (p. 20). The relevant decisions to reduce costs should, according to the report, include the reshaping of a force's workforce, revising business processes, redeployment of officers to frontline roles, and increasing the visibility of officers.

The report also determined that outsourcing certain services was a strategy that had not often been used by forces. Outsourcing was found to be capable of delivering resource efficiencies and providing redeployment opportunities and could assist in retaining patrol officers (p. 20). Eighty percent of police funding was spent on personnel costs, and it was this area that was the first to be examined to realize savings in order to meet any reduction in the budget. To operate with a reduced level of funding, police would need to increase productivity, reduce operating and administration costs, improve the pay and conditions of staff, and examine how staff were deployed (p. 105).

Conclusion

Since the mid-1980s, policing in the United Kingdom has undergone extensive change. The service has implemented a large number of strategies, processes, and policies that have, arguably, increased its professionalism. Some may disagree and argue that the service is merely complying with government policy and delivering services to meet the performance measures determined by the Home Office.

The evolution of policing in the United Kingdom clearly shows that there is no one-size-fits-all reform process and that any proposed reorganization or restructuring of the service must be tailored to meet local circumstances and culture (Association of Chief Police Officers, 2008, p. 28). Evidence from research has clearly identified that community and neighborhood policing must be flexible, responsive, and adaptable and must be based on local conditions (Association of Chief Police Officers, 2008).

The intention of the more modern reports released by Her Majesty's Inspectorate of Constabulary was to ensure that assets would be used more efficiently and effectively and that there would be more of a strategic police response to address national and international crime. It was also intended that local policing would continue to be developed and that it would become capable of addressing volume crime (Association of Chief Police Officers, 2008).

If the government is to progress with any form of strategic mergers, it needs to do so with support from the public and in collaboration with the forces involved.

Strategies Employed to Improve Service Delivery in New Zealand

9

Introduction

Since 1984, New Zealand has implemented a radical series of economic and labor market structural and operational reforms, which have been designed to increase the efficiency and effectiveness of government agencies. These reforms were the most thorough in New Zealand's history, and the changes were ranked as being among the most radical and comprehensive undertaken anywhere in the world. The scope and scale of change was significant and involved commercialization, corporatization, privatization, the restructuring of numerous government departments, the introduction of a new form of public financial management, and major changes to industrial relations. The reforms were implemented with a view to providing a more responsive public service and were implemented within an extremely short time frame. The key outcomes sought by the government were

- To have a competitive labor market
- To reduce the amount of government spending

The machinery of government also underwent dramatic upheaval and change. A new public sector environment was created out of these reforms and was characterized by

- The separation of policy and advisor roles from administrative and operational roles
- Objectives that would be stated in such a way that all parties providing public goods and services would be absolutely clear as to their role
- Maximized accountability
- Competitive neutrality that would ensure a level playing field to minimize costs and provide appropriate incentives and sanctions to enhance efficiency
- Managers that would have the autonomy to manage
- The implementation of accrual accounting and private-sector accounting and audit principles throughout the public sector

- The shift in focus from inputs to outputs and outcomes
- The privatization and outsourcing of some government services (Boston, 1991; Deane, 1986)

New Zealand Reforms

Up until the mid-1980s, New Zealand had the most centrally controlled economy of all the member countries of the Organization for Economic Cooperation and Development (OECD) (Preston, 1996). The "entire economy was a network of controls and cross-subsidies, in which almost every sector did its best to live off every other sector" (Preston, 1996, p. 2). Prior to this period, New Zealand's economy was growing at a rate considerably below the OECD average (McGrath, 2011). The main reason for the slow national growth rate was that the government sector absorbed approximately 12% of the country's Gross Domestic Product (McGrath, 2011).

Commencing in 1984, and continuing for another two decades, successive "governments implemented a series of reforms notable for their scope" (Preston, 1996, p. 3). It had been argued that while these reforms were extremely controversial and that mistakes had been "made in their implementation, they succeeded in transforming the economic landscape almost beyond recognition" (Preston, 1996, p. 3).

The government reforms were implemented in two phases. The first phase, 1984–1999, was based on three concepts: corporatization, deregulation, and privatization. This meant that specific government departments would be corporatized and were to be self-funding, and some government services would be deregulated to encourage market competition or the services would be sold to private institutions. The second phase, 1999–2005, was based on improving outcomes through the introduction of effectiveness and efficiency measures (McGrath, 2011).

These changes were based on the economic theories of Public Choice and Agency and were part of the government's management reform program called New Public Management (NPM). New Zealand was described as a laboratory for an economic experiment (Scott, Bushnell, & Sallee, 1990), as such profound change had never been undertaken anywhere in the world and involved the transformation of New Zealand's welfare state into the world's first post-welfare state (Boston, 1991). The sweeping changes were encapsulated in the enactment of two pieces of legislation:

1. The State Sector Act 1988
2. The Public Finance Act 1989

It was proposed that this legislation would provide the framework to allow better business techniques to be applied and would enable funding to be allocated based on outputs and agency services to be measured.

The First Phase: A Performance and Accountability Framework

The changes that were introduced to the government sector were designed to clarify the objectives of each agency and match each agency's objectives with agency resources in a more efficient and effective manner (Deane, 1986). To match objectives and resources, management and financial authority was decentralized by statutory delegation from the government to individual agencies. This established a basis for "increased responsibility and improved accountability for individual [agency] managers" (Deane, 1986, p. 22). The aim was to increase the adaptability of agencies and reduce the inflexibility of agency management.

To support the decentralization of management and financial authority, the government implemented an accountability structure that required agencies to table an Annual Statement of Intent (SoI) in Parliament. A SoI outlines the strategic and corporate plans of an agency, financial measures and targets, and the scope and nature of an agency's operational activities (Deane, 1986). Both plans create a method of evaluation by allowing an agency's annual reports to be reviewed and compared to the performance outlined in the agency's SoI.

The final component of the accountability structure was the establishment of a distinction between agency outputs and government outcomes. In New Zealand, an agency's outputs are defined as the goods and services produced by that agency, while a government outcome is defined as the effect that an agency's outputs have on the community (Scott et al., 1990). The chief executives of the agencies were to be directly responsible for the outputs produced by their departments with the type of outputs being agreed to by the government minister responsible for the agency (Scott et al., 1990).

The Second Phase: Reorientation

By the late 1990s, the government agency reforms appeared to have achieved their original objectives. It was not known whether this was because the original reform elements had not been implemented correctly or because government agencies were adapting to the reform elements and to the change in the environment (Ayto, 2011). In response to the waning of the original NPM reforms, the government introduced a program called Managing for Outcomes (McGrath, 2011). The new program emphasized outcomes within every aspect of management and "also instilled a culture of learning from success and failure and modifying work programs depending on results" (McGrath, 2011, p. 76).

As a part of the review of the implementation of NPM, the government realized that the government agencies in Wellington "could no longer mandate what solutions should be" (McGrath, 2011, p. 76). In response, the government introduced legislation that made local councils more accountable to their communities (McGrath, 2011). In essence, the approaches taken by the government to the economic and social challenges became more localized, but the decentralized approach was reversed and it became more of a "centralised governance model in the interest of efficiency and effectiveness" (McGrath, 2011, p. 77).

New Zealand Police

The New Zealand Police are a national police service and are responsible for a full range of law enforcement services and investigations from minor criminal offending and traffic enforcement to major and organized crimes. In 2014, the organization comprised approximately 9063 sworn officers and 2969 civilian employees and was structured to include a national headquarter and 12 districts (New Zealand Police, 2014). The 12 districts are made up of 37 policing areas, which encompass more than 380 police stations (New Zealand Police, 2014).

Response of the New Zealand Police to the Environment

The reform of the 1980s in New Zealand was heavily influenced by the political discussions that were held in Australia and the United Kingdom. The New Zealand Government adapted the political and structural processes used in these countries and introduced them into the New Zealand public sector. Political emphasis was placed on government agencies to do more with less, and government agencies came under an increasing amount of pressure from the public to be more accountable for the use of public funds and to deliver better and more focused services.

A principal element of the reform was the way in which government agencies were to be funded. The New Zealand Government differentiated the role of the purchaser of the government agency service from the provider of the service. In other words, the government (the purchaser) was separated, in theory, from the police (the provider of the service). To achieve this separation, the police budget, which had been previously funded via a number of different funding streams, was integrated into a single fund for all police services.

The new single fund was termed VOTE POLICE and was managed by the New Zealand Treasury. In essence, the new financial regime was based on the government purchasing a number of hours of the police organization's time (which would contribute to the achievement of the government's outcomes) and the police selling those hours back to the government (in return for funding). Police time was aggregated into 14 organizational outputs, ranging from regulatory services and policy advice to responding to offences and nonoffense incidents. The outputs contributed to the outcomes sought by the government and it was the hours that the police delivered to produce the outputs that were purchased by the government. It also included arrangements to fund capital expenditure in addition to normal operating costs.

In order to implement the government's reforms, police managers were compelled to critique their structures, budgets, and service delivery processes. A number of management processes and frameworks, including corporate planning, strategic planning, NPM, performance measurement, organizational restructuring, and resource allocation, were implemented to enable managers to deliver services more effectively.

New Zealand Police Corporate Planning (A New Approach to Objectives and Outputs)

Police activity is defined in terms of the tasks that it undertakes, the range of tasks bound by the scope of the law, the demands made by the community, and the resources available. This creates duplication and is a problem for police when attempting to establish an efficient and effective organization. To counter this situation, police recognized that it had a limited amount of resources, and to make the best use of its resources, it needed to identify specific operational objectives.

The following elements are required to deliver police services efficiently:

1. Defined organizational objectives
2. Outputs that are specified to meet these objectives
3. The outputs that should be a state monopoly and those that are contestable are determined
4. Development of a structure that facilitates the reassessment of the first three steps (Gorringe, 2001)

The core objective of the police was defined as having a coercive (enforcement) function. It was also noted that the objective should reflect an ability to deliver other services of a noncoercive nature when these other services contribute to the effective and efficient performance of the core objective.

The police were not initially able to adopt an output-outcome model as proposed by the government. This was because the police were not able to distil a comprehensive list of outputs in terms of their activities in a format that met the government's monitoring requirements and that was compatible with its own financial and management information systems.

The New Zealand Police set its goals for the 1989/1990 period at a high level of generality and outlined strategies that would make their achievement possible. Two goals, for example, were as follows:

1. To implement a Community Policing system by June 30, 1993
2. To increase the level of public satisfaction with police services (New Zealand Police, 1989)

It was proposed that these strategic objectives would be translated into plans at the regional, district, and area levels. While the mix of strategies adopted varied between localities, the strategies were limited in detail and in their operational approach to improve service delivery.

As an understanding of the core components of, and the management of police service delivery improved, there was a shift away from the core enforcement outputs and a move toward a core, persuasive group of proactive policing outputs. Later, the police shifted its focus from achieving individual outputs to the achievement of strategic outcomes, which were set at a higher level, but were supported by what is termed as impacts. In 2010/2011, for example, the police had the following two strategic outcomes and impacts:

1. Outcome 1: Confident, safe, and secure communities
   a. Confidence in the police is maintained, and fear of crime and crashes is reduced.
   b. New Zealand is seen as a safe and secure place in which to live, visit, and conduct business.
   c. The public, especially victims of crime, expresses satisfaction with police service.
2. Outcome 2: Less actual crime and road trauma, fewer victims
   a. Less harm from crime, crashes, and antisocial behavior.
   b. Vulnerable people are protected and safe.
   c. Rate of increase in demand on the criminal justice system is abated (New Zealand Police, 2010).

New Zealand Police: Strategic Planning

In 1992, as a response to the government reforms and a desire to improve policing effectiveness, the police developed its first, comprehensive, five-year, strategic plan. The plan was based on a private sector, strategic planning model and defined the police mission, values, strategic goals, strategies, critical success factors, and a series of implementation programs. The overall vision of the police was to achieve "Safer Communities Together" by implementing 22 strategies through the Community-Oriented Policing program (New Zealand Police, 1992). The strategic plan was linked to the governments' 10-Year Social and Economic Strategy and the Annual Business Plan for Police. The business plan formed the foundation for negotiating outputs and the financial appropriation from the government.

The strategic plan took into account the advances made in technology and the increasing resourcing constraints coupled with the demand for better performance and greater accountability. It also took into account the growing appreciation of the importance of working in partnerships with the community and other agencies and the recognition that the police are only part of the broader public safety solution.

The development of the plan resulted in an integrated business transformational program, which was to be implemented in several phases over the following four years. The program provided a framework for frontline staff to deliver better, more effective services to, and with the community. The strategies that it encompassed used technology to reduce the amount of paperwork and administration, which would return staff resources to the streets, the adoption of a strong customer focus for policing, and the development of people skills and expertise to enable police to improve its performance (New Zealand Police, 1996b).

One of the key strategies in the strategic plan was to dramatically improve the police business and information systems infrastructure. By world standards, the police had a reliable and robust financial and criminal information system. These were, however, neither comprehensive nor sophisticated to a high enough level to meet the challenges of the government, the police, and the community in the twenty-first century. To support the implementation of its strategies, the police made a substantial investment in technology. The primary purpose of the investment was to support the business of policing and to provide information. The most widely publicized project in this area was the design and implementation of the Integrated National Crime Information System (INCIS) that was to support frontline policing and produce substantial gains in productivity.

The introduction of the strategic plan not only resulted in a major shift in business processes but also entailed a profound change in the police culture, which cut across all dimensions of police activity. The plan emphasized the following changes to the police culture:

- Empowerment of individuals
- Decentralization of decision-making

- Open, honest two-way communication
- "Bottom-up" innovation
- Genuine teamwork
- An absolute commitment to customer focus (New Zealand Police, 2001)

The results of the first strategic plan were traditional in the sense that there was a reduction in reported crime, the road toll had reduced, and there was an increase in crime clearance rates (New Zealand Police, 1996a). However, during the development of the plan and the implementation of the new systems, which supported the government's reforms, several problems emerged when attempting to apply the model to some aspects of policing and the broader criminal justice fields. The problems encountered were as follows:

- An absence of research upon which strategies could be developed
- Deficiencies in the information systems, which could not provide quality data to support analysis
- Inadequate research and evaluation infrastructure, which could be used to identify and evaluate new or alternate initiatives
- The impact of politics on the process of strategic development and implementation
- The limitations inherent in attempting to quantify social costs and benefits in economic terms and to establish clear causal links (New Zealand Police, 1997)

These problems were not related to determining the cost of delivering police services. Under accrual accounting and economic costing methodologies, the cost of delivering services could be established reasonably accurately. The problem was in calculating benefits and establishing clear links to the outputs that produced those benefits.

A second strategic plan was developed and implemented in 1996, which built on the achievements of the first plan. Since this time, the New Zealand Police have developed and introduced strategic plans approximately every five years.

Policing Excellence Program

In early 2008, owing to a change in national government and the newly elected government calling for a review of the organizational costs of the New Zealand Police, the police implemented the Policing Excellence program. This program comprised 11 work streams or initiatives that would enable police to be better placed in the future to deal with changing demand (New Zealand Police, 2012). Table 9.1 defines each of the 11 work streams.

Table 9.1 Policing Excellence Program Work Streams

Work Stream	Definition
Police model	A framework for redeploying the encapsulated program benefits to crime prevention
Case management	Aims to achieve efficiencies in the methods police use to manage reports of crime
Alternative resolutions	Develops alternative sanctions for low-level offending
Rostering to reduce demand	Increases the number of police available for deployment at key times
Crime reporting line	Establishes a national reporting channel for nonemergency crime
Cost recovery	Examines whether specific costs can be recovered for noncore police services
Mobility	Improves the technology available to frontline police, ensuring staff safety
Support services to the frontline	Examines how the police is utilizing its entire complement of staff
Policing act opportunities	Examines how support services are provided across the organization
Asset management	A program to improve the management of assets
Performance measurement	Examination of the current performance framework with a view to designing more comprehensive measures based on intended outcomes

Source: Adapted from New Zealand Police, Policing excellence report card, Unpublished, November 2012.

The work streams were intended to increase service delivery effectiveness, free up resources, and increase the use of technology to enable the police to spend more time on serving its communities (New Zealand Police, 2012). The aim of the program was to facilitate the transfer of officer time from performing administrative tasks and completing compliance paperwork to working more with the public and victims.

The program provided a comprehensive framework for the implementation of the new New Zealand Policing Model. This model positioned prevention at the head of police business and placed victims and witnesses to the occurrence of an incident or crime at the center of the police response (New Zealand Police, 2012). The approach was supported by continuous improvement in external relationships, excellence in leadership and the development of staff.

Conclusion

The majority of the elements contained in the original 1980s' reform structure remain intact today. McGrath (2011) proclaimed that "the model today is qualitatively different from the original design" (p. 76). Government agencies are on a journey of continuous organizational improvement. The original model concentrated on the outputs that individual agencies were to achieve, which would contribute to the achievement of government outcomes, of which had to be achieved with very little assistance from other government agencies. Today, this has been replaced with an interagency approach to the delivery of government services and "more emphasis on what might be called joined up governance" (McGrath, 2011, p. 76).

Since the reforms in the mid-1980s, rapidly changing social and economic conditions, concern about the increasing level of crime, and increasing public expectations led the police to reassess its role and the organizational processes and structures that it uses. The aim of the reassessment was to ensure that the police had the capability and organizational processes to deliver the best possible Community-Oriented Policing service to meet both the government and the community's expectations.

While the police have been able to improve the efficiency and effectiveness of its service delivery, it has become clear that the police cannot achieve all of the outcomes that the community and the government expect them to achieve. This is because of the considerable number of conflicting demands that are made of them. This conflict has created challenges in balancing police budgets and resources and suggests that outcome measurement alone is not a simple technique for assessing the achievement of the delivery of police services (Moore & Stevens, 1991). The need to measure outcomes has meant that the police have had to continually examine its strategies, structures, resources, and costs to identify better methods and processes to improve officer and organizational efficiencies and effectiveness.

Strategies Employed to Improve Service Delivery in the United States

10

Introduction

It is an understatement to say that local policing across the United States was adversely affected by the 2007 economic downturn (Melekian, 2012b). Hilsenrath, Ng, and Paletta (2008) described the economic downturn as the worst economic and financial crisis in 70 years. The downturn placed pressure on state and municipal budgets that subsequently resulted in cuts to police agency funding (Police Executive Research Forum, 2009, 2011).

While police agencies were endeavoring to deliver services with reduced funding, the demand for police services increased (den Heyer, 2013a, 2013b; Police Executive Research Forum, 2009, 2011). Police were being called to attend to incidents that would never have been conceived of in the past (New Jersey State Association of Chiefs of Police, 2007). They were interceding in events, which, in the past, would have been considered to be civil, social, or moral in nature, rather than being of a criminal nature. The New Jersey State Association of Chiefs of Police (2007) signaled that in order for the police to be able to respond effectively, different forms of service and an increasing number of services needed to be developed.

Reduced levels of funding have meant that difficult management and budget decisions have had to be made, which has had an impact on the level and the quality of service provided. It has been increasingly difficult for police agencies to deliver effective service, maintain operational and administrative staffing levels, and deliver special programs, such as Community Policing (Wilson & Grammich, 2012). In some cases, the reduction in funding has threatened the future of some local agencies (Melekian, 2012b).

As funding allocations to police agencies decreased, police management looked for other opportunities to reduce their organizational costs. Two options that were considered were the civilianization of sworn positions and the use of volunteers (Melekian, 2012b). Restructuring was another option, and in particular, the consolidation or merging of agencies and the sharing of administrative and support services (New Jersey State Association of Chiefs of Police, 2007).

The New Jersey State Association of Chiefs of Police (2007) emphasized that whatever service delivery model is selected, whether based on civilianization or restructuring, it should be the one that is the most appropriate for a particular community, as a standardized approach will not take into consideration the specific needs of a community. The diversified nature of American policing makes it clear that taking a single approach to increase police agency effectiveness will not work in all police agencies and that an approach that works in one part of the country may not work in another part (Melekian, 2012b). The impact of the implementation of a consolidation, merging, or sharing program should be analyzed and evaluated to see whether operating costs increase or decrease and whether the program affects Community Policing. The New Jersey State Association of Chiefs of Police (2007) advocated that comprehensive, individually designed, consolidation, merging, or sharing plans that are specific to a community may have the ability to make budget savings.

The change in the economic operating environment has been viewed by most agencies and commentators as being temporary, and therefore to date, there has been no fundamental strategic change as to how police agencies across the United States deliver their services. While many agencies have downsized, the majority have not changed the way that they deliver their services, or the business model that they use (Melekian, 2012b). This has created tension for police managers as they have had to prioritize between delivering patrol services and maintaining Community Policing programs.

This chapter discusses the elements that affect the environment in which police agencies operate, the management of police agencies, Community Policing, and the approaches undertaken by police agencies in the United States to reduce their operating costs. This chapter also examines police agency amalgamations and consolidations and the problems experienced in implementing these types of reform.

Economy

Dial (2012) maintained that the 2007 financial collapse was not without warning and had been foretold as early as 1973 and that the collapse triggered a "revolution of change in many police agencies across America" (p. 106). Most police agencies were affected by a decline in city revenues, and austerity budgets became a standard part of baseline municipal operations rather than the exception. The reduced level of funding experienced by police agencies contrasted to the funding levels that police agencies had enjoyed over the past 25 years. Previously, police agencies had received adequate funding to employ extra staff and had enough funding to pay for whatever resources were required. The downturn placed pressure on the police to improve their management of resources if they were to maintain their services while experiencing decreases in funding.

As a result of the financial downturn in 2011, more than 12,000 sworn officers were laid off, approximately 30,000 law enforcement positions were left vacant and approximately 28,000 sworn personnel faced work furloughs of at least one week. The situation was similar for civilian personnel (Melekian, 2012b).

Since the financial collapse, police chiefs in the United States have been discussing how to modify their service delivery and how to determine the type of structural changes needed if service delivery levels are to be maintained while keeping within resourcing levels. As a response, police agencies have reviewed the way that they handle investigations and the prevention of crime (Duncan, 2012). More than 26% of respondents to a survey conducted by the Major Cities Chiefs Association stated that their agencies had decreased follow-up investigations into property crime, nonfelony domestic assaults, and drug and traffic offending (Melekian, 2012b). In surveys conducted by other major research institutions, agencies reported that they had responded to decreasing resourcing by reducing staff and recruit training and deferring the purchase of equipment and new technology (Melekian, 2012b). There are less police officers on patrol or available to undertake investigations as a consequence of the cutbacks in service and organizational capability. The officers that are available may not be as well trained as previously and may be using older equipment. This has the potential to compromise an officer's safety and the safety of citizens and may have a negative impact on the public's confidence in the police.

Management

The management approach taken by police agencies has developed over two specific periods. The first approach was Command and Control, and this style of management was used from the 1940s until the 1970s (Middleton-Hope, 2007). The paramilitary approach of Command and Control was replaced with the management models of Problem-Oriented and Community Policing, which were introduced in the 1980s and 1990s. The Problem-Oriented and Community Policing management models were then overshadowed by a more comprehensive approach that included the concept of intelligence-led policing. Devolved financial responsibility was introduced in conjunction with intelligence-led policing (Middleton-Hope, 2007), which called for police decision-makers to be more strategic when managing their resources and to be more accountable. The new management approach was readily accepted by police managers, and there were two reasons why managers embraced the concepts. The first was a result of the evolution of the management methods adopted from the 1940s, which culminated in the philosophy and practicality of Community Policing. The second reason was the call for police managers to be fully accountable for the management of the sizably funded organizations and to respond to culturally and ethnically diverse communities.

Community-Oriented Policing

In a 2004 article, William Oliver argued that there had been three generations or stages in the development of Community Policing. The first stage was the creation of a number of service delivery innovations, the second was the acceptance of those innovations, which was evident from the commitment displayed by police administrators, and the third, which began in 1995, was one of growing recognition. After more than 10 years of implementation, Community Policing became the preferred method of service delivery (Oliver, 2004). Oliver's views, however, were not widely shared. In a 2011 survey of 300 police departments that reported that they had implemented a Community Policing program, not one of the 300 departments reported that they had implemented all of the Community-Oriented Policing elements. Only modest versions of the policing program had been adopted (Mayo, 2012).

The partial implementation of Community Policing may not result in the most effective delivery of services, as Community Policing is a general approach to police service delivery. Community Policing works well when combined with traditional police management and operational approaches.

Three major studies in the United States, which examined the effect that the 1990s' Community-Oriented Police Services (COPS) hiring grant programs had on crime rates in 6100 agencies between 1995 and 1999, indicated a significant reduction in local crime rates in cities with populations over 10,000 citizens (Schieder et al., 2012). The drop in the level of crime was supported by the research conducted by Zimring (2012), who claimed that "the rate of reported crime in the United States has dropped each year after 1991, for nine years in a row, the longest decline ever recorded" (p. v). The crime rate in the United States in 2009 was roughly the same as it was in 1968, with the homicide rate being at its lowest level since 1964 (United States Department of Justice, 2009). The reasons for the decrease in reported crime remain a mystery and are still being debated.

While lower levels of reported crime have been maintained for more than 15 years, pressure is being placed on police agencies to further reduce reported crime rates and to increase the efficiency of their delivery of services.

Staffing of Police Agencies

In an attempt to reduce organizational costs, police agencies from across the country, ranging in size and structure, have implemented staffing cuts

(Wilson, 2012). In 2008, a survey of police chiefs conducted by Fischer (2009) found that more than 63% of the respondents were planning to implement funding cuts, with just under one-third of the agencies involved in the study intending to reduce the funding for sworn staff. This was despite the implementation of a number of budget reduction strategies, such as the elimination of sworn officer overtime, freezes on hiring new sworn and civilian staff, less academy recruit classes, attrition and layoffs or incentives for early retirements (Wilson, 2012). To keep within their funding allocation levels, more than 29% of the responding agencies anticipated discontinuing their special units (Fischer, 2009), while other agencies were planning to cut specific police programs such as grounding helicopters and returning SWAT officers to patrol (Lewis, 2009).

Amalgamation, Mergers, and Regionalization

It is well known that police agency jurisdictions are not well matched to geographical areas and that the decentralized geographical structure of police agency jurisdictions does not align with the occurrence of crime. Crime has no respect for the presence of borders or the imposition of legal jurisdictions. Treverton, Wollman, Wilke, and Lai (2011) claimed that not only does the jurisdictional structure of police agencies not correspond with the occurrence of crime, but the composition of the jurisdictions makes little sense.

Police agencies have attempted to minimize the weaknesses of decentralized, organizational structures by establishing task forces and fusion centers (Fuentes, 2012), and from the sharing of information of specific offences, although routine information sharing is rare. It is even more uncommon for agencies to share their resources, their assets or their support services, which has created gaps in the enforcement of the law, of which criminals are using to their advantage.

One approach to minimize the gaps in law enforcement is to amalgamate or merge agencies. Two issues should be considered before amalgamating or merging with another agency. The first is that the amalgamation must either maintain or improve service delivery effectiveness, meaning that it must either decrease or maintain current reported crime levels, and the second is that the amalgamation must be cost-neutral or decrease an agency's expenditure.

There is an influential, but perhaps not well supported, strand in American organizational thinking that institutional consolidation achieves operational budget savings and improves police agency service delivery through the elimination of redundant support services (Burack, 2012). Police agencies, owing to decentralization, cannot, other than in the larger-sized city agencies, absorb large budget cuts without making extensive changes to their organizations, their processes, or their structures, and, as a result, amalgamation becomes an important policy issue in the discussion relating to police agency expenditure. However, the research that is available as to whether the amalgamation of police agencies delivers cost savings is contradictory. A number of researchers who have conducted evaluations on police agency mergers claimed that in merged agencies, the effectiveness of the service delivered had increased (Cooper & Koop, 2003; Krimmel, 1997, 2012; Kushner & Siegel, 2005a; Lithopoulos & Rigakos 2005; McDavid, 2008). While other researchers, such as Gyimah-Brempong (1987, 1989), suggested that amalgamations are inefficient as "police output is produced under decreasing returns to scale, inferring that jurisdictions should consolidate to produce police services" but only if the preference for amalgamation justifies the increased cost (Finney, 1997, p. 121).

Inconsistencies of Consolidations

The consolidation of police agencies has long been the subject of discussion and debate among police managers, decision-makers, policy makers, and politicians. The 2007 fiscal decline bought "greater urgency to these discussions and has underscored the need to increase collaboration in a number of areas that might not have been considered under other circumstances" (Melekian, 2012b, p. 18). There has been very little systematic research undertaken to examine the consolidation programs of police agencies owing to the acceptance of Community Policing. It is the involvement of local communities in Community Policing that has suppressed the implementation of police agency consolidation programs (Shernock, 2004). This is owing to the perception that Community Policing has improved the delivery of police services at the local level.

Consolidation usually involves merging police agencies that are contiguous or within the same county (Peak, 1993). Police agencies usually merge in order to increase their effectiveness and lower their operational costs, and the merging of police agencies usually takes one of two forms. The merging of two or more separate police agencies into a regional or metropolitan police agency that forms an acceptable government is the first form (Treverton et al., 2011). The second comprises a small-sized police agency contracting with a county sheriff's department or a municipality to provide police services (Treverton et al., 2011).

The system of policing in the United States is complicated, owing to the large number of local agencies and the number of management layers within an agency. While decentralized structures allow for autonomy and the catering to specific communities, practitioners and academics must understand the impact that this type of structure has on the delivery of service. Understanding the impact that the form of organizational structure has on an agency is important owing to the changing interaction between demographic, social, financial, and criminal variables that are experienced at the local, state, and national levels (den Heyer, 2013a, 2013b).

The cost of establishing a consolidated police agency is a major problem, especially given the current economic downturn, and may be unaffordable (Wilson, Weiss, & Grammich, 2012). It may take a number of years before the costs are recovered. Despite the upfront costs, a survey conducted by researchers at the School of Criminal Justice at Michigan State University revealed that, as of September 2011, more than 150 agencies across the United States had experienced some form of consolidation (Wilson & Grammich, 2012). However, this research defined consolidation as being between local police and fire departments and not between two contiguous police departments.

In seeking to identify the costs involved in consolidating police agencies for the period 1988–2008, the Pennsylvania-based Institute for Public Policy and Economic Development examined the statistics from two consolidations. The first was based on the individual agency per capita figure, and the second was the per capita figure when compared across the state. The institute noted that communities with consolidated police departments experienced lower costs than traditional police departments and that departments that had consolidated had a lower per capita cost per service delivery type (The Institute for Public Policy and Economic Development, 2010). In an intracounty comparison undertaken by the institute, it was found that consolidated departments in one county had more than a "two-thirds cost advantage over stand-alone departments," and in four other counties, consolidated departments enjoyed "a three-quarters cost advantage" (The Institute for Public Policy and Economic Development, 2010, p. 4).

Using the 2006 state-level economic information that was available, the institute found "that the cost of most [consolidated] regional departments was below the 2006 state-wide stand-alone per capita police department service cost" (The Institute for Public Policy and Economic Development, 2010, p. 4). Since the Pennsylvania study was completed in early 2010, a further 23 regional (consolidated) departments have been formed in the Commonwealth (The Institute for Public Policy and Economic Development).

According to Finney (1997), in the late 1980s, an estimated 6% of cities in the United States consolidated in some form to reduce costs. Moreover, 90% (39 of 43 police agencies) of Los Angeles area jurisdictions that had incorporated since 1954 had implemented formal intergovernment arrangements (Finney, 1997). Finney (1997) expanded on these findings by noting that the reason for the large number of police agency consolidations in the Los Angeles County may be because governmental sharing in the region is economically efficient.

The Department of Community and Economic Development (DCED) publication *Regional Police Services in Pennsylvania, A Manual for Local*

Government Officials lists one advantage of municipalities forming regional police departments as:

> **Reduced Costs**. The cost of providing police services is lower in communities served by consolidated police departments. This was established in an analysis of the ten consolidated police departments existing in Pennsylvania in 1988–89 conducted by the former Department of Community Affairs. Nine of the ten consolidated departments operated at an average 24 per cent lower cost when compared to nearby traditional police departments serving communities comparable to those served by the consolidated department. Generally, lower costs result from the need for fewer officers, fewer vehicles, fewer ranking positions and fewer police headquarters facilities
>
> **Cited in The Institute for Public Policy and Economic Development (2010, p. 9)**

Ambiguities of Regionalization

As a response to limited or decreasing levels of resources, of which will become more frequent in the future (Etue, 2012), a number of regionalization projects are being undertaken across the United States. While still in its early stages of development, regionalization has provided efficiencies in police administration, increased the availability of patrols, and enhanced the working relationships of police agencies with their communities (Etue, 2012). However, regionalization programs are being undertaken before there has been any comprehensive agreement as to the standards that should be met or how performance will be measured (Treverton et al., 2011).

Despite previous attention focusing on the benefits of the regionalization of police agencies, La Grange (1987, p. 7) claimed that "these have seldom materialized." However, Melekian (2012b) contended that there is an increasing awareness for collaboration and a willingness to look at regionalization as an option for improving the efficiency and the effectiveness of service delivery. In a study conducted by the former Department of Community Affairs, it was found that "in nine out of ten situations and, if properly managed, regional departments [may] save an average of 24% when compared to traditional police departments serving the same municipalities" (Pennsylvania Governor's Center for Local Government Services, 2012, p. 10).

There are a number of advantages and disadvantages in establishing a regional police agency. The National Executive Institute Associates, in 2002, highlighted several benefits of having a regional police force. These state that

> Regional police forces, theoretically, would have the resources to provide the region with better service in the areas of protecting citizens against criminal behaviours, quality investigation of criminal acts, faster response times, adequate

manpower [sic] to handle most emergency situations, and a host of other non-traditional services. Properly deployed, a regional police force would provide each community with far more service/protection than they presently enjoy"

Cited in The Institute for Public Policy and Economic Development (2010, p. 24)

The advantages and disadvantages and the reasons for not implementing a regional police service have been summarized and are presented in Table 10.1.

The likelihood of a regionalization program reducing organizational costs must be placed within the context of the research undertaken by Ostrom, Parks,

Table 10.1 Advantages, Disadvantages, and the Reasons for Not Implementing Regional Police Services

Advantages of Regional Police Services	Disadvantages of Regional Police Services	Reasons for Not Implementing Regional Police Services
Improvement in the uniformity and consistency of enforcement	Loss of local services	Small-sized police agencies are often content with their operation, the services provided, and the quality of their personnel.
Improvement in the coordination of law enforcement services	Loss of local control	Citizens view regionalization as responsible for increasing their taxes.
Improvement in the recruitment, distribution, and deployment of police personnel	Loss of citizen contact	Regionalization has commenced in some areas with merging of jails, communications, etc.
Improvement in training and personnel efficiency	Initial establishment costs	The increased use of technology is viewed as being too expensive.
Improved management and supervision	Increased costs for less service	Population demographics are in a state of rapid change.
Reduced costs		
Improved career enhancement opportunities		
Should provide better and improved quality of services		
Elimination of jurisdictional issues		

Sources: Adapted from Kirschner, J., *Northampton county regional police study Hellertown Borough and Lower Saucon Township*, Governor's Center for Local Government Services, Pennsylvania, PA, 2012; Pennsylvania Governor's Center for Local Government Services, *Southern York County regional police study: Borough of Stewartstown*, Governor's Center for Local Government Services, Pennsylvania, PA, 2012, pp. 9–11; Tully, E.J., Retrieved on December 8, 2002 from http://www.neiassociates.org/-consolidation-law-enforcement/, 2012, pp. 1–5.

and Whitaker (1978). These researchers examined the performance of 1159 local police agencies across the United States and the findings of their research discredit "the notion that small police services make less efficient use of their employees than large departments" (cited in Lithopoulos & Rigakos, 2005, p. 341).

In 2010, doctoral student Julie Schnobrich-Davis (2010) examined an alternative to consolidation to reduce operating costs. Schnobrich-Davis (2010) claimed that increasing the cost-effectiveness of police agencies could be achieved by establishing Law Enforcement Councils (LECs), similar to the collaboration of 43 law enforcement agencies that operate to the south of Boston, Massachusetts. The organization was incorporated as a nonprofit entity in 2002, and its goal is to provide mutual aid programs and services to area law enforcement agencies (Schnobrich-Davis, 2010). The motivation for the collaboration came from the realization that there are many incidents that exceed the resources or capabilities of any one single agency and that by sharing resources, "law enforcement agencies would more efficiently and effectively handle such situations" (Schnobrich-Davis, 2010, p. 1).

The success of the LEC in Southern Massachusetts has led to the establishment of a regional LEC in local municipal police agencies in Northeastern Massachusetts (Schnobrich-Davis, 2010). Regional LECs provide a mechanism for coordinating the activities of multiple law enforcement agencies, which can assist in an incident, and create a structure for robust strategies and resource deployment capabilities on a geographical basis (Schnobrich-Davis, 2010).

Another alternative to consolidation is the extension of a multijurisdictional task force (MJTF) (Shernock, 2004). According to Shernock (2004) and Phillips (1999), MJTFs are a de facto form of consolidation, incorporate all of the components attributed to consolidation, and are compatible with Community-Oriented Policing. Its compatibility with Community-Oriented Policing may be because of the increasing number of MJTFs that have been established (Shernock, 2004). As Weisheit, Falcone, and Wells (1996) observed, "the community policing movement has been defined by some as a movement away from consolidation and toward decentralization" (p. 77). In the International Association of Chiefs of Police's 2011 survey, more than one-quarter of the responding agencies stated that they were participating in multijurisdictional sharing of resources, "such as dispatch services, SWAT, hazmat, crime technicians, crime laboratories, and training" (International Association of Chiefs of Police, 2011, p. 9).

Examples of Consolidation and Regionalization

This section presents a brief summary of the consolidation practices of police agencies in the United States. While there is a general lack of information about the consolidation of police agencies in the United States, a number of

Table 10.2 Consolidated Police Agencies 1984–2014

	Year	Police Agencies Involved	State
1.	1984	Houma Police and Terrebonne Parish Sheriff	LA
2.	1988	Lynchburg Police and Moore County Police	TN
3.	1991	Athens Police and Clarke County Police	GA
4.	1992	Lafayette Police and Lafayette Parish Sheriff	LA
5.	1992	City and Borough of Yukatat Police	AK
6.	1993	Charlotte City Police and Mecklenburg County Police	NC
7.	1996	Augusta Police and Richmond County Police	GA
8.	1998	Augusta County and Richmond County Police	GA
9.	2001	Hartsville Police and Trousdale County Police	TN
10.	2001	Broomfield City Police and County Police	CO
11.	2002	Haines and Haines Borough Police	AK
12.	2003	Louisville City Police and Jefferson County Police	KY
13.	2003	Cusseta Police and Chattahoochee County Police	GA
14.	2006	Georgetown Police and Quitman County Police	GA
15.	2007	Tribune Police and Greeley County Sheriff	KS
16.	2008	Statenville Police Echols County Sheriff	GA
17.	2009	Preston Police and Webster County Police	GA
18.	2010	Unified Police Department of Greater Salt Lake	UT
19.	2011	Ossinning and Westchester County Police	NY
20.	2014	Macon Police and Bibb County Police	GA

Source: Author.

consolidations have been undertaken since 1984. Table 10.2 presents a schedule of 20 police agencies that implemented a consolidation program between 1984 and 2014. The remainder of this section discusses the consolidation of police agencies in Pennsylvania, and Table 10.3 summarizes the consolidation of police and other agencies in 10 other states.

Consolidation of Police Agencies in Pennsylvania

The first regionalized police department in Pennsylvania was established in 1972. Since this time, 34 agencies have undertaken a regionalization program. The Pennsylvania Governor's Center for Local Government Services (2012, p. 1) claimed that the objective for the establishment of the majority of the regionalized police agencies was "to strengthen existing police services, including the areas of effective administration, supervision, training, investigation, patrol, and specialty services."

There are more than 1100 police agencies currently operating in Pennsylvania (Miller, 2006). Most of these agencies are small in size and many have often been unable to provide the full range of police services (Pennsylvania

Table 10.3 Consolidation Programs and Initiatives in Other States

State	Reform Program	Reform Initiative
Florida	N/A	Since 1976, eight separate counties have attempted to consolidate law enforcement services at the county level. The counties are Duval, Hillsborough, Escambia, Leon, St. Lucie, Alachua, Okeechobee, and Volusia.
Georgia	1997—Service Delivery Strategy to identify gaps or overlaps between county and city agencies.	N/A
Indiana	N/A	2007—Commission for Local Government Reform recommended the provision of services at a broader, county level.
Maine	2007—Began massive school district restructuring.	N/A
Michigan	2007—Centers for Regional Excellence (CREs) have made grants to encourage local governments to work collaboratively.	N/A
Minnesota	1993—Created the Government Innovation and Cooperation Board to improve efficiency in the delivery of government services.	N/A
New Jersey	2006—Convened Joint Legislative Committee on Government Consolidation and Shared Services. 2007—Created the Local Unit Alignment Reorganization and Consolidation Commission (LUARCC).	The LUARCC has recommended more efficient operations, including structural and administrative streamlining.
New York	The Aid and Incentive Municipalities Program provides financial incentives for municipalities to consolidate.	Working on legislation to reduce waste created through the confusion of New York's laws for local government consolidation.
Ohio	2008—Passed legislation creating the Commission on Local Government Reform and Collaboration to develop recommendations to increase efficiency and effectiveness of local government.	Established the Fund for Our Economic Future to increase the economic competitiveness of Northeast Ohio.

(Continued)

Table 10.3 (*Continued*)   Consolidation Programs and Initiatives in Other States

State	Reform Program	Reform Initiative
Wisconsin	State's Department of Administration exists to assist agencies with collaboration and consolidation.	Established the Local Government Institute of Wisconsin to conduct research, enhance collaboration, and educate the public and policy makers on ways to improve local government.

Sources: Adapted from McLaughlin, P. et al., *Legislative approaches to right-sizing municipal services*, Pennsylvania, Institute for Public Affairs Temple University, Philadelphia, PA, 2009; Myers, P., Consolidating police services: Local control vs. Financial choice, Retrieved on October 30, 2012 from http://www.fdle.state.fl.us/Content/gctdoc/258b0143-2da0-4dfd-b9e6-37979df84528/Myers-Rick-research-paper-pdf.aspx, n.d.

Governor's Center for Local Government Services, 2012). Budget constraints forced municipalities to consider the introduction of regionalization as a cost-saving measure (Miller, 2006; Pennsylvania Governor's Center for Local Government Services, 2012); however, there are many other advantages to be gained from consolidating or regionalizing police agencies or services, such as

- An improvement in the uniformity and consistency of police enforcement
- An improvement in the coordination of law enforcement services
- Better distribution and deployment of police personnel
- Reduced organizational and administrative costs
- Possible achievement of economies of scale through the reduction of the total number of police officers, the number of police vehicles and other equipment, as well as the consolidation of departmental headquarters (Miller, 2006)

In Pennsylvania, the advantages of regionalization were substantiated by the research undertaken by the Institute for Public Policy and Economic Development (2010) and McLaughlin, Atherton, and Morrison (2009). Both of these research groups found that

- Both the per capita cost by delivery type and the per capita averages for the counties indicated significant advantages for consolidated departments over stand-alone departments.
- The stand-alone per capita values did not gauge the quality of a police force as measured by its deployment of full-time officers over part-time officers to reduce operating expenses.
- The consolidated force continues to have a cost advantage over the stand-alone force.

- The cost of contracting for police services based on municipal need is also significantly lower than the stand-alone department.
- The intracounty comparison of per capita costs showed a more than two-thirds cost advantage of consolidated over stand-alone agencies.

Consolidation of Police Agencies in Other States

A number of state and local agencies in the United States are examining or have introduced programs or initiatives to consolidate local government agencies and services to reduce costs and increase service delivery effectiveness. The consolidation programs and initiatives that have been implemented or are being considered by other states are presented in Table 10.3.

Conclusion

There is extensive pressure on police agencies in the United States to change the way that they deliver their services and structure their organizations. The pressure emanates primarily as a response to the downturn in local economic conditions, but it has also come about from police managers realizing that there is a need to change how police services are delivered, especially the delivery of patrol services (Melekian, 2012b). Melekian (2012b) claimed that the need for change in the delivery of patrol services was driven by the loss of organizational capacity—the number of officers available for patrol—and from "recognition of the fact that patrol visibility does not need to touch 100 per cent of a jurisdiction's streets and neighborhoods" (Melekian, 2012b, p. 90).

To ensure that there is confidence in, and acceptance of the police by the public during periods of change, police agencies will need to ensure that they have created robust partnerships and relationships with nongovernment organizations, citizen groups, and politicians (Duncan, 2012). To survive and prosper, the structure of the future police organization must be "mobile, flexible and regional" (Duncan, 2012, p. 75).

Regionalization, merging, or sharing are approaches that police agencies should examine to ensure that they are in a position to increase the effectiveness of their service delivery. Smaller-sized police agencies may consider one of two variations within the regionalization, merging, or sharing framework. The first variation that should be considered is the combination of specific services with other police agencies in a local area without merging entire departments. Combined police services are often referred to as functional consolidations and can comprise administration services or special crime investigation squads (La Grange, 1987). The second alternative that should be considered is a combined service that has been described by Burack (2012) as a hybrid model.

The hybrid model focuses on high-cost, specialized functional areas of police agencies, such as training facilities, crime laboratories, and communications networks or infrastructure. The model may comprise a functional consolidation or may include a contract between agencies to deliver services. The model of service delivery and how it affects the structure of an agency and its deployment of resources must be considered if police agencies wish to ensure that they have the capability to adapt to the changing environment.

To be able to adapt to change and to maintain the extensive gains made in Community Policing over the past two decades, Melekian (2012a) suggested that police agencies undertake an extensive restructuring of their service delivery model. Melekian (2012a) also suggested that there may be some benefit in expanding Community Policing programs in challenging economic times. Community Policing is an enabler for police agencies when implementing an organizational restructuring program, as Community Policing is not an alternative strategy to traditional or reactive policing (Melekian, 2012a) but is one that is capable of complementing other police service delivery approaches. A further reason as to why police agencies need to maintain a Community Policing capability is that it is an important method for sharing crime information with citizens and business owners (Melekian, 2012b), and, as a result, is one way of ensuring trust and confidence in the police as they implement changes in their service delivery.

This chapter has examined the approaches adopted by police agencies in the United States to reduce their operating costs or to increase their service delivery efficiency or effectiveness. The major problem in this examination is that no research has been conducted to identify whether a strategy that has been introduced actually works, or, if it does work, what effect it has had on service delivery processes or the relationship of an agency with its community.

Part 2: Conclusion

The most salient observation about the Canadian approach to, and their experience of, police agency amalgamations and regionalizations is that a rigid either/or approach has not been needed (Vancouver Police Department, 2008). The UK and the Canadian case studies both illustrate that the more modern approach to amalgamations includes an allowance or process for local control over police service delivery while ensuring that policing is coordinated at a regional level.

The approach to regionalization taken by the English and the Welsh forces is similar to that of the Canadian approach. English and Welsh forces have devolved the management and administrative authority to the Basic Command Unit level but have retained control at the centralized headquarter level.

The two approaches are "recognition of the different kinds of problems confronting the police, which in turn require different kinds of organizational responses" (Wood, 2007, p. 294).

The examination of the various programs that each country has introduced has identified that in some cases there is a preference for implementing New Public Management (NPM) over regionalization, amalgamation, or outsourcing. Rationalization overcomes the either/or approach as to whether to amalgamate with another agency. The benefit of NPM is that it does not require an extensive project, which may take two to three years to implement, nor does it generally involve staff redundancies. The strength of an NPM program is that it can be introduced as one comprehensive program or various elements of the program can be introduced incrementally over time.

Case Studies III

Establishment of Police Scotland
A Reform to Increase Effectiveness

11

Introduction

Police organizations and policing in western societies are undergoing profound change (Jones & Newburn, 2002). These changes are reactions to a range of developments, such as the privatization of security, the occurrence of transnational crime and terrorism, and the advances made in technology. Since the early 2000s, and as a result of the economic recession in 2007, one of the principal catalysts for the change has been the drive for police forces to increase the efficiency and effectiveness of their service delivery (Butterfield, Edwards, & Woodall, 2004; Cope, Leishman, & Starie, 1997; den Heyer, 2013a, 2014). To improve police service delivery and to preserve the confidence of the public, governments and police managers have examined alternative methods to maintain and enhance service delivery levels within their existing operational and administrative staffing levels.

Some of the strategies that governments and police agencies have explored to improve the delivery of their services have been consolidation, regionalization, and amalgamation; organizational centralization/decentralization; new public management; enhanced performance management systems; civilianization; and restructuring.

One of the preferred approaches to police reform is mergers and consolidation. Police force mergers and consolidation are not a new occurrence. An examination of policing from the late nineteenth century through to the twenty-first century shows that there has been a steady decrease in the number of constabularies in the United Kingdom (Jones & Newburn, 2002). In 1870, there were 220 constabularies in England and Wales, which decreased in number to 131 by 1946, and then decreased again to 43 by 1972 (Jones & Newburn, 2002).

Police force mergers were replicated north of the border in Scotland. In the 1850s, there were over 90 local police forces in Scotland (Fyfe & Scott, 2013). This number halved by the 1950s and by the 1970s had halved again to 22 (Fyfe & Scott, 2013). In 1975, new regional and island councils were established, which bought the number of police forces in Scotland to eight.

Policing in Scotland has traditionally been different from policing in England and Wales, and since the early 2000s, Scotland has taken a different approach to police reform. Police forces in England and Wales have used collaboration and partnerships to improve the efficiency and effectiveness of their service delivery and have largely discounted the merging of forces. In comparison, Scotland has embraced the concept of reform through the use of mergers and, in April 2013, merged eight forces to establish a single national force: Police Scotland.

This chapter is a case study that examines the planning and the development of the merger of the Scottish Police and presents an evaluation as to whether the merger achieved the original aims and objectives of the Scottish government. Against this background, this chapter critically examines the basis for the decision leading to the establishment of Police Scotland. Drawing on government documents and reports, and interviews with key actors (including serving and retired senior police officers and national and local political representatives), this case study endeavors to provide insights into the decisions leading to the reform one year after the merger took place.

The case study does not evaluate Police Scotland's performance in its first 12 months but focuses on the reasons for the adoption of the single force option and whether the reform provided the foundation that would improve policing in Scotland.

The background of policing in Scotland and the governance framework of Scotland's police prior to April 2013 form the basis of the case study. The major issues leading to the reform, the documents on which the reform was based, and the case for change are also discussed. Finally, the conclusions drawn from the interviews held with a number of the key actors in the reform process will be presented and discussed.

Background to the Reform

From the beginning, policing in Scotland was more of a preventative process rather than a reactive law enforcement process. Policing was not only about responding to the occurrence of crime but emphasized elements of accountability for the welfare of the community. The focus on a community-based approach acknowledged the importance of local police involvement by the establishment of police boards and a local property rates-based financial structure, which gave the local community a vested interest in making local policing work (Donnelly & Scott, 2008).

The emphasis of community within policing was also demonstrated by the legal description of the duty of constables, which was, in essence, to guard, patrol, and watch to prevent the commission of offences, preserve order, and protect life and property (Police (Scotland) Act 1967, s. 67). The emphasis placed on the community provided for the ready acceptance of Community-Oriented Policing by the police forces in Scotland. Donnelly and Scott (2008) maintained that by the 1990s, Community Policing had been established in all eight of the Scottish Police forces and was the catalyst for the majority of successive administrative and operational policing strategies.

History of Policing in Scotland

The first major police force in Scotland was established in Glasgow in 1800 by the Glasgow Police Act of 1800, which was 30 years before the establishment of Sir Robert Peel's London Metropolitan Police (Donnelly & Scott, 2008). The passing of the Glasgow Police Act was followed by the passing of the General Police Act of 1833, which instituted police forces in other Scottish cities and burghs, while the Police (Scotland) Act of 1839 facilitated the establishment of police forces in rural counties.

By the 1850s, there were more than 90 local police forces. Through the merging and amalgamation of local bodies, the number of forces decreased to 45 by the end of the 1950s (Fyfe, 2013). The number of forces decreased again by the 1970s to 22, with each of the major cities having established its own police force. In 1975, the restructuring of local governments established new regional and island councils and realigned police force boundaries to create eight new territorial police forces: Central Scotland Police, Dumfries and Galloway Constabulary, Fife Constabulary, Grampian Police, Lothian and Borders Police, Northern Constabulary, Strathclyde Police, and Tayside Police (Fyfe, 2013). This structure remained in place until the establishment of Police Scotland on April 1, 2013.

The establishment of the territorial-based system resulted in eight very different police forces, not only in relation to size but also in relation to the size of the jurisdictional area, the population size per officer, and the number of crimes per 10,000 people. The eight police forces were governed by six separate joint police boards. This structure proved to be problematic, as the boundaries of the eight forces did not align with the boundaries of the six joint boards.

The differences between the eight forces have been highlighted in Table 11.1. As the table depicts, there were a number of differences between the forces, with Strathclyde Police having more officers than the other seven forces combined, and the Northern Constabulary covering a geographical area of more than double that of the other seven forces while having the second to smallest number of officers.

The varying sizes and capacity of the eight police forces meant that different collaborative arrangements arose, which enabled forces to deliver some of the specialist services that were required to deal with increasingly

Table 11.1 Details of the Eight Scottish Police Forces (prior to April 1, 2013)

	Population Served	Area (miles²)	Number of Officers (February 2011)	Number of People per Officer	Crimes per 10,000 People (2009/2010)	Clearance Rate (%) (2009/2010)
Central Scotland Police	291,760	1,020	846	345	562	60
Dumfries and Galloway Constabulary	148,510	2,469	508	292	464	71
Fife Constabulary	363,460	531	1082	336	581	55
Grampian Police	544,980	3,373	1546	353	567	48
Lothian and Borders Police	939,020	2,500	2990	314	692	43
Northern Constabulary	288,840	12,000	792	365	490	62
Strathclyde Police	2,217,880	5,371	8382	265	725	47
Tayside Police	399,550	2,896	1225	326	570	58

Source: Author.

sophisticated criminal elements (HMCIS, 2009). To increase the coordination of specialist police services, on April 1, 2007, the Scottish Executive/ Government created the Scottish Police Services Authority (SPSA). The Scottish Criminal Record Office, the Scottish Police Information Strategy, and the Scottish Police College at Tulliallan combined to form the SPSA, which provided technical, scientific, and training support services to the eight territorial forces.

To coordinate the investigation of drug offences, the Scottish Drug Enforcement Agency (SDEA) was established on April 1, 2001. The Police, Public Order and Criminal Justice (Scotland) Act 2006 renamed the SDEA as the Scottish Crime and Drug Enforcement Agency (SCDEA) and provided the agency with statutory recognition. The SCDEA was to be funded through the new SPSA and on April 1, 2013, it was incorporated into Police Scotland.

Initially, serving police officers were seconded to the SDEA, but with the establishment of the SCDEA, officers were able to be recruited directly. The SCDEA worked alongside the eight police forces and was answerable to the Scottish government through the SPSA. The director of the agency was responsible to the ministers and the Scottish Parliament for financial and administrative matters.

Governance of Police prior to April 1, 2013: "Tripartite Structure"

Similar to the structure established in England and Wales (and prior to the introduction of the Police and Crime Commissioners in 2012), Scotland, prior to April 1, 2013, had a tripartite structure of police governance and accountability (Fyfe, 2013). The tripartite structure was established by the Police (Scotland) Act 1967 and saw the responsibility for the police service being "shared by the tripartite partnership of the chief constable of each force, Scottish ministers and the police authority in the form of the local police board" (Donnelly & Scott, 2008, p. 196). The tripartite structure created by the Police (Scotland) Act 1967 established that

- The central government, with overall responsibility for policing policy in Scotland, was to contribute 51% of the costs of policing, approve the appointment of Chief Constables, and agree to force establishments and police numbers.
- Local government interests in policing would be represented in police boards that were made up of locally elected councilors. The responsibilities of the councilors included the setting of the budget for their local force (and contributing 49% of the costs of policing),

> providing the Chief Constable with the resources necessary to police
> the area and appointing senior officers.
> - The Chief Constable of the local force, while answerable to the
> local police board and to Scottish ministers, was able to exercise
> operational independence in relation to the management and the
> utilization of police officers (Donnelly & Scott, 2008; Fyfe & Scott,
> 2013).

The constitutional role of the Chief Constable was defined in the Police
(Scotland) Act 1967, which determined that the Chief Constable had the
responsibility for the direction of the police force and "full operational discretion for the delivery of policing in the force area" (Donnelly & Scott,
2008, p. 197). As is consistent with the majority of British Law countries, the discretion of the Chief Constable is a principle of constabulary
independence.

Donnelly and Scott (2008) claimed that doubts were raised as to whether
the police boards were able to influence local policing. This claim was based
on the ambiguity of the role of police boards, as they had an advisory role
to the SPSA and an authoritative role to the Chief Constable. The ambiguous role of the police boards was accentuated further by their responsibilities decreed in the Local Government in Scotland Act, 2003. Under the Act,
police boards were to procure the best value in resources to ensure the efficient and the effective delivery of police services and were to monitor the
performance of the force and determine whether the force had implemented
a continuous improvement program. However, this statutory governance
requirement was difficult to achieve because police boards were made up of
part-time members from local councils, who may, or may not have had, an
interest in policing (Donnelly & Scott, 2008).

Her Majesty's Inspector of Constabulary for Scotland had the statutory responsibility for inspecting the eight police forces (Donnelly & Scott,
2008). The thematic inspections undertaken and the resulting reports developed by the Her Majesty's Inspectorate of Constabulary Scotland became
the medium for raising crime-related topics across the forces and provided a
basis for developing coordinated policy.

While the responsibilities of the tripartite members were authorized by
legislation, accountability was weak, especially in the communication process. This resulted in the roles and the responsibilities of the tripartite members becoming less clear.

The complexity of the Scottish Policing governance arrangements and
relationships is presented in Figure 11.1. The eight forces were accountable
primarily to a specific joint board, council or authority, but also had repre-
sentation responsibilities with the Scottish Police Board and the Association
of Chief Police Officers in Scotland (ACPOS) Council.

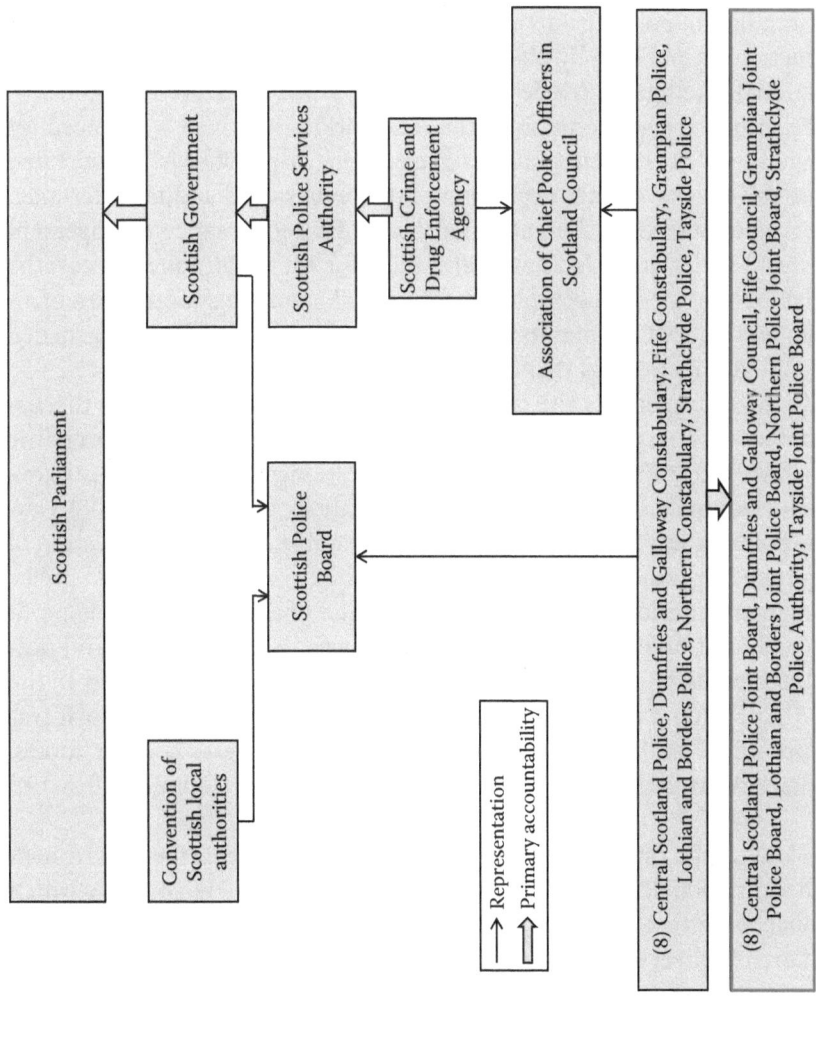

Figure 11.1 Scottish Policing governance arrangements prior to April 1, 2013. (*Source:* Author.)

Major Issues Leading to the Reform

There were a number of triggers that led to the reform of policing in Scotland. The first was, according to Donnelly and Scott (2008), the emphasis that the 1980s Conservative Government placed on government agencies to provide value for money services. The emphasis placed on improving the performance of governments was the catalyst for the need for a more strategic understanding of policing and police management in Scotland and led to the introduction of "policing by objectives, New Public Sector Management and the National Intelligence Model" (Donnelly & Scott, 2008, pp. 194–195).

The second trigger came from the recognition that there was a need for a change in police accountability as the existing tripartite system operated in three stove pipes. A later expansion of the reviews and audits undertaken by the Auditor-General, the implementation of a performance management framework, which included national targets for the eight police forces, the establishment of a police complaints framework, and the appointment of an independent Police Complaints Commissioner for Scotland all strengthened the accountability process (Donnelly & Scott, 2008).

The third trigger was the changing political landscape and the discussion that was taking place pertaining to nationalism and independence. The establishment of the Scottish Parliament questioned the role of local government (Donnelly & Scott, 2008). It was Donnelly and Scott's (2006) view that, as policing was a locally delivered, accountable, service, the creation of the Scottish Parliament provided a basis for the debate to go beyond police force mergers and look to a single force for the entire country. This point was expounded upon in a discussion, which was held in parallel, and pertained to increasing the efficiency and the consistency of service within the expanding policing agenda and on subjects ranging from common infrastructure and "mutual aid arrangements through access to other forces' specialist resources to national policies and strategies" (Donnelly & Scott, 2008, p. 192).

Following the establishment of the Scottish Parliament, the government identified 5 national, high-level objectives and 15 national outcomes to which the police were to contribute. Two national outcomes that are principally related to the delivery of police services were Outcome 9: We live our lives free from crime, disorder, and danger; and Outcome 15: We have strong, resilient, and supportive communities where people take responsibility for their own actions and how they affect others (Sustainable Policing Project, 2011).

The five high-level objectives are presented in Table 11.2.

An expanding policing agenda followed the introduction of the Local Government in Scotland Act in 2003. The Act introduced a number of changes in the way in which public agencies were to work together, principally

Table 11.2 Five High-Level Objectives of Scotland

The strategies are to create a country that is
- Wealthier and fairer
- Healthier
- Safer and stronger
- Smarter
- Greener

Source: Adapted from Sustainable Policing Project, *Phase two report: Options for reform*, Retrieved on February 2, 2014 from http://www.scotland.gov.uk/Resource/Doc/254432/0115237.pdf., 2011.

that the police were to develop community planning partnerships in collaboration with local authorities (Scottish Government, 2011b). The planning process resulted in the police delivering Single Outcome Agreements for each local authority. The agreements detailed prioritized outcomes that were to be achieved and would contribute to the national outcomes (Scottish Government, 2011b).

The final trigger leading to police reform came from the financial pressure that the Scottish government was facing (Sustainable Policing Project, 2011, p. 3). Owing to the need for the government to make savings, a fundamental review of how police delivered their services was needed. According to the Sustainable Policing Project report (2011), the financial pressure forced the "question of whether the existing policing model, based around eight forces with limited inter-force collaboration, [was] the most effective and efficient model for Scotland" and whether a single force with national coverage would be more efficient and effective (p. 3).

The principal weakness in the eight force policing structure, according to the Sustainable Policing Project (2011), was that the force boundaries did not match those of partner agencies. The views of the Sustainable Policing Project were based on two reports written by Her Majesty's Inspectorate of Constabulary Scotland, which suggested that Scotland's eight force structure may not be the appropriate policing system for the new fiscal environment.

Table 11.3 presents the highlights of two of Her Majesty's Inspectorate of Constabulary Scotland reports and the four reports prepared by the Sustainable Policing Project (SPP) and the Scottish government, which provided the case for the reform of police in Scotland.

In looking for efficiencies in the delivery of police services, the Scottish government, in June 2010, established a project called the SPP, which was tasked with developing a sustainable policing model. To ensure that the SPP provided robust and realistic options, the government stipulated a detailed mandate and a timetable for the deliverables of the project.

Table 11.3 Background Documents Leading to the Reform

Organization	Date of Report	Report Title	Highlights of the Report
Her Majesty's Inspectorate of Constabulary Scotland	December 2007	Annual Report of Her Majesty's Inspector of Constabulary for Scotland	The report argued that while most policing in Scotland should be locally based and accountable, there was a small number of police responsibilities for which a "strong and competent national level of capability is required so that people in every part of Scotland receive the same level of professional service."
Her Majesty's Inspectorate of Constabulary Scotland	January 23, 2009	Independent review of policing in Scotland: A report for the Cabinet Secretary for Justice	This review was concerned with identifying the action required to ensure that Scottish police forces are properly supported and could continue to deliver effective policing as a response to a wide range of demands and within available resources.
Sustainable Policing Project	November 2010	Sustainable policing project: Interim report	The aim of the interim report was to identify the key principles that must underpin a sustainable, locally responsive, accountable, police service, to identify the scope and scale for further cost savings in policing that will protect frontline policing and the delivery of outcomes for communities, and to identify and appraise options for reform that would deliver identified further cost savings.
Scottish government	February 2011	A consultation on the future of policing in Scotland	The document assessed the strengths and weaknesses of the pre-April 2013 model of policing under three headings: • Local engagement and partnership • Accountability • Efficiency
Sustainable Policing Project	March 2011	Phase 2 report: Options for reform	The report sought to identify a model of policing that will be sustainable in the long term, delivering policing services to a high standard in the most cost-effective way possible.
Scottish government	September 2011	Police reform program: Outline Business Case	The case appraised three options for the reform of policing in Scotland: eight forces, with enhanced national delivery; a regional force model; and a single national service model.

Source: Author.

Table 11.4   Sustainable Policing Project Mandate

Aim

To develop rigorously appraised options for further cost savings that will enable frontline policing outcomes to be sustained in 2013–2014 and beyond, in the face of anticipated spending reductions.

The key initial product of the SPP was a report delivered to the December meeting of the Scottish Policing Board. This report included

- A rigorous analysis of the current costs in policing
- The identification of options for savings beyond 2012–2013

Roles and Responsibilities

- The Scottish government would chair the SPP and would make decisions on the next steps following the delivery of the final report.
- The Scottish Policing Board would receive and consider the findings of the SPP work and determine how to progress the formal implementation of the findings.
- The SPP would gather and assess evidence, identify options for achieving additional cost savings, appraise those options using a rigorous methodology, and present findings and proposals for the next steps to the Scottish Policing Board.

Source: Sustainable Policing Project Team, *Sustainable policing project: Interim Report*, November 2010, pp. 1–2, Retrieved on 20 February 2014 from: http://www.scotland. gov.uk/Resource/Doc/254432/0110858.pdf.

Table 11.4 presents the details of the aim and the roles and responsibilities contained in the SPP mandate.

In order to identify a more efficient and effective policing model from the policing models proposed, the SPP developed a framework or template that was based on seven layers of common policing functions (Sustainable Policing Project, 2011). The layered template was subsequently used to develop the Target Operating Model (TOM), which formed the basis for evaluating the proposed policing models (single force, regionalization, or enhanced eight forces). The evaluation was to determine which model provided the highest benefit-to-cost ratio. The template is presented in Table 11.5.

Table 11.5   Seven-Layer Template Common to Policing Functions

1. Customers and stakeholder relationships (including partnerships)
2. Outcomes of policing
3. People—allocation and management of officers and staff to deliver policing
4. Data and information critical to the delivery of policing
5. Process—the key processes to deliver policing and interface with others in the wider process
6. Technology to support information management and policing process
7. Assets required to support the delivery of policing

Source: Adapted from Sustainable Policing Project, *Phase two report: Options for reform*, Retrieved on February 2, 2014 from http://www.scotland.gov.uk/Resource/Doc/254432/0115237. pdf., 2011, p. 17.

The SPP created the philosophy and the framework for the future reform of policing in Scotland. During the early research phase of the project, the team proposed that the government establish a coordinated change program to ensure that the stated social outcomes would be achieved given the proposed budget constraints and to ensure that there was transparency in the identification of any future policing options. The change program proposed by the team was based on their belief that changing the structure of the eight police forces would not in itself drive police service delivery efficiency or effectiveness but determined what was critical for the government to be able to achieve its outcomes.

As a result of the early reports produced by the Her Majesty's Inspectorate of Constabulary Scotland and the later reports prepared by the SPP, the Scottish government considered the eight force structure untenable and that reform was necessary (Scottish Government, 2011a). The Scottish government commented that the eight forces had remained the same since 1976, while the policing environment had undergone significant change (Scottish Government, 2011b). It was the view of the government that an extensive reform of the police would provide the platform to improve accountability and responsibility and to devolve governance to local areas (Sustainable Policing Project, 2011).

Case for Change

Financial Backdrop

In 2011, the government's budget was forecast to remain at the same level or would enter a period of decline until 2015/2016, and the budget was not expected to reach 2009/2010 levels again, in real terms, until 2026 (Sustainable Policing Project, 2011). This meant that the policing budget would be approximately 15% less or would be reduced by £1.72 billion in real terms (Sustainable Policing Project, 2011). The Scottish public sector, including police, had benefited from real term increases in their funding allocations and had experienced increases in their staffing levels during the previous 10 years (Sustainable Policing Project Team, 2010). It was envisaged that there would not be an improvement in the financial environment in the foreseeable future, which meant that the Scottish government needed to examine their expenditure and improve public sector efficiencies (Sustainable Policing Project, 2011). However, the government was also aware that while there was a need to decrease public spending, a large investment could be required in the short term to improve the efficiency of police service delivery.

How the effectiveness of the police could be improved without increasing their funding was the first area to be examined by the government.

The government determined that the public sector partnership activity could be improved without increasing funding. The government proposed that agencies could achieve better outcomes and reduce the duplication of functions across the agencies and maintain effective service delivery by improving their partnerships with each other and the community (Scottish Government, 2011a).

The government suggested that the police could make some efficiency gains through the collaboration of the eight forces. According to the Her Majesty's Inspectorate of Constabulary Scotland (2009), there was little evidence that collaboration between the eight forces was occurring and that the police needed to place an emphasis on collaboration to deliver specialist policing across Scotland (Scottish Government, 2011a). However, the government did note that increased collaboration would not necessarily deliver the improvements needed to improve the service delivered by police (Scottish Government, 2011a). The principal concerns held by the Her Majesty's Inspectorate of Constabulary Scotland were that there was limited information about the costs and the standards of collaboration and that a national body to provide oversight and governance did not exist (Her Majesty's Inspectorate of Constabulary Scotland, 2009).

A second area of weakness identified by the government was accountability (Scottish Government, 2011a). While there had been significant growth in police capability at the local, regional, and national level since the establishment of the eight-force structure in the 1970s, an accountability framework for policing at the national level did not exist (Scottish Government, 2011a). The eight-force structure had a complicated approach to service delivery (Her Majesty's Inspectorate of Constabulary Scotland, 2009) with service delivered through a mixture of lead force and collaborative agreements (Scottish Government, 2011a).

While joint police boards and police authorities provided a formal governance and oversight framework between the eight forces, Her Majesty's Inspectorate of Constabulary Scotland (2009) claimed that if the boards and authorities were to work together effectively, a system that provided further support and coordination was required. To clarify, Her Majesty's Inspectorate of Constabulary Scotland (2009) stated that there was "a lack of independent support provided to police boards or authorities, to enable them to properly deliver the degree of scrutiny, challenge and accountability required" to ensure appropriate democratic oversight (Her Majesty's Inspectorate of Constabulary Scotland, 2009, p. 6).

Sustainable Policing Project

The SPP team was to expand on the work completed by the ACPOS in 2010. The ACPOS laid the foundation for the discussion for the reform of the Scottish Police and highlighted the potential for cost savings, which would protect frontline policing and deliver outcomes for the community (Sustainable Policing Project Team, 2010). The SPP was to determine its response and "identify a model of policing that will be sustainable in the long term, delivering policing services to a high standard in the most cost-effective way possible" (Sustainable Policing Project, 2011, p. 3). The approach adopted by the project team was based on a first principles* approach, which established "a clear framework within which to take Scottish policing forward" (Sustainable Policing Project Team, 2010, p. 5).

The framework, however, was founded on an improved delivery of service. To enable the SPP to develop the framework, they completed a scope for efficiency. Table 11.6 presents the elements of the scope for efficiency† that was adopted by the project team.

In compliance with their mandate, the SPP presented an interim report to the Scottish Policing Board on December 15, 2010 (Scottish Government, 2011a). The report centered on three options for policing in Scotland: a single force, three or four regionalized forces, or enhancing the eight forces that were currently in place. Each option was considered against the following three key criteria:

1. Improving services for the delivery of better outcomes at local and national levels.
2. Accountability to, and close engagement with, local communities in every part of Scotland is essential.

Table 11.6 SPP Approach Used to Identify Scope for Efficiency

- Identification of the full range of efficiency levers
- Identification of the most appropriate lever or levers that can be applied to each policing function
- Identification of the current functional view of policing in Scotland and a new functional model (which could be applied to any structure) that safeguard local policing but recognizes that many functions currently delivered regionally could be delivered nationally, with some regional deployment
- Identification of the range of efficiencies that might be achieved within functional groups
- Assessment of the scale of efficiency likely to be delivered at a low, medium, and high confidence level for each function to give a range of potential savings

Source: Adapted from Sustainable Policing Project Team, *Sustainable policing project: Interim report*, Retrieved on February 20, 2014 from http://www.scotland.gov.uk/Resource/Doc/254432/0110858.pdf, November 2010, pp. 6–7.

---

* A foundational proposition or assumption that cannot be deduced from any other proposition or assumption
† Identification of the range of efficiency that may be achieved with a functional area, group, or section

3. Efficiencies must be delivered while protecting frontline services as far as possible* (Scottish Government, 2011a, p. 23).

The report suggested that efficiencies and savings of between £81m and £197m per annum could be made by rationalizing and reducing duplication in administrative and operational processes across the eight forces (Scottish Government, 2011a). However, the report noted that there were two provisos to these figures. The first was that the figures were "a high level assessment and further work" was "needed to test deliverability" (Scottish Government, 2011a, p. 22). The second proviso was that the estimates were "based on high-level financial data provided by the eight Scottish police forces and SPSA, and identification of the range of efficiencies that might be achieved within each policing function, [were] based on benchmarking data from elsewhere" (Scottish Government, 2011a, p. 22).†

The report indicated that significant savings could be made, but the government realized that any savings made from the reform program may have needed to be reinvested in operational policing to ensure the achievement of agreed social outcomes (Scottish Government, 2011a).

Police Reform Program: Outline Business Case

In September 2011, the Scottish government released a second report for the reform of Scotland's police, which was compiled by the SPP and was titled the Outline Business Case. The first report by the SPP suggested 12 efficiency reform options within the following five broad structural alternatives:

1. A single service model
2. A regional police force model
3. An eight forces model with additional efficiencies
4. A "blue light" service model
5. A 32-unit model, based on the existing local authority boundaries (Scottish Government, 2011b)

These options were subsequently refined to three options, which were appraised and documented in the Outline Business Case: the existing eight

---

* The three key criteria became known later as the key drivers for reform and were changed to
  1. Improving local services and the delivery of outcomes
  2. Strengthening governance and accountability
  3. A financially sustainable police service
† The SPP research was based on 10 key functions: local policing; dealing with the public (customer contact); criminal justice; road policing; special operations; intelligence; specialist investigations; investigative support; support services; and national policing (Sustainable Policing Project, 2011, p. 3).

Table 11.7   High-Level Business Case Analysis Framework

- The strategic case for change—the current structure and strategic context for the Police Reform Program and the details of the key drivers for change
- The reform options—based on the "Target Operating Model" methodology, develops the reform options into models for analysis
- Options appraisal—includes economic appraisal; strategic assessment of options; and financial appraisal (detailed cost profiles, opportunities for savings, and estimated transition costs)
- Risk assessment—identified key risks and assessed the likelihood of their occurrence under each reform option
- The preferred option—a comparative analysis of the three options for structural reform based on a review of monetary, nonmonetary, and risk factors
- Progressing the preferred option—the proposed way forward for managing the change process (including business continuity, project and change management, benefits realization, risk management, and postproject evaluation)

Source: Adapted from Scottish Government, *Police reform programme: Outline business case,* Retrieved on February 1, 2014 from http://www.scotland.gov.uk/Resource/Doc/357534/0120783.pdf, 2011b, pp. 10–11.

forces, with enhanced national delivery; a regional force model; and a single service model (Scottish Government, 2011b). The appraisal was designed to consider efficiency savings for each of the three options and to ensure that the benefit of any change exceeded any costs. The appraisal also considered whether there would be any impact on outcomes and determined the option that provided the greatest financial net benefit (Scottish Government, 2011b).

Table 11.7 presents the high-level framework that was used to develop the business case for the need for police reform.

The analysis of the three options was based on a template called the Target Operating Model (TOM), which was developed by the SPP. The model was developed from a review of the policing functions of the eight forces and was capable of providing "a comprehensive review of monetary and non-monetary benefits, transition costs, and risk factors associated with the three reform options" (Scottish Government, 2011b, p. 8). A major strength of the model was that it was more comprehensive than the earlier models that had been used by the Scottish government to analyze the organization of the police. It took into account three new functional levels (local policing, national policing, and national support) and recognized the movement between the proposed policing functions from the local to the national level (Scottish Government, 2011b).

The template was a generic framework, which could be applied to each of the three proposed functional levels and provided a pictorial presentation of each option, its resources and processes. The template conveyed how each option would deliver its services (Scottish Government, 2011b). The Scottish government (2011b) claimed that the model described "an optimum model for service delivery, allowing an informed assessment of the costs, benefits and risks associated with each option" and represented "a model of the most effective and efficient way to deliver services, but is not a blueprint for any new service" (p. 8).

The Outline Business Case ranked the three options using the cost of implementation and affordability as criteria and recommended the adoption of the single service model. The primary differences between the three models related to

1. The scale of benefits that could be achieved under each structural model
2. The challenge in managing the transition to each new model
3. The complexity of delivering services in the different models once the transition was complete (Sustainable Policing Project, 2011, p. 5)

Although the single force model represented the most significant change, it also provided "the greatest opportunity to manage change, drive efficiency, and in delivering operations when the change is complete" (Sustainable Policing Project, 2011, p. 5).

The three options ranked on the criteria of cost are presented in Table 11.8.

The Scottish government (2011b) determined that a single service would provide the best option to reduce duplication and would "ensure consistency, and rationalize existing systems and structures" (p. 69). A single service would also be capable of realizing efficiencies from economies of scale, devolving funding from the national level to the local level, improving accountability, and experiencing greater engagement with each local authority (Scottish Government, 2011b). The Outline Business Case identified four other benefits that a single service would provide, and these have been presented in Table 11.9.

Table 11.8   Ranking of the Three Options on Monetary Factors

	Option 1: Eight Forces Enhanced	Option 2: Regional Force	Option 3: Single Service
Net present value (15 years)	1057m	1193m	1364m
Net efficiencies (year 5)	118m pa	132m pa	151m pa
Total transition costs (5 years)	132m	145m	161m
Affordability (year 5)	85m pa	97m pa	106m pa
Ranking	3	2	1

Source: Adapted from Scottish Government, *Police reform programme: Outline business case*, Retrieved on February 1, 2014 from http://www.scotland.gov.uk/Resource/Doc/357534/0120783.pdf, 2011b, p. 68.

Table 11.9   Benefits of a Single Police Service

- Protection of, and improvement in, local community policing
- The best opportunity to reinvest to improve local policing outcomes
- The highest potential for long-term financial sustainability
- The best opportunity to coordinate change, optimize benefit, and minimize risk

Source: Adapted from Scottish Government, *Police reform programme: Outline business case*, Retrieved on February 1, 2014 from http://www.scotland. gov.uk/Resource/Doc/357534/0120783.pdf, 2011b, pp. 69–70.

Consultation on the Future of Policing in Scotland

Following the release of the initial research undertaken by the SPP, on February 10, 2011, the Scottish government published "A Consultation on the Future of Policing in Scotland" to gather the public's views on the proposed reform of the police (Bryan et al., 2011).

The document presented three options for public consideration: eight services, but with enhanced collaboration; a rationalized regional structure; and a single service. It also outlined the strengths and weaknesses of the options and asked participants to consider whether each option

- Improved police services and outcomes
- Increased police accountability and engagement, especially in relation to local communities
- Delivered efficiencies while protecting frontline services (Bryan et al., 2011, p. 1)

In response to the consultation document, the government received 219 replies, 90 of which were from individuals and the remaining 129 were submitted by organizations (Bryan et al., 2011). The majority of the replies "were generally set within the context of a service that is currently perceived to be working well" and that any reform of policing needed to focus on the impact of the option on local communities (Bryan et al., 2011, p. 1).

In answer to the question pertaining to which reform option was more favorable, "there was limited support [from 22 respondents] for a single police force," while 59 of the 219 "respondents preferred the option to retain 8 forces with increased collaboration, and 45 supported a rationalised regional model" (Bryan et al., 2011, p. 3). However, approximately one-third (77 respondents or 35%) of the respondents could not decide on an option owing to "the lack of detailed evidence and information" presented in the consultation document (Bryan et al., 2011, p. 3).

The Reform Bill

On January 16, 2012, the government introduced the Police and Fire Reform (Scotland) Bill to the Scottish Parliament. The bill established the framework for the reform, the policing principles and the broad structures, and arrangements necessary for a new police service (Scott, 2012). The bill received royal assent and was passed into legislation on August 7, 2012.

The passing of the Police and Fire Reform (Scotland) Act 2012 marked "a significant advance for policing in Scotland" by providing the structure and detail of the "substantial requirements for the modernization of Scottish policing" and, for the first time, provided a statement of policing principles (Scott, 2012, p. 140). The legislation established a set of policing principles, a procedure for delivering policing at the local level and a national policing governance and accountability framework (Scott, 2012).

The act contained five significant clauses to enable the creation of a capable and sustainable single national police service:

1. A national police force would be established.
2. Local policing would be a statutory requirement and would be organized at the level of Scotland's 32 local councils.
3. The new police service would develop a national strategic plan and local policing plans and would publish annual policing plans in order to secure continuous improvement in policing.
4. A new body called the Scottish Police Authority would provide the governance for the new police service.
5. That policing in Scotland would be based on two policing principles:
    a. Policing is to be accessible to, and engaged with, local communities.
    b. Policing will promote measures to prevent crime, harm, and disorder (Fyfe and Scott, 2012; Scott, 2012).

Methodology

The purpose of this research was to examine the planning and the development of the Scottish police merger and to evaluate whether the merger achieved the government's original aims and objectives. In particular, the research sought to examine:

1. Why was a merger of all police forces adopted? What were the main drivers?
2. What alternative options to a merger were considered?

3. What activities and budget analyses were undertaken to plan for and implement the merger? What is the evidence for any change in the efficiency and effectiveness of the delivery of services by the new Police Service of Scotland?

To answer these questions, the study took a cross-sectional approach by interviewing and surveying serving and former police officers and other governmental officials from Scotland who had been involved in the reform in an official capacity. The interviews were semistructured and were based on a questionnaire of 16 questions that were used to guide the discussion. The questions that were used as a basis for the interviews are presented in Table 11.10.

Twenty-five serving and former police officers and government officials were contacted to obtain their permission to be included in a semistructured interview for this research. Twelve officers and officials (48%) agreed to be involved in the research, of which seven are serving police officers and five

Table 11.10 Semistructured Interview Questions

- What was your role in the reform?
- Did you think that the eight forces were successful in policing Scotland, and if so, what were the key measures of success?
- What was your initial response to the declaration that the eight forces were to reform as a single force?
- Did you initially agree with the single force concept? If so, why? If not, why not?
- Why do you think the government adopted the single force option?
- What do you think were the main drivers for the government to reform the forces?
- Why do you think the government did not accept the "enhanced collaboration" or the "regionalization" options?
- What activities and budget analyses were undertaken to plan for and implement the single force option?
- Was there a document identifying the outcomes of the reform and how the reform was to achieve these outcomes?
- What do you think were the major challenges to the implementation of the single force/ Police Scotland?
- Do you think the reform has been successful (especially in regard to achieving savings, better engagement with the community, improved partnerships, etc.)?
- Do you think policing in Scotland has improved as a result of the establishment of the single force? Why or why not?
- What do you think should be the reform's measures of success and what progress (if any) has there been in achieving these?
- What is the evidence of the improvement in policing in Scotland?
- Can Police Scotland be improved? How?
- What is the greatest challenge facing Police Scotland? Why?

Source: Author.

are government officials. Of the five government officials, three were former police officers who, at the time of this research, held senior positions in other Scottish government agencies. Eight of the twenty-five participants agreed to participate in a face-to-face interview, and owing to operational commitments, four agreed to answer the questionnaire by telephone interview.

Results

It was envisaged that the research would either confirm that the government and the police had undertaken extensive research and analysis prior to implementing the reform of policing in Scotland or would verify that there had been a formal procedure leading to the political decision to establish a single force. It was also predicted that the establishment of a single force would have been based on extensive research and analysis and that an implementation plan for a single force would have been developed and documented.

The interview phase of the research took place between mid-July and mid-August 2014. The participants were advised as to the intent of the interview and that the interview would form the basis for an examination of the political decisions that led to the establishment of a single force and the effectiveness of the service that would be delivered by the single force.

The results of the interviews and surveys are discussed in the following under four research questions.

Why Was a Merger of All Police Forces Adopted?
What Were the Main Drivers?

All 12 participants noted that the eight forces had performed well, and, as one participant claimed, "in some cases, at the top of their game." According to the participants, public confidence in the police throughout Scotland was evidence of the high level of performance delivered by the eight police forces.

When the announcement was made that a single force was to be established, all participants said that they were disappointed that the force that they belonged to would be merged. All of the police participants were senior officers, and they were sorry to see the individual identity of their forces merged into one national police force. However, all of the police participants were positive about the idea of a new single force and were cognizant of the challenges that the implementation of a single force created.

Only 4 (33%) of the 12 participants initially agreed with the single force concept, while 6 (50%) participants expressed that they had preferred the eight force or status quo model, while 2 favored the regionalization model.

All of the 12 participants noted that the main goal of the reform was to save money and that the main driver for the single force option was for the

Scottish government to ensure that the same level of service could be maintained in the future with a decreasing level of funding. One participant also identified that the establishment of the single police service was the start of a wider Scottish public sector reform program and if the reform of the police was successful, the approach may be used in other sectors. Another participant believed that the merger was about ensuring sustainability in the police service and that the establishment of a single national police force was inevitable. As noted by one participant, the single force option was the only way to drive police service delivery efficiency and effectiveness.

The only criticism that one participant had in the early stage of the announcement of a single force was that there could have been a wider public and internal police discussion about the other two options: retaining the status quo or regionalization and how the creation of the single force would be undertaken. According to this participant, there had been very little public discussion as to the strengths and weaknesses of the other two options and no discussion within or across the eight police forces.

What Alternatives to a Merger Were Considered?

All participants believed that the Scottish government considered three police reform models: enhancing the existing eight forces, creating a three or four force regional model, and the single force model. All 12 participants noted that the status quo model and regionalization would probably not have made the savings needed and that the status quo was not sustainable in the new economic environment. Two participants also observed that regionalization would only be the first step toward creating a single force, as this option would create three or four powerful Chief Constables, which would require a comprehensive and possibly an expensive governance framework. One participant believed that regionalization probably would not have increased collaboration across the forces or improved the efficiency or the effectiveness of service delivery.

Three participants also noted that the reform was not only about the police but was also about the Scottish identity, and as such, a new single national force could be viewed both internationally and within Scotland as a symbol of a new united Scotland.

What Activities and Budget Analyses Were Undertaken to Plan for and Implement the Merger?

All of the participants were familiar with the Outline Business Case developed by the Sustainable Policing Project on behalf of the Scottish government. One participant described the Outline Business Case as an extremely "high-level" form of strategic analysis.

It was noted by one participant that the major issue in the analysis phase of the proposed reform was that the Outline Business Case and its analysis were not publicly debated. Another participant noted that the Outline Business Case analysis was not well understood by the public or the police, while three participants noted that the data used were not robust and that the financial information was mainly based on "guesstimates."

Has There Been Any Change in the Efficiency and Effectiveness of the Delivery of Services by the New Police Service of Scotland?

A number of questions were used to answer the fourth research question. The results of these questions are presented in Tables 11.11 through 11.13. The first question asked participants to identify the major challenges in implementing a single force. Six (50%) of the participants believed that there were three major challenges to the implementation of the single force: the different cultures of the eight forces; the scale, complexity, and the timeline of the reform; and being able to retain local support for the police. Table 11.11 presents four major challenges to implementing a single force that were identified by the participants.

Five of the 12 interview participants (approximately 42%) said that the reform had been successful, especially as far as the public were concerned.

Table 11.11   What Do You Think Were the Major Challenges to Implementing a Single Force/Police Scotland?

Major Challenge	Number of Times Challenge Identified by Participants[a]
The differing cultures of the eight forces	6
The scale, complexity, and timeline of the reform	6
Retaining local support for police	6
Internal resistance to the reform	2
Anxieties over centralization of the police	2
The law enforcement approach to policing rather than a community policing approach[b]	2
Meeting required reform savings	2

[a] Total is greater than 12 survey participants due to individual participant's identifying more than one challenge.

[b] This is often described as a "Strathclyde takeover (or Strathclydization) of Scottish policing." Due to the current Chief Constable of Police Scotland being the Chief Constable of the Strathclyde Police prior to the reform, there is a view that the Strathclyde approach to delivering police services is preferred over other forms of delivery, for example, a number of participants noted that it appeared that Police Scotland was using more of a law enforcement approach in some areas of service delivery rather than more of a community-oriented approach. A more law enforcement approach to service delivery, according to participants, is historically attributable to the previous Strathclyde Police.

Table 11.12   What Is the Evidence of an Improvement in Policing in Scotland?

Element of Improvement	Number of Times Improvement Identified by Participants[a]
That the savings have been made	6
Improved accountability of police	4
Greater access to specialist police	2
Level of crime/number of crashes	2
Better local service	2
More efficient and effective delivery of services	2

[a] Total is greater than 12 survey participants due to individual participant's identifying more than one element of improvement.

Table 11.13   What Do You Think Should Be the Measures of Success of the Reform and What Progress (if Any) Has There Been in Achieving These?

Measure of Success	Number of Times Measure of Success Identified by Participants[a]
Public confidence in the police	6
Keeping within budget	4
Measures identified in the legislation	4
The performance of Police Scotland	2
The reduction in the level of crime	2
Complaints against police	2

[a] Total is greater than 12 survey participants due to individual participant's identifying more than one measure of success.

According to four of these five participants, the public did not notice any difference in how police services were delivered or how the police responded to emergency calls and requests for assistance from the public, from day 1 of the merger. Five of the participants felt that policing in Scotland had improved as a result of the establishment of the single force. An improvement could be seen from the deployment of specialist officers to assist other police localities with operations and from the capability of Police Scotland to investigate sexual offending historic/cold cases.

Table 11.12 presents six elements, which have improved since the establishment of Police Scotland. The elements of improvement, which were identified by most of the participants, were the budgetary savings that had been made and the improvement in the accountability of the police from the establishment of the Scottish Police Authority and a Scottish Police Investigations and Review Commissioner and an increase in the audit responsibility of Her Majesty's Inspectorate of Constabulary Scotland. However, one participant disagreed saying that there had been no evidence of any improvement in policing in Scotland.

The participants identified six measures of reform success, and these have been presented in Table 11.13. The most frequent measures of success that were identified by the participants were "public confidence in the police," followed closely by Police Scotland keeping within budget and Police Scotland achieving the three objectives of the reform, which were decreed in the 2012 Act. The three objectives decreed in the 2012 Act were for the single police service to

1. Protect and improve local services despite financial cuts, by ceasing the duplication of support services and not reducing frontline services
2. Create more equal access to specialist support and national capacity—where and when they are needed
3. Strengthen the connection between services and communities, by creating new formal relationships with each of the 32 local authorities and better integrating with community planning partnerships (Scottish Government, 2012)

The 2012 Act policy memorandum also noted that any Scottish public sector reform program must ensure that

1. Public services are built around people and communities, their needs, aspirations, capabilities, and skills and work to build autonomy and resilience.
2. Public service organizations work together effectively to achieve outcomes.
3. Public service organizations prioritize prevention, reduce inequalities, and promote equality.
4. All public services constantly seek to improve performance and reduce costs and are open, transparent, and accountable (Scottish Government, 2012).

The final two questions related to the future of Police Scotland. The first question asked whether the delivery of services by Police Scotland could be improved. Participants identified four different forms of improvement for the future, and these have been presented in Table 11.14. There was little difference in the number of times that an improvement was identified by participants, but the most frequently mentioned strategy for future improvement was the approach to the delivery of policing services. Four participants identified "consistency versus flexibility of the delivery of services." This priority pertained to Police Scotland having the ability to develop policies at the national level, but ensuring that any policy that would be developed would

Table 11.14   Priorities for the Future Improvement of Police Scotland

Form of Future Improvement	Number of Times Improvement Identified by Participants[a]
Approaches to delivery of policing services	5
Restructuring of the organization	4
Consistency versus flexibility of delivery of services	4
Continuous improvement of Police Scotland	3

[a] Total is greater than 12 survey participants due to individual participant's identifying more than one form of future improvement.

Table 11.15   What Is the Greatest Challenge Facing Police Scotland?

Future Major Challenge	Number of Times Challenge Identified by Participants[a]
Level of Police Scotland's budget	8
Structure/staffing composition	4
Culture of the new organization	4
Public confidence in Police Scotland	4
The role of the Scottish Police Authority	4
Retaining the 17,324 officers	2

[a] Total is greater than 12 survey participants due to individual participant's identifying more than one future challenge.

take into account local issues and that the policies would be flexible by allowing local police commanders to design implementation strategies in consultation with local councils.

The final question asked was what was the greatest challenge facing Police Scotland? The participants identified six challenges, and these have been presented in Table 11.15. The most frequently cited challenge for the future was the level of funding and whether the current level of service could be delivered if further funding cuts were imposed.

Three participants noted that the reform had not been fully implemented and that a change program is a journey. Another participant commented that it will be some time before Police Scotland will have the organizational maturity to be able to fully comprehend and be able to react comprehensively to the changing Scottish political environment.

Discussion

There are two major problems when examining or evaluating the merger or reform of government sector institutions, especially police forces. The first is that any merger of a government institution will be a political decision (La Grange, 1987) and that the merger or reform is usually not a decision made by the agencies involved. According to Krimmel (1997) and Reiner (1986), the political dimension of any reform is the most important aspect as it is often the fear held by local politicians that they may lose control of local police agencies that usually derail any attempts to merge or regionalize police agencies. The political dimension of any police reform can make an evaluation of how an organizational structure was decided upon difficult, because the final decision may be political, and not based on any form of analysis to improve operational or service delivery efficiency or effectiveness. The second issue relating to the political dimension is, according to Lithopoulos and Rigakos (2005), that the final merger model is often decided upon early in the planning process and becomes a fait accompli and that any documentation developed for the merger tends "to rationalize rather than criticize its impacts" (p. 339).

In fact, as can be seen from this research, even though the eight Scottish police forces were performing well and that seven of the eight forces would have preferred either the "enhanced collaboration" model or regionalization, their views were not sought, and if the forces views were sought, they did not hold any weight in the final decision. However, it is not known in the Scottish case whether the voices of the seven forces were not heard because they were classed by the politicians as having a vested interest in the final outcome of the reform. Nor is it known whether the politicians relied exclusively on the Outline Business Case to make the final decision. If the politicians did base their decision solely on the Outline Business Case, any of the options preferred by the seven forces would be negated.

The second major problem encountered when evaluating whether merged police agencies are actually more efficient and effective than they were prior to merging is that there has not been any research conducted into this area of police management. While there have been two evaluations of the mergers of UK health providers (Braithwaite et al., 2005; Fulop et al., 2002), there is no accepted theory of police reform, no accepted method as to how such a reform should be evaluated, nor has there been any comparative studies of earlier police organizational mergers. The lack of research into the impact that reform has had on agencies and their delivery of services was underlined by Braithwaite et al. (2005), who noted that

> [t]he evidence for making a difference, let alone demonstrably improving productivity or outcomes, is surprisingly slender .... In truth, there are no randomized trials, no longitudinal studies of multiple restructuring events or time series designs and little scientifically acceptable cross-sectional work .... While there are studies, they challenge rather than support restructuring. (p. 542)

Similar conclusions are echoed by studies of other public sector agencies. Research into 25 UK National Health Service trusts, which merged between 1996 and 2001, for example, found evidence of negative effects on the delivery of services owing to a loss of managerial focus on services (Fulop et al., 2002).

As a result of the absence of an accepted theory of police reform and an accepted method to evaluate such a reform, researchers have looked for models, frameworks, or theories from other research areas that could be applied to specific case studies. Terpstra and Fyfe (2014), for example, draw on Kingdon's (2003) approach to the analysis of policy change and policy formation to examine similarities and differences between recent police reforms in Scotland and the Netherlands. However, Kingdon's approach to policy change and formation is not appropriate for this research because Kingdon's approach concentrates on the predecision processes (involving agenda setting and the consideration of policy alternatives); the importance of the coupling of problems, policies, and politics to create windows of opportunity in terms of policy change; and the role played by "policy entrepreneurs" in taking forward police reform. As highlighted by Terpstra and Fyfe (2014), understanding the evolution of public policy and, in particular, moments of significant policy change, is a key focus for political and administrative science researchers. This is despite that it is a field where there are several competing theories and perspectives (John, 2003) and that there are similarities in terms of what is understood to be the key elements in making sense of policy change.

Policy Analysis Framework

Public Choice theory has had a huge influence on modern thinking and the development of political science, public policy, and public administration (Boston, 1991). A number of different terms have been used to describe Public Choice theory, including Social Choice theory, Rational Choice theory, the Economics of Politics, and the Virginia School. The main principle of the theory is that people are believed to be rational and that they are dominated by self-interest (Gorringe, 2001). The theory also sought to minimize the role of the state, limit the discretionary power of politicians, and curb the functions of government (Boston, 1991). It was believed that because politicians had abused their power, this power could be minimized through the restructuring of budgets and performance arrangements (Pallot, 1991).

Modern research, based on Public Choice theory, proposes that any government reform program must consider the following: "(1) the preferences of citizens and other actors in the system; (2) the nature of the good or service desired; and (3) the structure of the institutions through which demands are expressed and production decisions made" (Bish, 2001, p. 5).

These three elements form the basis for examining the Scottish police reform. However, while the three elements may determine that the establishment of a single force was the appropriate option, this, within the three-element model, according to Bish (2001), could be "flawed nineteenth-century thinking and a bureaucratic urge for centralized control" (p. 1).

The study of police reform in Scotland has revealed two major issues and three issues of a more minor nature. The first major issue is that the Scottish government appeared to rely principally on the recommendations presented in the Outline Business Case to base their decision on—to accept the single force option. However, there are a number of weaknesses within the Outline Business Case. The first was that the financial data were not robust, and the majority of the figures were best guesses and not actually based on real cost figures. The second was that neutral language was not used to compose the Outline Business Case. It was written in such a way to emphasize that the single force option was the better of the three options.

The second major issue pertains to the reliance of the Scottish government on the 2011 public "Consultation on the Future of Policing in Scotland" survey. This was a public survey of which there were only 219 replies, 22 (approximately 10%) of which supported the establishment of a single force. The survey did not represent the population, as the number of respondents was too small, nor did the number of responses provide a convincing argument for implementing the single force option.

A minor issue that was noted was that there was a need for the Scottish government to look at methods for decreasing the costs of policing. The cost of policing in Scotland had increased over the past 10 years and there was very little incentive for police forces to look at ways of reducing costs or improving their service delivery efficiency and effectiveness (Fyfe, 2013; Fyfe and Scott, 2013). Another issue that was noted related to how the reform was undertaken. There was no evidence of any further analysis being completed following the publication of the Outline Business Case as to how the single force option would be implemented. The third issue was that there appeared to be an overreliance or overacceptance of all things Strathclyde. This overreliance in some ways makes sense as prior to the reform, the Strathclyde Police were the largest of the eight Scottish forces, and their approach to policing may have been more suitable for a single national force. An opposing view was that the Strathclyde service delivery approach should have been balanced with earlier local policing approaches, which would have ensured continued support for the police.

These issues are at the crux of the Scottish reform discussion. However, what will determine the future of Police Scotland is not the elements that the Scottish government were guided by during the reform but how policing is delivered by Police Scotland.

Conclusion

This study shows that while there was a need to improve the efficiency and effectiveness of the eight Scottish Police Forces, the decision to reform policing in Scotland does not appear to have been based on transparent decision-making, best evidence, or best practice. The decision to implement the reform appears to have been based on the joint actions of a large number of semiautonomous actors, each having their own interests, agendas, and views (Terpstra and Fyfe, n.d.). Second, the implementation process has been a mechanical process, relying on the enactment of legislation (the Police and Fire [Scotland] Act 2012) (Terpstra and Fyfe, n.d.), and not on the development of a comprehensive implementation plan. According to Terpstra and Fyfe (n.d.), as the government relied only on the legislation, there was no creativity for a robust and comprehensive governance and service delivery framework, which was capable of taking into account both national and local policing issues.

The need for police reform is not a windfall but builds over a period of time and is triggered by a number of precipitating factors (Brodeur, 2005). The need for the reform of policing in Scotland was clearly evident by the documentation of six background reports, which are presented in Table 11.3. However, a reform needs to be planned and implemented appropriately if it is to deliver any improvement in the effectiveness of service delivery, and any increase in productivity needs to be matched in parallel by a strategic, concerted, and sustained effort to improve the management of resources across the new institution (Her Majesty's Treasury, 2006).

In order to survive and prosper, Police Scotland must develop and maintain an acceptable alignment with its environment (Snow & Hambrick, 1980). Police Scotland must ensure that its organizational structure is not overly centralized and is able to ease the fundamental tensions between the pressure to centralize and standardize. The organization's executive must also ensure that Police Scotland is able to take account of the need for decentralization, local operational autonomy, and the sponsoring of local initiatives.

Ghosts of Policing Strategies Past

12

Is the New Zealand Police "Prevention First" Strategy Historic, Contemporary, or of the Future?

Introduction

In response to the changing environment, police agencies in recent years have adopted a number of different approaches to deliver their core services. The most common approaches that have been adopted have been Community-Oriented Policing, Problem-Oriented Policing (Thurman & Zhao, 2004), and Intelligence-Led Policing. However, these approaches have not made any fundamental change to the way that police agencies carry out their business to the extent that, for example, Compstat (see Willis, Mastrofski, & Weisburd, 2007) or the UK National Intelligence Model have.

Radical changes in the New Zealand economy in the late 1980s placed pressure on the New Zealand Police (NZP) to develop and implement three extensive change management programs. The first change management program, called Policing 2000, commenced in 1996. This was an integrated business transformational program, which comprised 10 major projects, which were to be implemented in several phases over the following four years (Doone, 1996). The second program, introduced in 2009, was called Policing Excellence and comprised 11 change management work streams (New Zealand Police, 2011a). The third program, introduced in 2011, subsequently encapsulated the Policing Excellence program and was called Prevention First (New Zealand Police, 2011c).

This chapter will use Mintzberg's (1978) strategic analysis framework to discuss and compare the extensive changes that the NZP have made since the late 1980s to increase their service delivery efficiency and effectiveness. The discussion will focus principally upon the initial change management program, Policing 2000, within the context of the changes within the New Zealand government sector and the organizational changes instituted later by the NZP. Organizational changes that were implemented in the 1990s will be compared to the post-2010 changes and whether the later changes provided a structure that would result in an increase in the efficiency and the effectiveness of the service delivered will also be examined. The comparison between the two major periods of change will highlight the strengths and weaknesses of each change program, as both were radical and may be viewed as being instrumental in changing the way that the police deliver its services. While it is not the purpose of this chapter to use a statistical approach to measure the success of the three programs, nor to suggest a generic detailed organizational change management program, the chapter will highlight and discuss a number of key issues in the design, development, and implementation of the three change management programs.

A Framework for Analyzing the New Zealand Police Change Management Programs

Every organization must adapt and maintain a relationship with its environment in order to survive and advance (Snow & Hambrick, 1980). To be able to adapt and maintain a relationship with the environment, organizations must design and implement relevant political and operational strategies. The development of strategies should be a regular part of managing an organization and should include the systematic scanning of the environment, an assessment of the organization's capacity and needs, and adapting the organization's actions in light of changing goals (Cohen & Eimicke, 2012). It must be acknowledged that not all strategies are deliberate plans that have been developed in advance of a managerial decision (Mintzberg, 1978). It must also be appreciated that there is a distinction between strategy formulation and strategy implementation (Snow & Hambrick, 1980) and that strategies can take many different types or forms.

Making a distinction between strategy formulation and implementation is advantageous as the design aspects of strategy formulation can be identified as a separate and distinct phase from the execution-focused, strategy implementation. Snow and Hambrick (1980) maintained that the "formulation/ implementation dichotomy is useful conceptually ... it implies that strategy is developed consciously and purposefully" (p. 527). While Mintzberg (1978) claimed that strategy can be viewed as a set of consistent behaviors by an organization within an environment and that a strategy may also be considered to be the organization's response to the changing environment. However, organizational strategies can emerge unintentionally.

Strategies, whether intentional or unintentional, are called emerging strategies (Mintzberg, 1978). Emerging strategies may be viewed as a pattern of sequential decisions in the strategy development process and in the actions of an organization. Snow and Hambrick (1980) noted that these strategic decisions will typically be directed at maintaining an organization's relationship or "alignment with its environment and managing its major internal interdependencies" (p. 528).

The second point that Snow and Hambrick (1980) made was that distinguishing between strategy formulation and implementation and intentional and unintentional strategies enables an organization to make decisions based on its organizational goals and to allocate the resources necessary to achieve its goals. Mintzberg (1978) claimed that strategy formulation follows the important pattern of management mediating between the two forces of "a dynamic environment and bureaucratic momentum" (p. 934). An organization looks for methods to maintain a relationship or mediate with the environment and to manage the "distinct change-continuity cycles" within the environment (Mintzberg, 1978, p. 934).

Strategic options are not made in a vacuum but reflect the dominant social, economic, and political paradigms of the time (Cohen & Eimicke, 2012). The possibility that patterns or cycles form within the formulation and implementation of strategies suggests that strategies may not "change in [a] continuous incremental fashion," but could change "in spurts, each followed by a period of continuity" (Mintzberg, 1978, p. 941). People in organizations do not respond to incidents continuously but react in discreet steps to events that are large enough in size for them to understand (Mintzberg, 1978). As a result of the continual changes in an environment, organizations form and implement strategies in continuous cycles.

The complex relationship between formation and implementation and between intentional and unintentional strategy can be examined by establishing phases of an intended strategy. This relationship is presented in Figure 12.1. As illustrated in the figure, there are two types of strategies: intended and realized. An intended strategy becomes a realized strategy upon implementation and maybe called a deliberate strategy (Mintzberg, 1978). However, during the implementation of an intended strategy, the

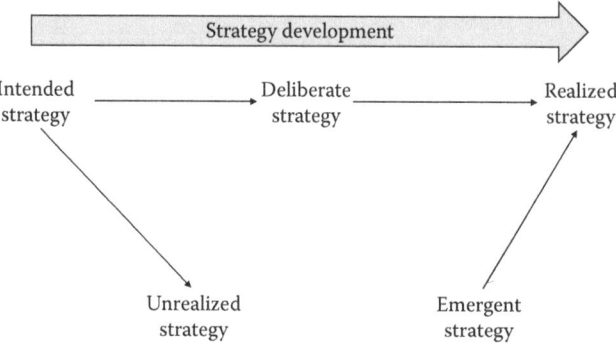

Figure 12.1 Types or forms of strategies. (Adapted from Mintzberg, H., *Manage. Sci.*, 24, 945, 1978.)

strategy may become unrealized due to a number of factors, but at the realized stage, further strategies can also emerge from unforeseen opportunities. Furthermore, strategies can change their form during realization and can become "formalized as deliberate," leading them to become identified as intended strategies (Minzberg, 1978, p. 946). This implies that strategies may have an incubation period during their formation as an emergent strategy.

The major problem with undertaking an analysis of the strategies that an organization has developed is that strategy is usually viewed as being purposely developed, and in advance of the decision that is made (Mintzberg, 1978). Problems may also emerge when attempting to identify as to whether an organization has developed a strategy, or whether an organization is responding to a particular change in the environment, or if it is responding in a familiar way and whether the response is "a continuation of, not a change in, strategy" (Snow & Hambrick, 1980, p. 528). Whether a strategy is an intended strategy appears to be based on what has worked previously (Minzberg, 1978).

New Zealand Public Sector Reforms (1984–1990)

From 1984, New Zealand implemented a radical series of economic and labor market reforms designed to eliminate government debt and create an internationally competitive economic environment. The government reforms were the most thorough in New Zealand's history, and the changes were ranked as among the most radical and comprehensive undertaken anywhere in the world (Boston, Dalziel, & St. John, 1999; Boston, Martin, Pallot, & Walsh, 1991). The scope and scale of these changes was significant, involving commercialization, corporatization, privatization, the restructuring of numerous government departments, the introduction of a new form of public financial management, and major changes to industrial relations (Boston et al., 1991, 1999). It was also intended that the reforms would result in a more responsive public service (Gorringe, 2001).

At this time there was pressure from the public for the police to become more accountable for the use of public funds and to deliver better and more focused services. The police also faced additional pressure from the political emphasis placed on the public sector to do more with less (Gorringe, 2001) and the importance placed on government programs being more effective (Salamon, 2000). This created the backdrop for the three change management projects: Policing 2000, Policing Excellence, and Prevention First. In each of these programs, the structures, budgets, and service delivery processes of the organization were examined, and it was intended that the implementation of these programs would improve the service delivery of the police while reducing operational costs.

Initial Response by the New Zealand Police to the Environment of the Late 1980s

The NZP are a national police service and are responsible for a full range of law enforcement services and investigations from minor criminal offending and traffic enforcement to major and organized crimes. In 2015, the organization comprised approximately 9063 sworn officers and 2969 civilian employees and was structured to include a national headquarter and 12 districts (New Zealand Police, 2015). The 12 districts are made up of 37 policing areas, which encompass more than 380 police stations (New Zealand Police, 2015). Table 12.1 presents the number of police officers and nonsworn staff and the number of officers per 100,000 population from 1996 to 2014.

In the late 1980s, a community-oriented and problem-solving strategy of policing, with decentralized management and the delegation of operational responsibilities to the area level, was implemented by the police, which was

Table 12.1 Number of New Zealand Police Officers and Nonsworn Staff Members and Officers per 100,000 Population 1996–2014

Year	Number of Sworn Officers[a]	Number of Nonsworn Staff[a]	Ratio of Officers per 100,000 Population
1996	6914	1830	185.17
1997	6876	1840	181.78
1998	6973	2133	182.78
1999	7061	1717	184.01
2000	7081	1815	183.44
2001	7045	1804	181.26
2002	7165	2017	181.34
2003	7257	2176	180.18
2004	7328	2288	179.23
2005	7385	2346	178.55
2006	7577	2564	181.04
2007	8113	2771	191.97
2008	8453	2960	198.33
2009	8776	3105	203.86
2010	8789	3099	201.91
2011	8856	3128	201.90
2012	8940	3039	202.69
2013	8783	2891	197.52
2014	9063	2969	202.30

[a] New Zealand Police Annual Reports 1996–2014.

entitled Project Blueprint.* However, metropolitan policing remained centralized and a full implementation of Community-Oriented Policing and problem solving remained some distance away. Despite the slow implementation of Community Policing, by 1996, 15% of the police resources were devoted to crime prevention and noncrime community problem-solving initiatives (Doone, 1996).

In 1992, the police developed a comprehensive strategic plan. This plan was set in the context of the ongoing public sector reforms and was developed in response to rising crime trends and a desire to improve the effectiveness of service delivery. The plan was based on a private-sector strategic planning model and defined the police mission, values, strategic goals, strategies, critical success factors, and a series of implementation programs. The overall vision was the achievement of "Safer Communities Together" through the implementation of a series of 22 strategies and a Community-Oriented Policing model (New Zealand Police, 1992). The plan was linked to both the government's 10-year social and economic strategy and the annual business plan (New Zealand Police, 1993). The business plan provided the basis for output negotiation and the government appropriation of funds.

The strategic plan included a sophisticated business change model, which was to transform the way that policing was undertaken in New Zealand and was designed to be implemented over the following four years. The model of change that the organization selected was an integrated business process reengineering (BPR) and change management model with a heavy emphasis on people skills, business redesign, technology, and performance measurement. The police expected significant improvements in performance with additional resources from within the organization being made available for frontline policing and, in particular, for crime prevention, community, and other problem-solving policing initiatives (New Zealand Police, 1992).

One of the key strategies documented in the strategic plan was to dramatically improve the business and information systems infrastructure. By world standards, the police had reasonably reliable and robust financial and criminal information systems. These were, however, neither comprehensive nor sophisticated enough to meet the challenges posed by the government, the police or the community to lead the police into the twenty-first century (Small, 2000). To support frontline policing and to upgrade the technological systems, the organization, in 1994, obtained the government's approval to invest $200 million in capital and operating expenditure to develop an

---

* Project Blueprint comprised establishing a number of Community Police Centers (CPCs) or small police stations. The organization and staffing of each were replicated across the country. By the late 2000s, the majority of CPCs had either closed or had been downgraded to patrol bases. As a result, the NZP has only implemented a limited version of Community Policing into its policing approach.

Integrated National Crime Information System (INCIS) over the following eight years (New Zealand Police, 1993). This was a major undertaking, and the police approached the challenge as a business transformation program, using project management, business tools, and change management techniques.

The initial results of the strategic plan were successful in a traditional sense, with a reduction in reported crime, a reduction in the road toll, and an increase in the clearance of a number of different types of crimes (New Zealand Police, 1994). The level of reported crime, the number of crimes resolved, the percentage resolved, and the number of road fatalities from 1990 to 2013 have been presented in Table 12.2. During the development of the strategic plan and the implementation of new systems to support

Table 12.2   Level of Reported Crime, Number Resolved, Percentage Resolved, Number of Road Fatalities, and Fatalities per 100,000 Population from 1990 to 2013

Year	Reported Crime	Crime Resolved	Percentage of Crime Resolved	Number of Road Fatalities	Number of Fatalities per 100,000 Population
1990	405,867	161,256	39.73	729	21.4
1991	449,462	163,416	36.36	650	18.8
1992	461,523	169,873	36.83	646	18.5
1993	458,830	167,546	36.52	600	17.0
1994	447,525	171,453	38.31	580	16.2
1995	465,052	170,649	36.69	582	16.0
1996	477,596	175,751	36.80	514	13.8
1997	473,547	176,299	37.23	539	14.3
1998	461,677	175,176	37.94	501	13.2
1999	438,074	170,299	38.87	509	13.4
2000	427,230	177,034	41.44	462	21.1
2001	426,526	179,007	41.97	455	11.8
2002	440,129	184,465	41.91	405	10.3
2003	442,489	192,540	43.51	461	11.5
2004	406,363	181,344	44.63	435	10.7
2005	407,496	176,362	43.28	405	9.9
2006	424,137	185,227	43.67	393	9.5
2007	426,384	194,768	45.68	421	10.0
2008	431,383	201,419	46.69	366	8.6
2009	451,405	215,618	47.77	384	8.9
2010	426,345	202,545	47.51	375	8.6
2011	406,056	190,820	46.99	284	6.4
2012	376,013	178,853	47.03	308	6.9
2013	360,411	158,042	43.85	253	5.7

Source: New Zealand Police Annual Reports 1990–2013.

the wider government reforms, several problems emerged when attempting to apply the model to some aspects of policing and the broader criminal justice field. These problems were as follows:

1. The absence of an unambiguous research base, upon which to make choices and to develop strategies
2. Deficiencies in the information systems, which did not provide sufficient quantity, quality, or consistency of data to support strategic analysis
3. Inadequate research and evaluation infrastructure to identify and evaluate new or alternate initiatives
4. The impact of politics on the process of strategic development and implementation
5. The limitations inherent in attempting to quantify social costs and benefits in economic terms and to establish clear causal links (Doone, 1996)

In regard to point number 5, the problem was not related to cost per se. Under accrual accounting and economic costing methodologies, costs could be established to a reasonably accurate degree. However, the problems that the police faced was in calculating the benefits to be gained and establishing clear links to the outputs, which produce social benefits (Doone, 1996).

As well as the problems encountered in implementing the plan, the environment was changing rapidly and extra reporting requirements had been imposed on government agencies by the government. Significant change had occurred in the environment since the plan was developed, such as major advances made in technology, resource constraints coupled with increasing demands from the government and the public for better performance and greater accountability. There was also a growing appreciation of the importance of working in partnership with the community, NGOs, and other government agencies and a recognition that the police were only part of the broader public safety solution (New Zealand Police, 1996a).

As a consequence of the problems and the changing environment, in 1994, the police realized that the strategic plan needed to be redeveloped and updated. During the development of a new strategic plan, the police identified the need for a fundamental but more comprehensive and targeted change management program. The result was Policing 2000, an integrated business transformational program, which covered 10 major projects, which was to be implemented in several phases over the following four years (New Zealand Police, 1996a). The program was to provide the framework for frontline staff to deliver better, more effective services to, and with the community. The program encompassed strategies that used technology to reduce paperwork

Table 12.3   The 10 Policing 2000 Projects

1. Structures and resources
2. Information and technology
3. People
4. Culture and values
5. Business processes
6. Partnerships
7. Customers
8. Services
9. Performance measurement
10. Change management and communications

Source: Adapted from Small, F., *Ministerial inquiry into INCIS*, New Zealand Government, Wellington, New Zealand, 2000.

and administration, return staff resources to the street, the adoption of a strong customer focus, and the development of people skills and expertise to enable the police to improve their performance (New Zealand Police, 1996b). The 10 projects included in the program are presented in Table 12.3.

The 10 strategies were developed from extensive consultation with customers, staff, and the strategic partners of the organization. The program was led by an executive member of NZP (at Deputy Commissioner rank), with a full-time resource of approximately 100 staff and a part-time resource of approximately 50 operational staff who provided frontline input into both the strategic development and the design of new systems (Small, 2000).

Creation of Policing 2000

As a result of the rapidly changing social and economic conditions, concern about increasing crime, and the expectations of the results of the government reforms of the mid-1980s, the police realized in early 1994 that there was a need to reassess its role, its organizational processes, and its structures. The aim of the reassessment was to have the police deliver the best possible Community-Oriented Policing service to meet government and community expectations (New Zealand Police, 1996a).

The program covering the reassessment of the strategic direction of the police was called Policing 2000. This program replaced the 1992 strategic plan and provided a framework for performance improvement and change. A key feature of Policing 2000 was the BPR application to policing. BPR adopted a customer-centric perspective and concentrated on redesigning work processes. It was envisaged that the approach would dramatically alter the way that policing was undertaken and would provide an environment for optimizing the use of resources and for doing more with less (Doone, 1996). The reengineering process spanned the entire organization and the strategy of doing more with less extended across all operational and administrative functions (Small, 2000).

Investment in Technology

To support the implementation of the Policing 2000 strategies, a substantial investment in technology was made. The primary purpose of the investment was to support the business of policing and to provide critical management and crime information. The most extensive technological project was the design and implementation of the Integrated National Crime Intelligence System (INCIS), which was developed to support frontline policing and to produce substantial gains in individual and organizational productivity.

Profound Change in Culture

It was envisaged that the implementation of Policing 2000 would result not just in a major change in organizational processes but would result in a profound change in the police culture that would cut across all dimensions of NZP activity (New Zealand Police, 1996b).

It was proposed that the culture of the new policing environment would be based on the following:

1. The empowerment of individuals
2. Decentralization of decision-making
3. Open, honest two-way communication
4. Bottom-up innovation
5. Genuine teamwork
6. An absolute commitment to customer focus (New Zealand Police, 1996a)

However, Policing 2000 was not fully implemented. On April 6, 1998, the Minister of Police announced a review of the administrative and management structures of the police in response to the overspending of the INCIS implementation budget, and because Policing 2000 was not meeting its original timelines and milestones (Report of Independent Reviewer, 1998), it would not be able to deliver the estimated efficiency gains and the program was not implemented.

Post 2000 New Zealand Police Organizational Change Programs

Policing Excellence

In early 2008, a newly elected government, in response to the 2007 international fiscal crisis, imposed a review of the police with the view of reducing organizational costs. To reduce costs, the police commenced the development of the Policing Excellence program, which was a major change program comprising 11 work streams or initiatives, owned and driven by individual District Commanders. The work streams were designed to enable the police to "become more effective and more focused on prevention," and to be better placed to deal with changing demands (New Zealand Police, 2011a). The program's 11 work steams are defined in Table 12.4.

The work streams were intended to increase service delivery effectiveness, free up resources, and increase the use of technology, which would

Table 12.4   The 12 Policing Excellence Program Work Streams

Work Stream	Work Stream Definition
Police model	A framework for redeploying the encapsulated programs benefits to crime prevention
Case management	Aims to achieve efficiencies in the methods police use to manage reports of crime
Alternative resolutions	Develops alternative sanctions for low-level offending
Deployment model (rostering to reduce demand)	Increases the number of police available for deployment at key times
Crime reporting line	Establishes a national reporting channel for nonemergency crime
Cost recovery	Examines whether specific costs can be recovered for noncore police services
Performance management	Provides a framework to monitor and track the performance of the Prevention First operating strategy and priorities
Continuous improvement	Finding, sharing, and acting on more efficient and effective ways of doing police work
Victim focus	Preventing repeat victimization and ensuring crime victims receive a better service from police staff
Mobility	Improves the technology available to frontline police, ensuring staff safety
Support services to the frontline	Examines how the police are utilizing its entire complement of staff
Policing act opportunities	Examining how support services are provided across the organization

Source: Adapted from New Zealand Police, 2013c.

enable the police to spend more time on serving their communities. The aim of the program was to facilitate the transfer of officer time from administration and compliance paperwork to working more with the public and victims, and preventing problems from escalating (New Zealand Police, 2011a).

It was also intended that the implementation of the work streams would provide benefits across a number of other justice sector agencies. It was proposed that the project would "deliver better outcomes for victims, reassure communities and help stem the flow of cases into the criminal justice pipeline, and provide better and more consistent services throughout the country" (New Zealand Police, 2011a, p. 10).

The program provided a comprehensive framework to enable a new New Zealand Policing Model to be implemented. The model positioned prevention at the front of the business of policing and placed victims and witnesses at the center of the police response to an incident or event. The model was supported by the strategies of Continuous Improvement in External Relationships, Excellence in Leadership, and the Development of Staff (New Zealand Police, 2011c).

The majority of Policing Excellence work streams were implemented during 2012/2013 and were expected to start delivering benefits from July 1, 2013 (New Zealand, 2011a). As the Policing Excellence program overlapped the introduction of the Prevention First program, elements of Policing Excellence were incorporated into the Prevention First program. It was also anticipated that the benefits gained from the introduction of the Policing Excellence program would be reinvested into prevention policing to drive the implementation of the Prevention First operating strategy and the New Zealand Policing Model (New Zealand Police, 2011c). It was envisaged that an emphasis would be placed on reducing the number of "repeats" (victims, offenders, and locations) (New Zealand Police, 2011c).

Prevention First

The Prevention First strategy was initiated shortly after the appointment of a new Commissioner of Police in April 2011. Prevention First was designed to be the operating strategy for the police and would place prevention and people at the forefront of the organization (New Zealand Police, 2011b). The strategy was implemented to operationalize policing actions and enable the police to deploy resources to manage calls for service, understand and respond to the drivers of crime, and to foster a change in mind-set to put prevention and the needs of victims at the forefront of policing. The strategy was designed to ensure that prevention was the responsibility of every police employee (New Zealand Police, 2011c). Prevention First was premised on ensuring that all police employees understood their role and would establish a link between operational information and an intelligence-driven resource management and deployment model and the five drivers of crime* (New Zealand Police, 2013). It was believed that the drivers of crime did not act in isolation but intersected, overlapped, and impacted upon one another (New Zealand Police, 2013). The strategy included three tasks for police employees, which were as follows:

1. Be aware of and leverage community services and networks to protect vulnerable people, particularly repeat offenders
2. Act with urgency against prolific offenders
3. Develop innovative and sustainable, practical solutions using problem-solving approaches to manage crime hot spots and priority locations (New Zealand Police, 2011c)

At the same time that the police were developing the Prevention First strategy, the government, in mid-2011, implemented new performance outcomes for the justice sector, of which all justice agencies were to work jointly toward achieving (Ministry of Justice, 2012). The major targets that the government set for the police to achieve by June 2017 (as measured against 2008/2009 rates) were the reduction of the

- Crime rate by 15%
- Youth crime rate by 5%
- Violent crime rate by 20%
- Rate of reoffending by 25% (Ministry of Justice, 2012, p. 1)

To support the justice sector performance targets, the police determined that they would achieve a

- Four percent increase in prevention outputs (by 2014/2015)
- Thirteen percent fewer recorded crimes
- Nineteen percent fewer non-traffic apprehensions resolved by prosecutions (by 2014/2015) (New Zealand Police, 2011c)

A pivotal element that enabled the Prevention First strategy to succeed was the deployment model† (New Zealand Police, 2011b). The model was designed to deploy staff, and manage calls for service, and comprised four major components: critical command information, tasking and coordination, workforce management, and operational delivery (or execution). Critical command information described the information that decision-makers needed to consider before making decisions about the deployment of resources, and tasking

---

* The five drivers of crime were identified as alcohol, families, organized crime and drugs, road policing, and youth.
† The Deployment Model has often been referred to as the "New Zealand Police Model."

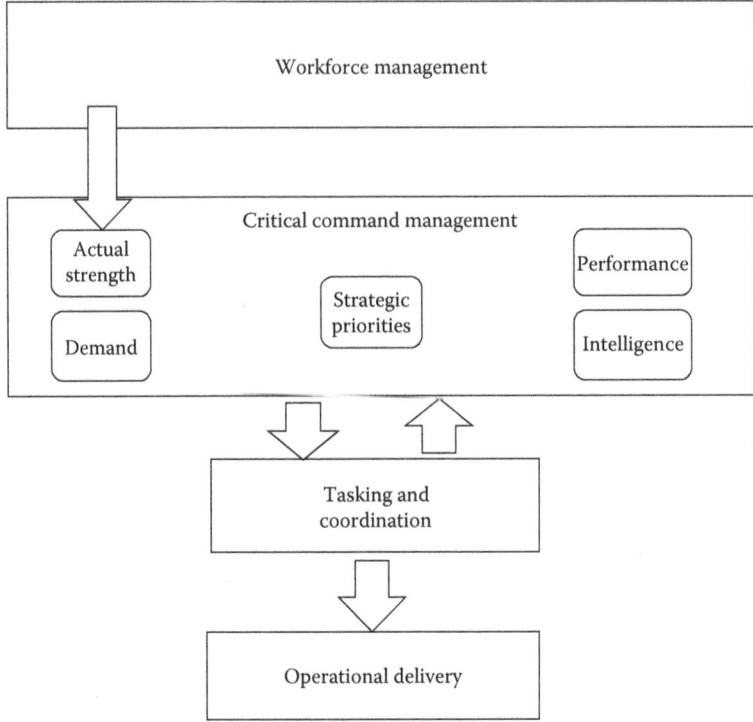

Figure 12.2 New Zealand Police prevention first deployment model. (Adapted from New Zealand Police, *Prevention first: National operating strategy 2011–2015*, New Zealand Police, 2011c; *The New Zealand police deployment managers guide: Right people, right place, right time, right result: Prevention first—national operating strategy 2011–2015*, New Zealand Police, 2011d; 2011e.)

and coordination is the process by which the critical command information* prioritizes operational activity (New Zealand Police, 2011d). The management of human resources was analyzed to determine whether effective management was taking place and that crime reduction targets would be achieved. The crime reduction targets were included in the workforce management component. The major components of the deployment model and the linkages between its four major components are presented in Figure 12.2 (New Zealand Police, 2011c, p. 4).

The deployment model was founded on three principles: well-informed and well-directed tasking of resources, a better understanding of demand and organizational capabilities, and a clear focus on achieving the right results (New Zealand Police, 2011d). The purpose of the model was to enable

---

* Critical Command Information has five parts: intelligence products, demand for services, performance, strategic priorities, and actual strength (New Zealand Police, 2011d, p. 8).

Table 12.5   Total New Zealand Police Budget and the
Number of Public Calls for Service from 1999 to 2013

Year	NZP Budget (,000)	Public Calls for Service
1999	861,673	319,817
2000	848,504	352,513
2001	898,793	368,144
2002	919,368	429,729
2003	966,980	472,234
2004	1,012,685	495,989
2005	1,059,443	533,487
2006	1,018,642	613,263
2007	1,131,342	660,278
2008	1,246,453	704,866
2009	1,369,441	675,708
2010	1,415,392	708,079
2011	1,469,075	721,106
2012	1,471,433	713,917
2013	1,481,158	714,397
2014	1,491,177	772,928

Source: New Zealand Police Annual Reports 1999–2014.

decision-makers to deploy resources in a consistent approach across the organization, which would focus these resources on the local crime and crash
environment (New Zealand Police, 2011d).

By early to mid-2012, it became apparent to the executive that the police
needed to better understand how its resources should be redirected, how its
resources should be tasked, and what this actually meant on a day-to-day
basis at the operational and tactical levels of the organization. As can be seen
in Table 12.5, the operational demands made on the police had increased
substantially, the police budget had increased from $861m to $1,461m, an
increase of approximately 73% from 1999 to 2012, and calls for service from
the public had increased from 319,817 to 772,928, an increase of approximately 142% during the same period. The police executive needed to know
how to move existing resources from being utilized in a reactive manner to
being used in a proactive manner and how to achieve a 4% increase in prevention outputs. To redirect available resources to handle prevention tasks,
the police established District Coordination Centers (DCCs). The initial role
of the DCCs was to use the information gained from telephone calls made
by the public to the three national Communication Centers to identify crime
trends and hot spots and direct the attendance of prevention resources.

The title of the DCCs changed in mid-2013 to District Command Centers
to reflect the evolving role in real-time management and the dispatch of

resources to attend events and incidents. It had become clear to decision-makers that the DCCs were fundamental to the implementation of the deployment model and to the work streams within the Policing Excellence change management program and that the DCCs were a vital operational component of the deployment model. The deployment model was vital as it ensured that police staff were deployed to the right place, at the right time.

Discussion

The reforms of the New Zealand Government in the mid-1980s, in conjunction with the rapidly changing social and economic conditions, the concern about increasing levels of crime, and the increase in public expectations led the police to reassess its role and its organizational processes and structures. The aims of the Policing 2000 change program were to ensure that the police had the capability and the organizational processes to deliver the best possible Community-Oriented Policing service to meet both the government and the communities' expectations for the new millennium. Owing to Policing 2000 not reaching the implementation stage, the aims of the later organizational change management programs changed to include components of Community Policing and became more philosophical in nature, with the intention of changing the behavior and actions of officers and employees.

As Policing 2000 was not implemented, the police appeared to be reluctant to change its approach to strategy development and sought a familiar solution to a new problem, which is consistent with Mintzberg's (1978) theory of organizational strategy development. Alterations to the aims of the change management programs eventuated as a response to the changing direction of different governments (social or conservative), the response of the government to the 2007 fiscal crisis, and as a result of the police learning more about its business and the effects of change, as components of Policing Excellence and Prevention First were implemented. It is uncertain as to the understanding and the knowledge that the police held as to how the 11 Police Excellence work streams would increase the effectiveness of its service delivery, as research had not been undertaken, nor had a project been designed or a plan documented. The deficiency in evidence-based research, upon which to form strategy, is a theme common to all three change programs.

Langworthy (1986) claimed that the reformation or the reorganization of police agencies is "both controversial and mystical" (p. 1) and asserted that from the time of the establishment of the London Metropolitan Police in 1829 to the present, there has been little in the way of firm evidence to use when selecting one type of organizational reform over another. Since Langworthy's observations in 1986, there has been very little research and no evidence-based research that has examined how police agencies design and implement organizational reform programs to increase efficiency and effectiveness (den Heyer, 2009, 2013b; Maguire, 2003).

The absence of research in police reform places police managers in a no-win situation. Police reformers are not able to base their reforms on any accepted theory or best practice. They are also in the position of not being able to justify their change management program or answer their critics. This means that "police managers and critics are perpetually entangled in a debate that has no objective solution" (Langworthy, 1986, p. 2).

While the police have been able to increase the efficiency and the effectiveness of its service delivery (based on the decreasing level of crime and increasing services within its current funding), what has become clear over time is that due to conflicting demands, the police cannot achieve all of the outcomes that the community and the government require of them. This has created a challenge for police managers to be able to balance their budgets and their resources and suggests that output measurement alone is not a simple answer to assess the achievement of the delivery of police services (Cohen & Eimicke, 2012; den Heyer, 2009; Moore & Stevens, 1991). It has also created a situation where the strategy, structures, resources, and costs have been continually examined by the police to identify better methods and processes that may increase officer and organizational efficiencies and effectiveness. It was the continual examination of organization processes that resulted in the development of Policing 2000, Policing Excellence, and Prevention First.

Comparison of Policing 2000, Policing Excellence, and Prevention First

Policing 2000 was a police-initiated, police-centric, customer-focused comprehensive change management program conceived to streamline management and administration and to transfer effort and resources to frontline policing (Commissioner of Police, 1998), primarily at the area level. The program was based on the principles of decentralization and Community-Oriented Policing and was led by a Deputy Commissioner. It was designed to facilitate the operational strategies of firm and targeted enforcement, increase crime prevention, and work collectively with others to reduce crime, the fear of crime, and the road toll (Commissioner of Police, 1998). The objectives of the program were to ensure that the police were more efficient in delivering quality policing services, more accountable for the delivery of those services, and to be supportive of the government's public safety objectives (Commissioner of Police, 1998). This meant that the focus of the program was on efficiency and accountability, not on the effectiveness of services, although it was expected that greater efficiency and accountability would lead to the achievement of greater effectiveness in terms of public safety outcomes (Commissioner of Police, 1998).

The Policing 2000 program was not based on any research findings but was designed to examine how organizational processes could be improved and to identify potential areas that could become more efficient. BPR was used to examine the areas of potential improvement. The program was a comprehensive and broad approach to analyze the processes used by the organization and went from analyzing the complete process of how an officer orders a replacement pair of socks to how they are supplied to analyzing the process of a Traffic Offence Notice, from the point of issue to when it is finalized, either by payment or by prosecution. As a result of the size and multitude of the BPR task and to ensure that BPR would identify the required outcomes, the police created a coordinating body comprising Policing 2000s project leaders. However, because of the number of BPR projects and the detail involved in the analysis of each project, the project coordinating body became overwhelmed by the project management process. As a result, project leaders and analysts concentrated on the project management reporting requirements rather than on undertaking the actual BPR analysis, causing timelines to be extended and milestones to be missed. This created problems across the Policing 2000 program and eventually led to its demise and government intervention in 1998.

In comparison, Policing Excellence and Prevention First were designed to not only accommodate cost pressures within a static budget but to reduce operating costs and to assist the police with achieving the government's outcomes of reducing youth and violent crime, total crime, and the reoffending rate. In other words, the programs were driven by the achievement of the identifiable performance measures of reducing crime by 13%, increasing prevention outputs by 4%, and decreasing apprehensions by 19%.

The two programs were more targeted than Policing 2000, in that they were to address the five drivers of crime: alcohol, families, organized crime and drugs, road policing, and youth. Addressing the drivers of crime was to be achieved by concentrating on three drivers of change:

1. Productivity—getting the most benefit from policing, with emphasis on prevention
2. Sustainability—maintaining cost-effective service delivery with available resources
3. National consistency—embedding the same police model, practices, and standards in each district (New Zealand Police, 2011c)

Owing to the linking of the combination of these programs across the wider justice sector, the visibility of the performance measures and the focus on the practical drivers of crime have made Policing Excellence and Prevention First easier for police staff to accept than they did of Policing 2000. The fact that the programs were driven by the Commissioner and a Deputy

Commissioner, together with the achievement of performance measures by November 2013 (New Zealand Police Association, 2013) and the approach taken of implementing components of the programs as its development was completed, gave staff the perception that the organization was capable of making changes.

The three change management programs have a number of differences, but they also have similarities and support Mintzberg's (1978) strategy development theory. Policing 2000 was about "doing more with less," which was the mantra of the 1990s New Public Management (NPM) approach for government agencies and for changing the culture of the organization to reflect honesty and a commitment to focusing on customers. In comparison, Policing Excellence was introduced with the view that the organization would become more effective and more focused on prevention. The program also placed an emphasis on victims of crime and the public. A summary of the comparison of the three programs is presented in Table 12.6.

It appears that the major difference between the programs is that the police learnt from the mistakes made during the development of Policing 2000.

Table 12.6 Components of Policing 2000, Policing Excellence, and Prevention First

Program Component	Policing 2000	Policing Excellence and Prevention First
Aim included increasing efficiency and effectiveness	Yes	Yes
Included a coordinated comprehensive approach	Yes	Yes
Included fundamental changes to service delivery	No	Yes
Police centric	Police only involved in the program	Change program was linked to wider justice sector
Included budgetary savings	Yes	Yes
Made use of technology	INCIS	Mobility project
Used recognized analytical processes	Business process reengineering	No
Based on research	No	No
Service delivery level	Area	District
Authority/management	Decentralized	Centralized
Underlying police theory	Community Policing	Problem-Oriented Policing
Program comprised separate projects/work streams	Yes—10	Yes—11
Project level of design and development	Centrally	Centrally, but work stream leadership delegated to District Commanders

Source: Author.

This is not surprising, given that the Commissioner, who supported the initiation of Policing Excellence in 2008, was one of the major architects of Policing 2000. A cautious approach was taken with implementing Policing Excellence, the program did not focus as much on changing processes to increase efficiency. While the police have taken a familiar approach to change, both Policing Excellence and Prevention First can also be identified as emerging strategies, which is in line with Mintzberg's (1978) typology.

The softer approach when developing the later change programs was a major strength, as was the fact that the work steams were implemented as they were completed. This was in comparison to the Policing 2000 approach of attempting to implement 10 projects concurrently. The second major strength of the later change programs was that they worked in unison. Policing Excellence laid the groundwork and provided the structure for the implementation of the Prevention First strategy. This ensured a successful implementation of the more tactical Prevention First strategy, which enabled the police to achieve the four government-specified outcome performance measures.

The softer approach adopted by the police to implement change in the organization, whether by planning or good fortune, supports Langworthy's (1986) claims that decisions about how policing is undertaken should not be made in a vacuum and without simultaneously considering the impact that decisions have on the rest of the functional structure.

Has the Service Delivery of the New Zealand Police Improved as a Result of Policing 2000, Policing Excellence, and Prevention First?

Policing 2000 was never implemented, and as a result, it is impossible to identify as to whether or not it had any effect on service delivery. From an examination of Table 12.2 and Figure 12.3, it appears that the Policing Excellence and the Prevention First programs have had an effect on the number of crimes reported, the resolution of crimes, and the number of road fatalities. Since the implementation of Policing Excellence and Prevention First, the percentage of crimes resolved and the number of police officers per 100,000 population has remained stable, but the number of road fatalities per 100,000 population has decreased by three fatalities per 100,000 population, the number of calls for service from the public has increased by more than 9% and the public's trust and confidence in the police has remained constant at 78%, with participants surveyed stating that they have full or substantial trust and confidence in NZP (Gravitas Research and Strategy, 2009, 2014). Over the same time period, the population of New Zealand has increased

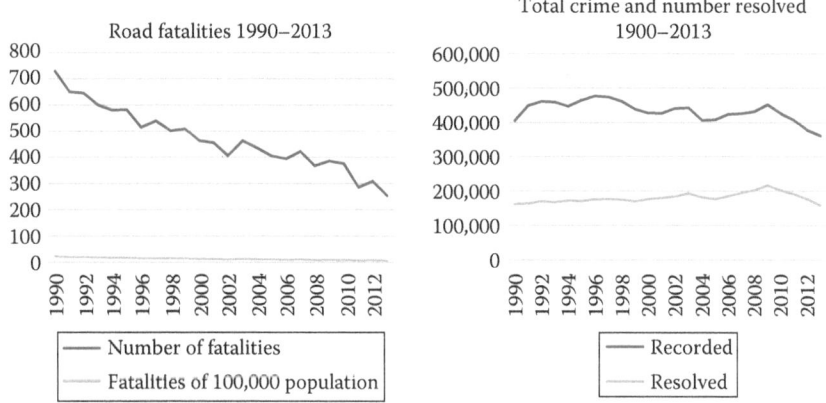

Figure 12.3 Number of road fatalities, total crime, and number of crimes resolved from 1990 to 2013. (*Source*: Author.)

by approximately 5%, while the ratio of police officers to 100,000 population has remained static. These results indicate that the programs have had a positive impact on the service delivered by the police.

Conclusion

Devising a successful strategy for the police depends upon defining the appropriate mission and goals and establishing robust external relationships in the operating and political environment. This approach will enable the police to develop strategy that should be successful in achieving its objectives (Ketchen & Short, n.d.). Ultimately, however, whether a strategy succeeds or not depends on whether the organization can be coaxed to perform as envisioned in the strategy.

Mintzberg's theory of strategy development emphasizes that familiar change management tools are often used by organizations to develop strategy. The principal instruments that members of the executive used in the three change programs to influence the improvement of the overall performance of the organization were familiar change management tools; streamlining administration, restructuring and reallocating resources, all of which were supported by a technological platform. It is the last point, technology, which may have been the savior of the Policing Excellence and Prevention First programs. Policing 2000 had been designed to be supported by an extensive technological capability, which was to provide an efficient working environment through the minimization of paperwork. However, the technology was unable to deliver the Policing 2000 objectives and led to the police suffering substantial financial difficulties resulting in the New Zealand Government taking court action against the technology suppliers.

An analysis of the three change programs suggests that the later programs were an improvement over the earlier program and that the changes in the environment and in the organization of the police gave rise to new opportunities and strategies. Policing Excellence and Prevention First are both leading police change management programs that have fundamentally changed the way that the police operate and deliver its services. However, the latter two programs have created semidecentralized, functionally dominated organizational structures that focus the attention of the organization on the development of specialized functional capabilities, encouraging staff to take a limited perspective on crime problems. Although the police have encouraged the continuation of Community Policing through the establishment of neighborhood policing, and the targeting of locations and problems of high risk through an intelligence model, the organization still evaluates itself largely in terms of crime-related indicators of success. All of these factors are consistent with a professional crime fighting strategy rather than a strategy that is oriented toward Community-Oriented Policing (Moore & Stephens, 1991).

The implementation of both Policing Excellence and Prevention First has ensured that the police is strategically placed to take advantage of the future environment and that the organization is capable of developing and implementing extensive change management programs that fundamentally affect how the organization delivers its services. Only time will tell whether Prevention First is a realized strategy and is able to build on its initial achievements and whether the revised service delivery structures and methods are capable of delivering the organizational efficiencies sought by government and the public.

Increasing Service Delivery Efficiency in Camden County Police Department, New Jersey

13

Introduction

Across the United States, decreasing levels of funding have made cities and municipalities consider consolidating or regionalizing some of their services, by combining their law enforcement services with neighboring cities or counties. A number of police agencies are sharing facilities or specialist services with other jurisdictions, while others have merged departments. The city that stands out is Camden, New Jersey. The city of Camden completely dissolved its police force to create a new police department. These actions were unprecedented in that no other major city had dissolved its police agency to create a new department. The creation of a new police department within the city of Camden was envisaged as being the first step toward the establishment of a regionalized police agency (Maciag, 2014).

During the discussions of creating a regionalized police agency, two questions arose. The first question was which parts of the existing agency will be regionalized and which parts will remain under local control? It was proposed that administrative functions such as payroll, benefits, purchasing, and IT could be centralized and that specialist units could be deployed from a central location, while the identification and response to local priorities would remain the responsibility of the respective local district or community (Camden County, 2011a).

The second question that arose was which model would best suit Camden city and Camden County? There is no one-size-fits-all approach to regionalizing municipal services. Smaller communities throughout California, for example, contract with counties for police services and in Pennsylvania, many regional police departments operate, but full mergers of large-sized departments are rare (Maciag, 2014).

The discussions held on the future of policing in Camden city and Camden County were tempered by the fact that any form of regionalization or consolidation agreement created political challenges as municipal governments are usually reluctant to relinquish local control of their police forces (Maciag, 2014). Furthermore, a number of social and deprivation issues had to be considered if a regionalized police agency was to be established in Camden. More than 50% of Camden residents, for example, live below the poverty line, while unemployment is double the national rate (Zernike, 2012). The city also has a high concentration of young adults who tend to be disproportionately poor and unemployed (Maciag, 2014).

This chapter comprises a case study that examines the establishment of the Camden County Police Department (CCPD), and specifically the Metro Division, and presents an assessment of the performance of the new agency in its first two years. Within this context, this chapter critically examines the discussions and debate leading to the establishment of the CCPD Metro. Drawing on media articles and municipal documents and reports, this case study endeavors to provide insights into the creation of the CCPD two years after it took place.

Background

Camden had, for more than a century, been a center of southern New Jersey industry, with a thriving and expanding economy. However, with the closure of a number of very large manufacturing and processing companies in the late 1960s and early 1970s, Camden experienced a decline in employment, industry, and population, which provided the catalyst for the deterioration of the city's infrastructure and an increasing crime rate. The loss of industry and the subsequent diminished tax base left the city with insufficient revenues to provide city government services, including policing. With low secondary school graduation rates and little industry remaining in the city to provide jobs for its residents, Camden became the center of the drug trade in southern New Jersey, a circumstance that was exacerbated by its close proximity to Philadelphia (New Jersey Office of the Attorney General, 2006). These factors contributed to Camden being consistently ranked among the cities with the highest crime rates.

The first year that Camden was identified as being the most dangerous city in the United States was in 2004, with more than 60 murders per 100,000 people (Morgan Quitno, 2015; New Jersey Office of the Attorney General, 2006). The city retained the title in 2005 and then again in 2009 (CQ Press, 2015). At that time, there was no question that Camden was facing a substantial and increasing crime problem and that Camden's Police Department, despite its substantial efforts, was facing very difficult challenges in dealing with the problem (New Jersey Office of the Attorney General, 2006). The murder rate in Camden city, in comparison to the murder rate in New York city between the years 2000 and 2008, is presented in Table 13.1. As a result of the deteriorating rate of crime, in early 2005, the then New Jersey Attorney General, Peter C. Harvey, established the Camden Commission on Public Safety to identify structural and organizational changes that could be made to improve the Camden Police Department (CPD) and reduce the occurrence of violence and serious crime in the city.

Table 13.1   Murder Rate in Camden City in Comparison to New York City 2000–2008

	2000	2001	2002	2003	2004	2005	2006	2007	2008
Number[a]	24	25	33	41	49	33	32	42	54
Per 100,000[a]	28.2	31.0	40.5	51.2	60.8	41.2	40.0	53.2	70.0
New York City per 100,000[b]	8.7	8.6	7.3	7.4	7.0	6.6	7.3	6.0	8.3

[a] City-data.com(2015a).
[b] City-data.com(2015b).

As concerns over the CPD's effectiveness emerged, a number of studies identified areas where the delivery of police services could be improved. According to the Commission's report, which was published in 2006, the principal reason that Camden had a long-standing major crime and drug offending problem was because the CPD had struggled to meet the challenges of its environment (New Jersey Office of the Attorney General, 2006). The report presented a history of the crime and policing problems in Camden and noted that as far back as 1986, due to the level of crime, the then mayor requested assistance from the New Jersey Attorney General. As part of the attorney general's response, the New Jersey Division of Criminal Justice conducted a review of the management and operations of the Camden Police Department. The report from this study included more than 150 recommendations, which were designed to improve the quality and delivery of police services (New Jersey Office of the Attorney General, 2006).

The New Jersey Division of Criminal Justice, 1986 report, was followed by a second review of the CPD that was undertaken by the attorney general. It also included a number of recommendations to improve the delivery of police services to Camden (New Jersey Office of the Attorney General, 2006).

A third review of CPD operations was held in 2002 and was directed by the state governor and undertaken by the attorney general. This review noted that the CPD had failed in its duty and responsibility to provide adequate policing services (New Jersey Office of the Attorney General, 2006) and led to the governor deploying New Jersey state police officers to provide support to the CPD. Support included the deployment of 93 state police to Camden and the establishment of the Anti-Crime Partnership program. The assistance provided by the state to the CPD was strengthened by an increased presence of other state and federal law enforcement agencies.

By 2003, it was evident that despite state and federal assistance, policing in Camden was not improving. According to the Commission's 2006 report, the reason for the lack of improvement in policing in Camden was owing to the failure of the CPD leadership to adopt the changes necessary to effectively police Camden (New Jersey Office of the Attorney General, 2006).

The apparent failure of the CPD to adopt the changes needed led to the attorney general placing the CPD under supersession* and in appointing the county prosecutor as a temporary state executive administer of the CPD (New Jersey Office of the Attorney General, 2006). The introduction of the supersession established the framework for the state prosecutor as the final authority to oversee and approve all administrative and management changes that the CPD may seek to introduce.

With the level of crime increasing in 2004 to that which made Camden the most dangerous city in the United States, in early 2005, the attorney general established the Camden Commission on Public Safety (CCPS). The CCPS was to identify the structure and organizational changes that the CPD needed to introduce in order to reduce the violence and serious crime in Camden (New Jersey Office of the Attorney General, 2006). While it was recognized that the CPD was not the only agency or institution responsible for the rising crime problem, they did have a major role, together with other social agencies, in addressing the level of crime.

The principal focus of the CCPS was to develop strategies that would improve both the effectiveness of the service delivered by CPD and the crime-reducing programs that would ensure that there was a foundation for a sustainable reduction of crime in Camden. For the CPD to be in a position to be able to continue with its own efforts to implement organizational reform and to improve its service delivery, it needed to implement the strategies identified by the CCPS. However, any reform implemented by the CPD needed to reflect national best practices.

The combination of the CPD working with other supporting law enforcement agencies and being supported by the CCPS provided the basis for the development and implementation of a new crime control strategy for Camden. At the same time that the new crime control strategy was being implemented, the New Jersey State Police, the U.S. Marshal's Office, and other state and federal agencies deployed additional resources to Camden to provide further support for the initiative. This cooperative effort became known as the 28-day plan and had a substantial positive impact, reducing the crime rate considerably during the first months of its implementation (New Jersey Office of the Attorney General, 2006). This indicated that with the right mix of operational strategies, resources, and assistance, the CPD could have a positive impact on the level of crime in Camden.

The CCPS made four contextual observations when searching for the right mix of elements that would have an impact positively on crime. The first was that the CPD had, for a number of decades, lacked the budget and

---

* The supersession of the Camden Police Department existed in the broader context of the state oversight of municipal government functions in the city of Camden undertaken pursuant to the "Municipal Rehabilitation and Economic Recovery Act" of 2002.

the resources to provide an effective service to the city of Camden. Second, for that same period of time, the CPD lacked the motivation, resolve, and the leadership necessary to implement and sustain the internal organizational frameworks that were necessary to have an effect on the level of crime in Camden (New Jersey Office of the Attorney General, 2006). Third, as a result of the organization being structured into operational units, each unit operated in a silo, which wasted and under-utilized resources and officers. Finally, and according to the CCPS, most importantly, the CPD lacked a strong partnership with the community (New Jersey Office of the Attorney General, 2006).

It appears that the recommendations made by the CCPS were not implemented, and therefore, the attorney general established the Advisory Commission on Camden's Public Safety (ACCPS) in 2006. In September 2006, the ACCPS released a report, which presented a number of recommendations for improving policing and public safety in Camden. The ACCPS noted that the implementation of the recommendations did not rest solely with the CPD but also with the Camden City Council and the leadership of New Jersey and that the recommendations should be undertaken immediately if the CPD was to move forward to improve public safety in Camden (New Jersey Office of the Attorney General, 2006).

Eighteen of the recommendations made by the ACCPS and the details of each recommendation have been presented in Table 13.2. The recommendations have been categorized into three areas: management and leadership reform; the development of a community policing model approach to crime control; and changes to the CPD's internal organizational structure. The recommendations proposed significant change for the CPD, and in particular, they identified the need for a fundamental change in the organizational structure of the CPD and in its operational philosophy, especially in regard to its relationship with the community. To ensure that the proposed changes to the CPD would be sustainable, the ACCPS also recommended that the supersession remain in place until the reforms were implemented and tested and that CPD develop a strategic plan to manage and measure the implementation of the recommendations (New Jersey Office of the Attorney General, 2006).

Implementing the 2005, 28-day plan and a number of the recommendations made by the ACCPS, together with the implementation of a number of other crime control tactics (surveillance cameras, improved street lighting and curfews for children), appear to have had some success in assisting with lowering the homicide rate in 2005, 2006, and 2007 and in the occurrence of violent crime generally (Zernike, 2012).

However, the fiscal crisis of late 2007 hit Camden hard, forcing the city to lay staff off and to reduce the CPD by more than 100 officers (Zernike, 2012). In response to the fiscal crisis, the governor granted Camden

Table 13.2   Recommendations of the Attorney General's Advisory Commission on Camden's Public Safety (2006)

Recommendation	Details of Recommendation
A. Management/Leadership Reforms	
1. Create a full-time civilian police director position.	Responsible for • Setting department policy • Issuing rules and regulations that govern the department Human resource management
2. Enact the legislative changes to allow the mayor to select a police chief from a larger pool of applicants.	Only the mayor could appoint a police chief from within Camden city Police.
3. Leave the position of police chief unfilled until existing leadership have the experience to be active members of the executive.	The police chiefs vacancy should not be filled until the enactment of the legislative change identified in Recommendation 2 and until the managerial and leadership capability is developed within the department.
B. Reforms Necessary for Adoption of Community Policing Model	
4. Continue to reduce the number of organizational silos.	Designate uniformed officers to neighborhoods, who work predictable shifts, and report to a District Commander who is responsible to a neighborhood.
5. Eliminate the use of ineffective policing tactics that are offensive to the community.	Tactics to be used to reduce crime but not alienate the public.
6. All field officers to complete training in problem-solving policing techniques.	Officers to be equipped with skills to effectively solve a wide range of neighborhood crime and disorder problems.
7. Vest District Commanders with full authority and responsibility to oversee and supervise all policing within their geographic areas.	District Commanders held responsible to and for their districts 24 hours a day.
8. District Commanders are to successfully complete sensitivity training.	This will enable District Commanders to take a broader view of the issues and to adopt a collaborative approach.

(Continued)

Table 13.2 (*Continued*) Recommendations of the Attorney General's Advisory Commission on Camden's Public Safety (2006)

Recommendation	Details of Recommendation
C. Internal Organizational and Strategic Changes	
9. Amendment of the 28-day plan to reflect the decentralized policing platform occurring under decentralized, accountable police managers.	The modified plan will allow for increased accountability for police performance on a neighborhood basis.
10. Improve internal communications so that all employees are fully informed of and understand the priorities and developments that impact their jobs.	Leadership must make itself highly visible and must interact regularly with officers at all levels of the department.
11. Recognize and strengthen the Compstat process to allow for the performance management of crime reduction efforts.	Reorganize the Compstat process into a strong and robust performance management tool.
12. Institute a managerial accountability system.	Enable managers to be engaged in monitoring and evaluating their subordinates' performance, training, retraining, rewarding, and discipline.
13. Adopt fixed-shift scheduling for officers.	Allows the department to better allocate its personnel to meet the crime prevention and policing needs of the community.
14. Improve communication between city government and the department.	The state of the city's financial position must be shared with the leadership of the department.
15. Establish district collaborative councils.	A collaborative relationship will build on the efforts of existing citywide public community organizations and serve as a resource to address public safety issues.
16. Restructure the Detective Bureau.	Reorientate the investigative functions to reflect the department's commitment to intelligence-led policing.
17. Schedule regular labor–management working meetings.	Foster an open, collaborative labor–management relationship that will facilitate the implementation of improved policing practices.
18. Raise the department's standard of performance by preparing and applying for accreditation.	The department should prepare and apply for accreditation, a process that will require the department to develop and adopt higher standards for professional objectives and procedures to meet those objectives.

Source: Adapted from New Jersey Office of the Attorney General, *Final report of Attorney General's Advisory Commission on Camden's public safety*, Retrieved on March 11, 2015 from http://www.state.nj.us/lps/com-report-camden.pdf, 2006.

$175 million in bonds and loans, plus a one-time $7.5 million appropriation from the state budget, in exchange for the appointment of a chief operating officer to run the city government and for gubernatorial control over the Camden School Board (Katz, 2009). It was proposed that the governor's plan would create jobs and business and lead to local employment opportunities.

Despite the governor's 2007 financial stimulus package, in 2011, there was a $26 million budget shortfall, which resulted in 46% of the staff being laid off in the city's police department (Gordon, 2014). This set the stage for the mayor and the council to examine alternative policing models for Camden. During the same period, crime continued to increase (see Tables 13.1 and 13.3), prompting the governor to deploy state police officers to conduct targeted patrols aimed at deterring criminal activity in identified crime hot spots and to strengthen the CPD efforts as the city and the county continued to examine the possibility of establishing a regionalized police force and metro division for Camden (Drewniak, 2011).

The important point to note is that, since 2005, the state police had maintained a presence in Camden and had provided the CPD with crucial policing assistance (Drewniak, 2011). According to Drewniak (2011), the state officers, who were members of the U.S. Marshals Fugitive Task Force, targeted high-risk criminals in Camden and helped the CPD to investigate more than 70% of the shootings that had occurred in the city.

In mid-2011, the mayor and the council of Camden, together with the county, developed a proposal for a countywide police force that would increase the number of uniformed officers and support personnel available for crime control in Camden (Zernike, 2012). This proposal would see the CPD dismantled and a new police agency established for the city.

The mayor had a number of reasons for dismantling the CPD. The continuing increase in the level of crime, police corruption, and the lack of willingness to restructure, which would have resulted in an improved service delivery, were some of the reasons for the dismantling of the CPD, but the principal reason was that the generous union contracts made it

Table 13.3   Camden Crime 2009–2011

Type of Crime	2009	2010	2011
Murders (per 100,000)	34 (43.0)	37 (46.8)	47 (60.6)
Rapes (per 100,000)	60 (76.0)	73 (92.3)	66 (85.0)
Robbery (per 100,000)	766 (969.9)	712 (900.3)	857 (1104.3)
Burglary (per 100,000)	1035 (1310.5)	1015 (1283.5)	1,436 (1835.4)
Motor vehicle theft (per 100,000)	649 (821.7)	519 (656.3)	800 (1030.9)

Source: http://www.city-data.com/.

financially impossible to employ enough officers to control crime in Camden (Zernike, 2012).

On August 2, 2012, the mayor of Camden and councilors from Camden County announced that the 141-year-old CPD, which was once the primary law enforcement agency in Camden and the second largest police force in southern New Jersey after Atlantic City, and once consisted of more than 460 police officers, would be disbanded in favor of a new county police department, the Camden County Police Department (CCPD). The CPD ceased operations on May 1, 2013, when the Camden County Police Department Metro Division took full responsibility for the policing of the city of Camden (Camden County, n.d.). In November 2012, Camden City Council began terminating the 273 officers employed by the CPD and began deploying officers from the CCPD (Zernike, 2012).

The concept of the development of the CCPD was based on a regionalized police agency. It was proposed that as individual municipalities attempted to respond to the increases in the number and severity of crimes in their areas, how and where they were being committed, and finding the resources to address the situation, they would view a regional approach as a more efficient and effective option.

There were more than 500 local law enforcement agencies across New Jersey that were affected by a 2% cap on municipal budgets that was imposed by the New Jersey. The cap on the municipal budgets would restrict the future growth of municipal budgets, and therefore, a regional police agency would be an essential tool for municipalities that are required to provide more services with fewer resources.

The state of New Jersey advocated the regionalization of CPD and that other municipalities in New Jersey consolidate or share services for two reasons. The first was that there was a possibility to realize savings through the achievement of economies of scale (Maciag, 2014), and the second was that there was a trend of crime cutting across municipal jurisdictional lines (Camden County, n.d.). It was also the view of the state that while each municipality is unique, their borders are a product of history and do not necessarily provide for the best or most efficient law enforcement framework, and nor do they bear any connection with contemporary management or administration needs (Camden County, n.d.).

Proposal to Establish the CCPD

Camden County has a population of 550,000 people and is policed by 37 local law enforcement agencies. According to the county, the law enforcement structure had 36 police chiefs too many, and the municipalities should join the countywide police agency to help cut municipality costs and maintain current staffing levels (quoted in Maciag, 2014).

The city wanted to reduce the cost to the taxpayer and improve neighborhood safety and felt that a regionalized law enforcement program was the best option to reduce the cost of providing a police service, improve the delivery of policing services, and allocate resources more efficiently by deploying more officers on patrol and on the streets (Camden County, n.d.).

The CCPD was designed to provide a professional police service with an efficient management structure, which would be able to efficiently and effectively deploy personnel who were able to work to consistent and efficient rules (Camden County, n.d.). The administrative processes of the new regionalized agency would be rationalized and would include a number of centralized specialist operational support and investigative units.

According to Camden County (n.d.), the sharing of services throughout the county is a practical, effective response to a diminishing level of resources and to the high cost of maintaining local government services. It was proposed that the CCPD would be structured to allow for centralized administration, booking, and evidence collection (Maciag, 2014). The implementation of a regional law enforcement restructuring program would give mayors and municipal governments a unique opportunity to reduce property taxes and to improve police services in an environment in which crime cuts across municipal jurisdictional boundaries (Camden County, n.d.).

The potential budget savings offered by the regionalization of law enforcement agencies would be identified in a detailed operational and financial assessment document (Camden County, n.d.). The proposal to establish the CCPD was based on a supposition that a regionalized police agency, divided into a number of coherent police districts, patrols, special operations, and investigative functions, had a number of efficiency and effectiveness benefits, which could be achieved by shrinking or removing a number of layers of management and administration. It was proposed that a new, more efficient organizational structure would enable a more effective deployment of personnel, reduce the number of senior officers and chiefs required, and allow for the efficient use of civilian personnel (Camden County). The city also expected that the sharing of equipment, the coordination of resources, and the elimination of overlapping positions and roles would result in a budget reduction and identify savings that could be used to employ more officers for uniform patrol and to purchase additional crime reduction equipment, such as surveillance cameras (Camden County).

The main strength of the proposed regionalization model was that the governance structure would allow for substantial input from designated leaders who represented the participating communities (Camden County, n.d.) and that other municipalities were free to join at any time. Joining the CCPD would be available to all municipalities in the Camden County on a voluntary basis, but no plans to join the regionalized police agency have been announced by other municipalities (Camden County). If municipalities did want to join, an assessment would be conducted with the input of the locality (Maciag, 2014). Staffing and participation costs would be made available to mayors to assist them to determine the cost of participating in the CCPD, and the potential cost savings would be projected. Transition plans, timelines, and staffing plans would be detailed for participating municipalities to ensure the continuity of policing services and to enable a seamless transition to the new agency (Camden County, n.d.). Camden County had been in negotiations in 2014 with two interested municipalities, but there was reluctance by local police chiefs to commit, and Maciag (2014) claimed that they were protecting their fiefdoms and that their actions were preventing their departments from growing.

Establishing the CCPD

On or about August 25, 2011, the city of Camden, the county of Camden, and the New Jersey state governor's office entered into a memorandum of understanding (MOU) to progress the establishment of the CCPD. According to the MOU, the city and county expressed a willingness to form a new regionalized police department, which would be available to provide police services to all municipalities in Camden County, if a specific municipality opted to join (Camden County, n.d.).

It was proposed by the city and the county that the successor police agency to the CPD would be the new regional Camden County police agency, CCPD. The CCPD would be the primary law enforcement agency for the city of Camden (Camden County, n.d.). The branch of the CCPD operating in the city of Camden would be referred to as the Metro Division, but unlike other metropolitan police agencies, it would not patrol outside of the city of Camden (Camden County). Table 13.4 presents the principles of the high-level plan to establish the CCPD.

It was envisaged that the establishment of the CCPD would save between $14 million and $16 million annually from the police budget of $60 million (Camden County, n.d.). The majority of the saving would be made from the civilianization of a number of former, uniformed-officer positions (Laday, 2014a) and from reducing the fringe benefits that had been required under the city's union contract with the police department (Camden County, n.d.). Unlike the CPD, the CCPD initially did not have a contract with the union.

The argument for disestablishing the CPD and creating the new regionalized CCPD was based on unionization and that the proposed administrative efficiencies would lead to an ability to deploy extra patrol officers to city neighborhoods, resulting in an improvement in the quality of police services

Table 13.4 High-Level Plan to Establish the Camden County Police Department

- The Camden County Freeholders, in cooperation with individual municipalities within the county, will create the CCPD.
- The CCPD will be under the jurisdiction of the county with substantial participation of community leaders.
- The CCPD will be divided into a number of police districts.
- The county will create the department and create appropriate work rules, compensation packages, and benefits for the newly created police department staff.
- The county will utilize uniforms, equipment, vehicles, etc., of the participating municipalities.
- Any Camden county municipality may choose to participate in the county police department.
- The direct cost of police services for each participating municipality will be passed on from the county to the municipality.
- The indirect cost of police services will be calculated and distributed to all of the municipalities participating in the CCPD.

Source: Adapted from Camden country, *Camden County (n.d.), White paper: The Camden County Police Department*, Retrieved on March 11, 2015 from http://www.camden-countypd.org/wpcontent/themes/ccpd/pdf/Police-White-Paper-6-7-11.pdf.

(Camden County, 2011a). However, some in the law enforcement community, especially academics and existing CPD officers, remained skeptical as to whether the regionalization plan was the right option and whether the establishment of a new police agency would provide the envisaged benefits (Maciag, 2014). One academic from New York City noted that there would be a loss of institutional knowledge and that building an entirely new police department would not solve Camden's problems, in fact it was "a completely misguided approach to effective policing" (quoted in Maciag, 2014).

No doubt the opinion of the academic was sought to balance the debate of the article, but the quote and the discussion pertaining to it display a shallowness of an understanding of the situation in Camden, the frustration of Camden residents, and how the CPD was removed from the reality of crime control in Camden. The quote also minimizes the skills of and the work put in by the city and county implementation team and implies that they did not appreciate that establishing a new regionalized police service from the ground up would be complicated and would involve a number of complex human resource, fiscal, and organizational development issues. The concept of how the CCPD was proposed to function initially is presented in Table 13.5.

To ensure that the establishment of the CCPD would achieve all of the principles of the high-level plan, the city and county contracted former Commissioner of Philadelphia Police Department, John Timoney. Former Commissioner Timoney, together with county and city public safety officials, developed a plan for the city of Camden's policing requirements as part of the proposed regionalized police agency. The plan was based on a partnership

Table 13.5   How the Concept of CCPD Was Proposed to Work

- Hiring of new police force and staff including administrative leadership and staff and supervisory and uniformed officers, using quality hiring standards.
- Civilian staff will be used for cost savings—countywide analysis of the functions that must be provided by uniform officers and the positions that may be civilianized will be undertaken.
- Any municipality wishing to participate will dissolve its police department by resolution/ ordinance—all municipal police staff will be laid off as part of the dissolution.
- There will be an established process for each municipality entering the county's police department—including a "Resolution of Interest" by the municipality, which would begin the process of a policing plan, financial analysis, and community consultation.
- The CCPD can and will hire former local police staff—priority will be placed on employing professional, skilled staff.
- Participating community leaders will actively take part in selecting management, supervisory staff, and police officers.
- Each police district will be assigned appropriate patrols, officers, and administrative support and services—municipalities will pay the direct cost of the service provided.
- Staffing will be allocated based on best practice for each participating municipality—with input from participating community leadership and professionals.
- A detailed transition plan will be developed by the CCPD and the municipality for each participating municipality.

Source: Adapted from Camden country, *Camden County (n.d.), White paper: The Camden County Police Department*, Retrieved on March 11, 2015 from http://www. camdencountypd.org/wpcontent/themes/ccpd/pdf/Police-White-Paper-6-7-11.pdf.

with the city, the county of Camden and the residents of the city of Camden, and included a new organizational structure and an implementation process. The plan suggested a change from the reactive model of policing in Camden city to a model based on a proactive approach to service delivery. The theory behind the plan was that a regionalized police agency would provide the emergency services necessary while engaging in proactive policing measures with the goal of improving the quality of life for the community (Camden County, n.d.). It was envisaged that the partnerships and the new approach to service delivery would be the foundation for the success of the regionalized police agency and the final documented plan became the draft organizational and functional plan for establishing the CCPD (Camden County).

CCPD Draft Plan

The organization of the CCPD contained within the draft plan was based on the public safety needs of the city of Camden (Camden County, 2011b). The draft plan proposed the number of officers that would be employed, but this was intended to be an aim and would not be the final number. The proposed staffing number was a model and would not be the full staffing complement on the first day of the operation of CCPD, as the actual staffing numbers would be finalized when the financial information had been fully analyzed by the city and county CCPD planning team (Camden County, 2011b). The proviso was that the budget for the CCPD would be based upon the expenditure of the city.

The positions and the numbers of staff required, which was documented in the draft organizational plan, are presented in Table 13.6, and the proposed major divisions are presented in Table 13.7. At the executive level, the CCPD was to be organized into the Office of the Police Commissioner, and two bureaus: the Chief Inspector of Operations and the Chief Inspector of Support Services. This structure would enable the Chief Inspector of Operations to move or deploy officers from any operational unit when demand and circumstances require (Camden County, 2011b).

The proposed structure was premised on four pivotal components, which would be essential for the success of the new CCPD Metro and for its acceptance by the residents of Camden. The first was the establishment of the Real-Time Tactical Operations and Information Center (RT-TOIC), within the Strategic Operation Management Division. The RT-TOIC is an intelligence-driven center that maintains a real-time awareness of conditions in the Camden city operating environment. Real-time awareness was achieved by coordinating technology and monitoring the tactical deployment

Table 13.6   Proposed CCPD Staffing by Position Type

Position	Number of Officers
Commissioner	1
Deputy Commissioner	1
Chief Inspector	3
Inspector	5
Captain	12
Sergeant	47
Officer	320
Total Full-Time Sworn	**389**
Special Law Enforcement Officer (SLEO) (I & II)	80
Police Aide	39
Analyst	5
Crime Scene Technician	5
Systems Administrator	1
Clerical Support	14
Telecommunicator	32
Total Full-Time Nonsworn	**176**
Total Staff of CCPD	**565**

Source: Adapted from Camden County, *Camden County Police Department: Proposed draft plan*, Retrieved on March 11, 2015 from http://camdencountypd.org/wp-content/themes/ccpd/pdf/Timoney-Draft-Plan-dated-9-26-11.pdf, 2011b.

Table 13.7   Proposed Structure for Essential Functions of the CCPD

1. Police Commissioner
2. Administrative Unit
3. Professional Standards Bureau
4. Deputy Police Commissioners
5. Support Services Bureau
   a. Support Services Division
   b. Strategic Operations Management Division
      i. RT-TOIC
      ii. SAU
6. Operations Bureau
   a. Emergency Response Division
   b. Community Policing Division
   c. Investigative Division

Source: Adapted from Camden County, *Camden County Police Department: Proposed draft plan*, Retrieved on March 11, 2015 from http://camdencountypd.org/wp-content/themes/ccpd/pdf/Timoney-Draft-Plan-dated-9-26-11.pdf, 2011b.

of all assets in the field to ensure compliance with the department's weekly crime reduction plan (Camden County, 2011b). The RT-TOIC also deploys, what the CCPD term, virtual patrollers by using the department's CCTV system to patrol target or high-risk neighborhoods. Police dispatch and 911 functions are also managed within the RT-TOIC (Camden County, 2011b).

The creation of the Strategic Analysis Unit (SAU) was the second pivotal component for the successful establishment of the CCPD Metro. The implementation of a unit such as the SAU was vital for the realization of the benefits of the RT-TOIC. The SAU is primarily responsible for the analysis of crime and organizational performance data and for criminal intelligence that predicts and advises law enforcement assets in the planning and the execution of the CCPD's crime control endeavors (Camden County, 2011b).

The third pivotal component is the Operations Bureau (OB). The OB is divided into three separate divisions: Emergency Response Division, Investigative Division, and the Community Policing Division. To ensure an appropriate patrol coverage of Camden city, the Emergency Response Division is divided further into two divisions: Day Patrol Division and Night Patrol Division (Camden County, 2011b).

The officers of the Day Patrol and the Night Patrol divisions each work 12-hour shifts, and each shift comprises two platoons. The minimum deployment is 20 patrol units per shift (Camden County, 2011b). The patrol divisions are responsible for general patrol functions and for responding to calls for service, including 911 calls (Camden County, 2011b).

The final pivotal component for the successful establishment of the CCPD Metro was the creation of a Community Policing Division (CoPD). The CoPD was kept entirely separate from the Emergency Response Division. The CoPD comprises four police districts that have the responsibility for geographical sections or neighborhoods of the city (Camden County, 2011b). The primary goal of the CoPD is to engage with the neighborhood and the community in order to address the quality of life issues. Each district is commanded by a Captain who is the central coordinator and the responsible authority for the district (Camden County, 2011b). It is also proposed that each district will have one Neighborhood Resource Officer (NRO) who will report directly to the District Commander and will work on addressing long-term, systemic problems that affect that district.

CoPD officers are expected to work effectively with neighborhood and community leaders and groups and are to become familiar with the problems and issues facing their assigned geographical area (Camden County, 2011b). The officers usually work alone on beats along commercial corridors, or on cycles patrolling neighborhoods, but they are also a part of a team that comes together to deal with serious crime or quality of life problems (Camden County, 2011b). It is envisaged that this comprehensive approach to Community Policing will lead to the development of strong and integral community partnerships.

The draft plan also proposed a governance framework to ensure that the CCPD Metro achieves the objectives determined by the city. The governance framework included the establishment of the CCPD advisory committee. This committee would meet biweekly to address issues such as the management of the CCPD, operations, special services, criminal justice implications, collective bargaining agreements, legal issues, and staffing (Camden County, n.d.).

CCPD Metro in 2014

To assist with the establishment of the CCPD Metro, the New Jersey provided Camden with a $5.5 million grant (Laday, 2014b), although this has been reported as being $10 million by one reporter (Kurdzuk, 2014). Savings of approximately $18 million have been made in the city by eliminating a number of personnel benefits such as long service pay and supplemental income for different shifts (Laday, 2014b). The grant and the previous city police budget of $62 million now pays the county for policing services in the form of the CCPD Metro. Under the previous unionized CPD, the cost of employing a police officer was approximately $180,000 and the city policing budget was able to pay for approximately 250 police officers, but now the cost of employing a police officer has decreased to approximately half of the previous cost, resulting in the budget extending to be able to pay for more than 400 officers (Kurdzuk, 2013).

The cost per officer, however, was not the only cost driver. According to Chief Thomson, the work roles and new collective bargaining agreement assisted the CCPD Metro in establishing a more efficient organization (Cornish, 2014). When the CCPD Metro was initially established, there were no binding work rules or confining contracts. The new contract and the fact that the CCPD Metro were able to civilianize a number of former uniformed positions meant that the CCPD Metro was able to make savings that was used to employ extra officers (Cornish, 2014).

With the budgetary savings, CCPD Metro, which unionized on October 1, 2013, was able to hire more officers and increase the actual number of officers, with the agreement of the city, to 411 or approximately 53 police officers for every 10,000 Camden city residents (Maciag, 2014). The CCPD Metro achieved the appointment of the 411th officer in late 2014. The increase in the number of officers has also enabled the CCPD Metro to be, or to be near, to having the highest police presence of any larger-sized city in the United States on a per capita basis. The point of interest is that the number of officers per 10,000 residents is more than three times the national average, according to FBI 2012 data of cities with populations exceeding 50,000. Cities of this size generally employed an average of 17 officers per 10,000 residents (quoted in Maciag, 2014). Only Washington, DC, recorded a higher number of officers per 10,000 residents in 2012, with approximately 61 officers per 10,000 residents (Maciag, 2014).

To assist the CCPD Metro to control crime in the city, on June 20, 2013, the Camden County Board of Chosen Freeholders approved the addition of a private force of 70–100 civilian ambassadors to provide community security and relationship building in the downtown shopping district of Camden. A contract was entered into with the private security firm Allied Barton to provide the ambassadors (Camden County, n.d.).

CCPD's Performance 2012–2014

According to the National Institute of Justice (2014), as a result of the establishment of the CCPD Metro, the number of police officers patrolling Camden's streets increased from 160 to 376 in the first year, and it reached its full complement of 401 sworn officers on June 7, 2013. As well as increasing the number of patrol officers, the CCPD Metro implemented a number of traditional Community Policing programs together with new technology. The department has, for example, reintroduced officers in walking the beat, a policing approach that disappeared from Camden streets in the 1960s, and this initiative has been supported by the installation of the department's 120 outdoor surveillance cameras, which are capable of reading license plate numbers and have shot-sensing microphones and a system that automatically alerts nearby officers to 911 calls.

Table 13.8 Camden City Levels of Crime January 1, 2012, to August 31, 2014

Type of Crime	January–December 2012	January–December 2013	Percentage Change	January 1–August 31, 2014[a]
Murder	61	49	−20	22
Rape	68	53	−22	29
Robbery	695	662	−5	362
Burglary	994	781	−21	528
Larceny—theft	2099	1827	−13	1117
Motor vehicle theft	658	437	−34	243

Source: Adapted from Camden country, *Camden County (n.d.), White paper: The Camden County Police Department*, Retrieved on March 11, 2015 from http://www.camdencountypd.org/wpcontent/themes/ccpd/pdf/Police-White-Paper-6-7-11.pdf.
[a] Laday (2014b).

The Camden city crime statistics to date appear to be promising. Camden's crime statistics are presented in Table 13.8. While the city still has a high level of crime, it has dropped significantly since 2012 (Camden County, n.d.). The major point that should be considered is that a decrease in reported crime occurred during a period when the CCPD Metro was still being implemented, and in a practical sense, when the agency was not fully staffed.

2013 Performance

The CCPD Metro's performance in reducing crime in Camden is presented in Table 13.8. As can be seen, for the 12 months from January to December 2012, there were 61 murders, which decreased to 49 murders during the same period in 2013 (a 20% decrease), and 22 murders for the first 8 months in 2014. The crime figures also show a decrease in rape, from 68 reported instances for the year 2012, to 53 for the year 2013 (a 22% decrease), to 29 for the first 8 months of 2014. However, it is not only the incidents of serious crime that has decreased, but crimes such as burglary and motor vehicle theft have also decreased significantly.

2014 Performance

The crime statistics in 2014 show a similar story. According to Wood (2014), total crime decreased from 1228 to 875 (just under 30%) in the first quarter of 2014 in comparison to the same quarter in 2013. This means that the effective crime rate dropped from 15.89 crimes per 1000 residents to 11.32 (Wood, 2014). There were three fewer homicides, bringing the total down to 10, from 13 during the same period last year. This reflects a 23% decrease. Assaults with a firearm decreased by more than 45% (Wood, 2014).

Since 2012, which was the city's most violent year in its history, and when it found itself being again, the most violent city in the United States, crime has decreased markedly. Shootings have halved in number, robberies and rapes are down by a third, and other violent crimes are down by more than one-fifth (R. W., 2014). Comparing the level of crime in 2014 with the level of crime in 2012 has seen a

- Fifty percent reduction in homicides
- Forty-nine percent reduction in rape
- Twenty-five percent drop in robberies
- Seventeen percent reduction in aggravated assaults
- Twenty-two percent drop in overall violent crime
- Thirty-one percent reduction in nonviolent crime (National Institute of Justice, 2014)

The downside to the decrease in the level of crime, however, is that a number of arrests have increased that have been mainly for quality-of-life infractions (R. W., 2014). The increase in arrests, which are in parallel to the prevention of crime effort, has been achieved by building and strengthening community relationships, which the CCPD insists is its main strategy (R. W., 2014).

While the performance of the CCPD Metro has to date been based on crime statistics and not on a survey of the residents of Camden, they do provide an insight as to the success of the establishment of the CCPD Metro. It would also be of value to view the statistics in relation to the complaints made by the public, as this would be one measure to determine the residents' satisfaction with CCPD Metro or their confidence in the new approach to service delivery. A second point that would be of value in assessing the performance of the CCPD Metro would be an in-depth analysis of the types of arrests being made by officers. Anecdotally, R. W. (2014) claimed that arrests have increased in Camden, but primarily for quality-of-life infractions. However, the claim is not supported by any analysis or statistics, and the CCPD Metro maintained that the reduction in the occurrence of crime has resulted from the extra officers on patrol and from building and maintaining community relationships. It is also possible that the decrease in crime in Camden is in line with the general trend of decreasing crime in most American cites.

CCPD Metro Approach to Crime Prevention

R. W. (2014) asks, what is the CCPD doing right? Looking at the crime statistics in Camden over the past two years, it gives the impression that crime has decreased significantly in the city. Is this decrease because Camden has introduced the traditional form of Community Policing with patrol officers

Table 13.9   Benefits of the CCPD Metro Approach

- Mitigated police layoffs in communities throughout the county.
- Coordinated deployment and administration of resources to reduce/eliminate redundant staffing and administration.
- Increased patrol officers on the street by eliminating redundant layers of bureaucracy and sharing of support resources and services (SWAT, Bomb Squad, etc.).
- Economies of scale and pooling of resources provide opportunities to use and share existing equipment, save on capital costs for all participating municipalities, and gain cost savings through shared purchasing and procurement of supplies, equipment, etc.
- Reduced insurance costs.
- Eliminated individual municipal staffing costs; county police department staff will be county employees.
- Addressed unsustainable cost increases in police compensation.
- Consistent with existing county all emergency services communications center operations.
- Countywide police forces are in existence elsewhere and are able to successfully maintain community programs throughout the country.
- Improved response times.

Source: Adapted from Camden country, *Camden County (n.d.), White paper: The Camden County Police Department*, Retrieved on March 11, 2015 from http://www.camden-countypd.org/wpcontent/themes/ccpd/pdf/Police-White-Paper-6-7-11.pdf.

walking or cycling their beats? Is it because the patrol officers knock on doors and introduce themselves and learn the names of people in a neighborhood (R. W., 2014)? Or is it because of the introduction of new technology and the targeted use of patrol resources?

The answers to these questions have been presented in Table 13.9. The table identifies a number of the benefits of establishing the CCPD Metro and at a more strategic level, some of the reasons as to why the approach taken by the CCPD Metro may be impacting the level of crime.

There are a number of major strategic initiatives that the CCPD Metro have implemented to improve the efficiency and effectiveness of its service delivery and to improve safety in Camden. The first initiative is in relation to the Camden community. As the chief of the CCPD Metro claims, the key has been in the establishment of Community Policing (Cornish, 2014). The central component to bridging any division between CCPD Metro officers and city residents has been to increase the interaction between the two groups (Maciag, 2014). According to Chief Thomson, to the residents of Camden, the color of the officer's skin, or the accent in their voice or where they grew up is not important. When residents call police for assistance, the officer's ethnicity is not important, it is the interaction between the member of the public and the police officer and the quality of the service provided. This means that the CCPD Metro has placed a considerable emphasis on the Community Policing strategy, which includes patrol officers walking the beat, listening to resident's concerns and hosting Meet Your Officers events to further engage residents (Maciag, 2014). The department is also reaching out to community leaders to organize meeting and events between officers and residents as a foundational approach that makes the CCPD Metro officers part of the neighborhoods they patrol and enforcing the idea that residents are partners in the effort to curb crime (National Institute of Justice, 2014).

The second strategic initiative has been the introduction of new technology and the creation of the RT-TOIC. According to Kurdzuk (2013), the RT-TOIC is the nexus of the CCPD Metro operation. The RT-TOIC is located at the CCPD Metro headquarters. There are walls in the headquarters building, which are lined with television and computer monitors that visually display the location of patrols and that detects gunshots within the city (Kurdzuk, 2013). The center is not only about state-of-the-art technology but is also supported by a section of intelligence analysts and command staff that are able to assess locations and situations to ensure the effective use of available patrol resources.

According to Chief Thomson, the RT-TOIC is indicative of the more with less emphasis placed on police agencies since the 2007 fiscal crisis and enables the targeting of crime hot spots by officers (Kurdzuk, 2013). The targeting of these high crime areas has meant that the CCPD Metro has been able to direct and coordinate patrol officer resources to lessen the effect of the occurrence of violence on residents and without conducting mass arrests (Kurdzuk, 2013).

Last, credit is due to the CCPD Metro officers themselves. According to Chief Thomson, the former CPD officers that joined the CCPD Metro were the most important part of the puzzle as they indoctrinated the new officers to Camden and to the neighborhood that they would be patrolling (Maciag, 2014). The CCPD Metro officers were deployed 25 at a time, while the CPD remained in operation and were trained on neighborhood streets in the hope that they could become a part of the neighborhood makeup and regain the trust of the city's residents (Zernike, 2013).

There have been problems and disagreements with individual officers. The ethnicity composition of the CCPD Metro is different from the CPD. More than two-thirds of the CPD officers were minorities; while in the CCPD Metro, minorities account for approximately 43% of sworn personnel in a city that is 95% minority (Maciag, 2014). This is an issue that the executive of the CCPD Metro will need to place an emphasis on rectifying, if they are to gain the confidence of the Camden community.

Conclusion

In the American policing sense, the establishment of the CCPD is an experiment in the true sense. It could even be called revolutionary. There are numerous examples of police agencies, large and small, across the United States that have or are in the process of implementing change initiatives to improve their service delivery efficiency and/or effectiveness. However, Camden stands out for the comprehensiveness of the program and for the depth of the change and the speed in its implementation.

What also needs to be considered in any discussion about the success of establishing the CCPD Metro is that policing was only one aspect of change that was introduced to improve the conditions of Camden residents. At the same time that the CCPD Metro was established, the Camden school district was undergoing reform. The state appointed a new superintendent of schools supported by a leadership team, which, in coordination with the community, took direct oversight in implementing the necessary reforms to deliver better results for Camden students and their families (National Institute of Justice, 2014).

Also during this period, the governor signed the bipartisan Economic Opportunity Act (EOA) to revamp the State of New Jersey Economic Incentive programs. The EOA specifically redirected New Jersey's incentive programs to create jobs and invest in the state's most distressed communities through the design and implementation of programs with lower qualification for assistance thresholds. As a result of the program, as early as 2014, the city of Camden was beginning to see a number of major economic development projects that were estimated to create more than 1250 new and permanent jobs (National Institute of Justice, 2014).

One view of the changes undertaken by the city and the county could be that it was union breaking and the negation of hard-won workers' conditions. However, the alternative debate is that, over time, the city had allowed corruption to set in and that the conditions that police officers enjoyed could be viewed as one aspect of this. The continual downward spiral that Camden was caught in could not continue.

The first two years of the CCPD Metro policing the city have seen the level of crime decrease. The decrease together with the framework of improved schooling and the prospect of developments and employment opportunities must be improving the city and the lives of residents. However, one aspect of the Camden County Police plan has not been achieved: the creation of a regionalized countywide police agency. The initial plan envisioned that other municipalities within the county would join the new CCPD, but to date, this has not happened (Maciag, 2014). Perhaps given more time and with the continued success of the CCPD Metro, other municipalities within the county may consider joining the CCPD.

Conclusion

14

One of the major findings of the research for this book is that the new environment is creating a force for change. The response to change calls for innovative practices, which can include the privatization, civilianization, and rationalization of the provision of police services. Within this environment is the contradiction that "[w]hile the role and capacity of public policing appears to be diminishing, policing scholars (Bayley, 1994; Bayley & Shearing, 1996; Murphy, 1998; Murray, 2000; Sheptycki, 1998) predict that global social and technological change will stimulate an ever-expanding requirement for policing and security in society" (Murphy, 2002, pp. 36–37).

Continuing change in the police operating environment makes it essential that police managers have a clear understanding of their responsibilities, the role of the police, and where they fit in the bigger picture of government and governance. It is essential that the police understand their role within government, as a number of changes that have occurred since the 1960s have been brought about, or led by government and government accounting or budgetary control agencies and not by the police themselves.

The police need to understand new public management (NPM) and its components and be able to adapt the strategy or components of the strategy for their specific circumstances. NPM is an adaptable and a tested approach to managing police agencies. The point that NPM has been implemented and used successfully in numerous police agencies around the world is important because the management and governance of police agencies is different from that of other government agencies and entities. Police agencies respond differently to their environment and deliver their services differently. They are often the only 24-hour emergency service that is usually immediately available. The differences between police agencies and other public sector entities are presented in Table 14.1.

The implementation of NPM or the implementation of aspects of the program will provide a platform for police agencies to raise their performance standards (Thomson, 2012) and improve their service delivery efficiency and effectiveness. However, without this foundational performance framework, police managers will not be able to develop measurement instruments, or be able to measure agency outputs and efficiency (Ostrom, 1973). The efforts by police managers to identify sound and relevant performance indicators "are

Table 14.1 Generic Differences between Police and Other Public Sector Entities

	Police Services	Other Public Sector Entities
Environment	Dynamic, risk based, violent, and possibly life threatening	Stable and mainly predictable
Services	Proactive and reactive. Protection of the community and promotion of safety	Support services or provision of policy. To provide a community service (e.g., health or education)
Objectives	To minimize costs and reduce the demand for expenditure	To recover costs (to an extent) by adopting a user-pays strategy
Revenues	Local, municipal, or state government funding	Fees, charges, taxes, and government funding

Source: Adapted from Hoque, Z. et al., *Account. Audit. Account. J.*, 17(1), 78, 2004.

essential for the evaluation of the effect of different organizational forms on the performance of the police" (Ostrom, 1973, p. 109).

Developing comprehensive organizational performance frameworks enables police managers to identify and compare options to make structural changes to their agency and to improve the delivery of their services. The ability to compare the capability of the performance framework will allow a proposed reform to be evaluated to determine its value (Ostrom, 1973).

The adoption of NPM in the early 1980s by UK police forces resulted in a new policing order (Cope, Leishman & Starie, 1997, p. 453). The new policing order comprised the implementation of NPM in its entirety, the greater centralization of the governance of policing and police agencies through collaboration and regional task forces while permitting the decentralization of the delivery of services (Cope et al., 1997). This model of centralization–decentralization has been readily accepted in the United Kingdom following the reluctance of the Home Office to implement a nationwide regionalization program that would have seen the number of local forces decrease from 43 to 13 regional forces. One of the major reasons that the UK Home Office withdrew the regionalization program was that they could not demonstrate that the proposed regional police services would be any more effective or efficient than a non-regional structure (Lithopoulos & Rigakos, 2005).

As discussed throughout this book, the findings from research as to the benefits of police agency amalgamation or regionalization are extremely contradictory. A number of researchers state that small- and medium-sized agencies are more efficient and effective (Loveday, 1995a, 1995b, 2006a, 2006b, 2007; Loveday and McClory, 2007; Ostrom, et al., 1978), while others state that regionalized agencies are more efficient and effective (Murphy, 2002; O'Bryne, 2001; Pennsylvania Governor's Center for Local Government Services, 2012).

The contradictory findings of the research into police agency amalgamations exist for a number of reasons. The first is that there is a lack of evaluative time series or pre- and postamalgamation research that examines a statistically significant number of agencies. The second reason is that owing to the lack of research, it is not known how the unsuccessful amalgamations were structured and implemented. Could an amalgamation have provided service delivery improvements if it was undertaken differently? The vacuum in research applies equally to the implementation of any of the strategies presented in this book, as none have been systematically evaluated.

The lack of information in regard to police agency amalgamations or the implementation of cost-reducing strategies may have led to an increased level of popularity of multijurisdictional collaborations and task forces as police managers look for alternatives to decrease operating expenses. According to Shernock (2004), multijurisdictional task forces have been evaluated positively and have been accepted by the criminal justice community. While Schnobrich-Davis (2010) identified that approximately "90 per cent of all agencies nation-wide give or receive emergency assistance, and [approximately] 50 per cent belong to formal mutual aid agreements" (p. 307).

Although collaborations and multijurisdictional task forces are a step in the alternative strategies direction, they are safe strategies. Schafer (2012) calls for bold and innovative ideas along with safe strategies to improve the public's confidence in the police. Bold ideas must be able to incorporate the best of policing's current service approaches such as Community, Problem-Oriented, and Intelligence-Led Policing.

In future years, police resources are likely to become even more constrained. Decreases in resources and budgets mean that it will become even more important for police managers to investigate methods to improve the delivery of community safety and implement strategies that assist and enhance the governance of their agencies. The challenge for police managers is to be able to identify the organizational structure and accountability frameworks that enhance local policing while also enabling police agencies to be able to respond to the newer trans-state or transnational and terrorism-related crimes (Loveday, 2006a).

In 1979, Dorothy Guyot published an article analyzing the then contemporary programs designed to change police departments in the United States. In this article, Guyot suggested that changing police organizations was akin to "bending granite" (cited in Palmer and Cherney, 2001, p. 47). If the police are to become more pliable, they must be able to use the service delivery improvement strategies that are available to shape their own future and to build strong mutually beneficial relationships with the community. It is hoped that this book will assist police managers, decision and policy makers in this process.

References

Ackroyd, S., Hughes, J., & Soothill, K. (1989). Public sector services and their management. *Journal of Management Studies, 26*(6), 603–619.

Advisory Commission on Intergovernmental Relations. (1971). *Measuring the fiscal capacity and effort of state and local areas.* Information Report M58. Washington, DC: U.S. Government Printing Office.

Amin, A., Gills, B., Palan, R., & Taylor, P. (1994). Editorial: Forum for heterodox international political economy. *Review of International Political Economy, 1*(1), 1–12.

Armstrong, A. (1998, June). A comparative analysis: New public management—The way ahead? *Australian Journal of Public Administration, 57*(2), 12–24.

Association of Chief Police Officers. (2008). *Police reform green paper: The future of policing.* Retrieved on October 30, 2012 from www.acpo.police.uk/documents/.../200803GENPRGP01.pdf.

Audit Commission (1990). *Annual report on police audits 1989/1990.* London, U.K.: Audit Commission.

Australian MAB-MIAC Task Force on Management Improvement. (1992). *Evaluating management improvement in the Australian Public Service: First report.* Canberra, Australian Capital Territory, Australia: AGPS.

Ayto, J. (2011). *The core elements of New Zealand's public sector management model as originally formulated State Services Commission.* Better Public Services Issues Paper. Wellington, New Zealand: The Treasury.

Bale, M., & Dale, T. (1998). Public sector reform in New Zealand and its relevance to developing countries. *The World Bank Research Observer, 13*(1), 103–121.

Baron, R., & Greenberg, J. (1990). *Behavior in organizations: Understanding and managing the human side of work* (3rd ed.). Needham Heights, MA: Allyn and Bacon.

Bayley, D. (1994). *Police for the future.* New York: Oxford University Press.

Bayley, D. (1998). *What works in policing.* New York: Oxford University Press.

Bayley, D., & Shearing, C. (1996). The future of policing. *Law and Society Review, 30*(3), 585–606.

Beaton, P. (1974). The determination of police protection expenditures. *National Tax Journal, 27,* 335–349.

Bish, R. (1999). *Local government service production in the Capital Region of British Columbia.* Victoria, British Columbia, Canada: British Columbia University of Victoria, Local Government Institute.

Bish, R. (2001, March). *Local government amalgamations: Discredited nineteenth-century ideals alive in the twenty-first* (The Urban Papers No. 150). Ottawa, Ontario, Canada: C.D. Howell Institute.

Boston, J. (1987, Winter). Transforming New Zealand's public sector: Labour's quest for improved efficiency and accountability. *Public Administration, 65,* 423–442.

Boston, J. (1991). The theoretical underpinnings of public sector restructuring in New Zealand. In J. Boston, J. Martin, J. Pallot, & P. Walsh (Eds.), *Reshaping the state: New Zealand's bureaucratic revolution* (pp. 1–26). Auckland, New Zealand: Oxford University Press.

Boston, J., Dalziel, P., & St. John, S. (1999). *Redesigning the welfare state in New Zealand: Problems, policies, prospects.* Auckland, New Zealand: Oxford University Press.

Boston, J., Martin, J., Pallot, J., & Walsh, P. (1991). *Reshaping the state: New Zealand's bureaucratic revolution.* Auckland, New Zealand: Oxford University Press.

Boyd, E., Geoghegan, R., & Gibbs, B. (2011). *Cost of cops: Manpower, and deployment in policing.* London, U.K.: Policy Exchange.

Braddon, D., & Foster, D. (1996). *Privatization: Social science themes and perspectives.* Aldershot, U.K.: Dartmouth Publishing.

Braga, A., & Weisburd, D. (2010). *Policing problem places: Crime hotspots and effective prevention.* New York: Oxford University Press.

Braithwaite, J., Westbrook, J., & Ledema, R. (2005). Restructuring as gratification. *Journal of the Royal Society of Medicine, 98*(1), 542–544.

Brandl, S., & Frank, J. (1994). The relationship between evidence, detective effort, and the disposition of burglary and robbery investigations. *American Journal of Police, 13*(3), 149–167.

British Columbia Chamber of Commerce. (2011). *Provincial issues—Justice.* Retrieved on January 10, 2012 from http://www.bcchamber.org/advocacy/policy/provincial_gov/justice/police_amalgamation.html.

Brodeur, J.P. (2005). Trotsky in blue permanent policing reform. *The Australian and New Zealand Journal of Criminology, 38*(2), 254–267.

Brown, K., Ryan, N., & Parker, R. (2000). New modes of service delivery in the public sector: Commercialising government services. *International Journal of Public Sector Management, 13*(3), 206–221.

Bryan, R., Granville, S., & Sizer, J. (2011). *Research support for a consultation on the future of policing in Scotland.* Edinburgh, U.K.: Queens Printers of Scotland.

Burack, J. (2012). Putting the "local" back in local law enforcement. In D. Cohen McCullough & D. Spence (Eds.), *American policing in 2022: Essays on the future of a profession* (pp. 79–84). Washington, DC: Community Oriented Policing Services U.S. Department of Justice.

Butterfield, R., Edwards, C., & Woodall, J. (2004). The new public management and the UK police service. *Public Management Review, 6*(3), 395–415.

Camden County. (2011a). *The Camden County Police Department: FQAs.* Retrieved on March 11, 2015 from http://www.camdencountypd.org/wp-content/themes/ccpd/pdf/Police-FAQ.pdf.

Camden County. (2011b). *Camden County Police Department: Proposed draft plan.* Retrieved on March 11, 2015 from http://camdencountypd.org/wp-content/themes/ccpd/pdf/Timoney-Draft-Plan-dated-9-26-11.pdf.

Camden County. (n.d.). *White paper: The Camden County Police Department.* Retrieved on March 11, 2015 from http://www.camdencountypd.org/wp-content/themes/ccpd/pdf/Police-White-Paper-6-7-11.pdf.

Carrington, R., Puthucheary, N., & Rose, D. (1997). Performance measurement in government service provision: The case of police services in New South Wales. *Journal of Productivity Analysis, 8,* 415–430.

Chapman, J., Hirsch, Z., & Sonenblum, S. (1975). Crime prevention, the police production and budgeting. *Public Finance, 30*(2), 197–215.

City-Data.com, Crime rate in Camden, New Jersey (NJ): Murders, rapes, robberies, assaults, burglaries, thefts, auto thefts, arson, law enforcement employees, police officers, crime map, 2015a, http://www.city-data.com/crime/crime-Camden-New-Jersey.html, accessed on 11 March 2015.

City-Data.com, Crime rate in New York (NY): Murders, rapes, robberies, assaults, burglaries, thefts, auto thefts, arson, law enforcement employees, police officers, crime map, 2015b, http://www.city-data.com/crime/crime-New-York-New-York.html, accessed on 11 March 2015.

Cloninger, D., & Sartorius, L. (1979, October). Crime rates, clearance rates and enforcement efforts. *American Journal of Economics and Sociology, 38,* 389–403.

Cohen McCullough, D., & Spence, D. (2012). *American policing in 2022: Essays on the future of a profession.* Washington, DC: Community Oriented Policing Services U.S. Department of Justice.

Cohen, S., & Eimicke, W. (2012, November 8–10). *Management innovation in improving response time at New York City's Fire Department.* A paper presented at the Fall Research Conference of the Association of Policy Analysis and Management, Baltimore, MD.

Commissioner of Police. (1998, November). *Final report on the review of police administration and management structures.* Wellington, New Zealand: New Zealand Police.

Committee for Economic Development (1972). *Reducing crime and assuring justice.* New York: Committee for Economic Development.

Cooper, B., & Koop, R. (2003). Policing Alberta: An analysis of the alternatives to the federal provision of police services (Public Policy Sources, No. 72). A Fraser Institute Occasional Paper, Vancouver, British Columbia, Canada.

Cope, S., Leishman, F., & Starie, P. (1997). Globalization, new public management and the enabling state futures of police management. *The International Journal of Public Sector Management, 10*(6), 444–460.

Cornish, A. (2014). *How a new police force in Camden helped turn the city around.* Retrieved on March 11, 2015 from http://www.npr.org/2014/09/02/345296155/how-a-new-police-force-in-camden-helped-turn-the-city-around.

CQ Press. (2015). *City crime rankings.* Retrieved on March 11, 2015 from http://www.cqpress.com/pages/cc2005.

Curry, B. (2014, December 23). Federal study to probe whether "civilianization" cuts policing costs. *The Globe and Mail.* Retrieved on March 12, 2015 from: http://www.theglobeandmail.com/news/politics/federal-study-to-probe-whether-civilianization-cuts-policing-costs/article22215496.

Darrough, M., & Heineke, J. (1978). Multi-Output Translog Production Cost Function: The Case of Law Enforcement Agencies. In J. Heineke (Ed.), *Economic Models of Criminal Behavior* (pp. 259–302). Amsterdam: North-Holland Publishing Company.

Deane, R. (1986). Public sector reform: A review of the issues. In M. Clark & E. Sinclair (Eds.), *Purpose, performance and profit: Redefining the public sector*, Wellington, New Zealand. Studies in Public Administration, No. 32. Proceedings of the 1986 Convention of the New Zealand Institute of Public Administration.

Delone, G. (2009). Organizational cooperation: Law enforcement agencies working together. *The Police Journal, 31*(1), 34–49.

den Heyer, G. (2008). *The United Kingdom national intelligence model: An assessment for the New Zealand police* (Unpublished master's thesis). Victoria University, Wellington, New Zealand.

den Heyer, G. (2009). *Econometric modelling and analysis to support operational policing: A New Zealand police case study*. Saarbrucken, Germany: VDM Verlag.

den Heyer, G. (2011). Is new public management a useful strategy for democratic policing? *Policing: An International Journal of Police Strategies and Management, 34*(3), 419–433.

den Heyer, G. (2013a). American policing in an age of austerity and globalization: An option to face the challenge. *Critical Issues in Justice and Politics, 6*(2), 1–26.

den Heyer, G. (2013b). Shape or adapt? The future of policing. *Salus Journal, 1*(1), 41–54.

den Heyer, G. (2014). Examining police strategic resource allocation in a time of austerity. *Salus Journal, 2*(1), 63–79.

Dial, D. (2012). Social unrest, drug abuse, cyber-crimes, and no money. In D. Cohen McCullough & D. Spence (Eds.), *American policing in 2022: Essays on the future of a profession* (pp. 105–108). Washington, DC: Community Oriented Policing Services U.S. Department of Justice.

Dixon, J., & Kouzmin, A. (1994). The commercialization of the Australian public sector: Competence, elitism or default in management education? *International Journal of Public Sector Management, 7*(6), 52–73.

Dixon, J., Kouzmin, A., & Korac-Kakabadse, N. (1998). Managerialism: Something old, something borrowed, little new: Economic prescription versus effective organisational change in public agencies. *International Journal of Public Sector Management, 11*(2/3), 1–19.

Domitrovic, B. (2013). *The worst economic crisis since when?* Retrieved on March 12, 2015 from http://www.forbes.com/sites/briandomitrovic/2013/02/05/the-worst-economic-crisis-since-when/.

Donnelly, D., & Scott, K. (2008). Policing in Scotland. In T. Newburn (Ed.), *Handbook of policing* (2nd ed., pp. 182–203). Devon, U.K.: Willan Publishing.

Doone, P. (1996). *Conference of commissioners' of police of Australia and South West Pacific region: Transforming police beyond 2000*. Unpublished presentation.

Douglas, M., & Tweeten, L. (1971). The cost of controlling crime: A study in economies of city life. *The Annals of Regional Science, 5*, 33–49.

Drake, L., & Simper, R. (2000). Productivity estimation and the size-efficiency relationship in English and Welsh police forces: An application of data envelopment analysis and multiple discriminant analysis. *International Review of Law and Economics, 20*(1), 53–73.

Drake, L., & Simper, R. (2004). The economics of managerialism and the drive for efficiency in policing. *Management and Decision Economics, 25*, 509–523.

Drewniak, M. (2011). *Governor Chris Christie deploys State Police resources to aid law enforcement efforts in Camden*. State of New Jersey Governor Chris Christie. Retrieved on March 11, 2015 from http://www.state.nj.us/governor/news/news/552011/approved/20111212c.html.

Duncan, B. (2012). Producing a positive return on investment. In D. Cohen McCullough & D. Spence (Eds.), *American policing in 2022: Essays on the future of a profession* (pp. 75–78). Washington, DC: Community Oriented Policing Services U.S. Department of Justice.

Eck, J. (1983). *Solving crimes: The investigation of burglary and robbery*. Washington, DC: Police Executive Research Forum.

Eck, J. (1992). Criminal investigation. In G. Cordner & D. Hale (Eds.), *What works in policing* (pp. 19–34). Cincinnati, OH: Anderson.

Eck, J. (1999). *Problem-solving detectives: Some thoughts on their scarcity*. Seattle, WA: Seattle Police Department.

Eck, J., & Maguire, E. (2000). Have changes in policing reduced violent crime? An assessment of the evidence. In A. Blumstein & J. Wallman (Eds.), *The crime drop in America* (pp. 207–265). Cambridge, U.K.: Cambridge University Press.

Eck, J., & Spelman, W. (1987). *Problem-solving: Problem-oriented policing in Newport News*. Washington, DC: Police Executive Research Forum.

Ehrlich, I. (1973). Participating in illegitimate activities: A theoretical and empirical analysis. *Journal of Political Economy, 81*(3), 521–567.

Etter, B. (1993, March). Future directions of policing in Australia. *The Australian Police Journal, 47*, 43–54.

Etue, K. (2012). No-boundaries policing. In D. Cohen McCullough & D. Spence (Eds.), *American policing in 2022: Essays on the future of a profession* (pp. 49–52). Washington, DC: Community Oriented Policing Services U.S. Department of Justice.

Fairweather, S. (1978). *Review of regionalized policing in Ontario*. Toronto, Ontario, Canada: Ontario Police Commission.

Farmer, D. (1978). The future of local law enforcement in the United States: The federal role. *Police Studies: International Review of Police Development, 31*, 31–38.

Farmer, D. (1984). *Crime control: The use and misuse of police resources*. New York: Plenum Press.

Fijnaut, C. (1999). Observations concerning recent police service reorganisations in Western Europe. In G. Bruinsma & C. van der Vijver (Eds.), *Public safety in Europe* (pp. 129–135). Enschede, the Netherlands: International Police Institute Twente, University of Twente.

Finney, M. (1997). Scale economies and police department consolidation: Evidence from Los Angeles. *Contemporary Economic Policy, 15*(1), 121–127.

Fischer, C. (2009). *Violent crime and the economic crisis: Police chiefs face a new challenge*. Washington, DC: Police Executive Research Forum.

Fisk, J. (1974). *The police officer's exercise of discretion in the decision to arrest: Relationship and organizational goals and societal values*. Unpublished, University College, Institute of Government and Public Affairs, Los Angeles, CA.

Fleming, J., & Lafferty, G. (2000). New management techniques and restructuring for accountability in Australian police organisations. *Policing: An International Journal of Police Strategies & Management, 23*(2), 154–168.

Fleming, J., & Scott, A. (2008). Performance measurement in Australian police orga-nizations. *Policing, 2*(3), 322–330.

Forst, B. (2000). The privatization and civilianization of policing. In P. McDonald & J. Munsterman (Eds.), *Boundary changes in criminal justice organizations: Criminal justice 2000* (Vol. 2, pp. 19–79). Washington, DC: National Institute of Justice.

Frazier, M. (2012). Quality and performance management: An innovative approach to future police management. In D. Cohen McCullough & D. Spence (Eds.), *American policing in 2022: Essays on the future of a profession* (pp. 23–28). Washington, DC: Community Oriented Policing Services US Department of Justice.

Fuentes, R. (2012). Austerity breeds prevention. In D. Cohen McCullough & D. Spence (Eds.), *American policing in 2022: Essays on the future of a profes-sion* (pp. 63–66). Washington, DC: Community Oriented Policing Services US Department of Justice.

Fulop, N., Protopsaltis, G., Hutchings, A., King, A., Allen, A., Normand, C., & Walters, R. (2002). Process and impact of mergers of NHS trusts: Multi-centre case study and management cost analysis. *British Medical Journal, 325,* 246–249.

Fyfe, N. (2013). Different and divergent trajectory? Reforming the structure, gov-ernance and narrative of policing in Scotland. In J. Brown (Ed.), *The future of policing: Papers prepared for the Stevens Independent Commission into the future of policing in England and Wales* (pp. 493–506). London, U.K.: Routledge.

Fyfe, N., & Scott, K. (2013). In search of sustainable policing? Creating a national police force in Scotland. In N. Fyfe, J. Terpatra, & P. Topa, (Eds.), *Centralizing forces? Comparative perspectives on contemporary police reform in Northern and Western Europe* (pp. 97–109). Den Haag, the Netherlands: Eleven International Publishing.

Gill, D. (2000). New Zealand experience with public management reform—Or why the grass is always greener on the other side of the fence. *International Public Management Journal, 3,* 55–66.

Gillespie, J. (2006). *Policing performance management systems: Identifying key design elements within a 'new' public management context* (Unpublished master's the-sis). School of Business Management, Edith Cowan University, Perth, Western Australia, Australia.

Glensor, R., & Peak, K. (2012). New police management practices and predictive software: A new era they do not make. In D. Cohen McCullough & D. Spence (Eds.), *American policing in 2022: Essays on the future of a profession* (pp. 11–16). Washington, DC: Community Oriented Policing Services U.S. Department of Justice.

Godfrey, J. (2007). None of the above: Lessons to be learnt from the police force structures debate. *The Police Journal, 80*(1), 55–78.

Golding, B., & Savage, S. (2008). Leadership and performance management. In T. Newburn (Ed.), *Handbook of policing* (pp. 725–759). Portland, OR: Willan Publishing.

Goldstein, H. (1990). *Problem-oriented policing.* New York: McGraw-Hill Publishing:

Gordon, C. (2014). *Camden: A new policing model for America's most violent cities.* Retrieved on March 11, 2015 from http://america.aljazeera.com/watch/shows/america-tonight/america-tonight-blog/2013/10/24/camden-a-new-policing-modelforamericasmostviolentcities.html.

Gorringe, P. (2001). *Economics for policy: Expanding the boundaries.* Wellington, New Zealand: Institute of Policy Studies, Victoria University.

Gravelle, J., & Rogers, C. (2011). Research and policing in times of austerity. *The Police Journal, 84*(3), 222–233.

Griffiths, C., Palmer, A., Weeks, L., & Polydore, L. (2006). *Civilianization in the Vancouver Police Department.* Vancouver, British Columbia, Canada: Vancouver Police Department.

Gyapong, A., & Gyimah-Brempong, K. (1988). Factor substitution, price elasticity of factor demand and returns to scale in police production: Evidence from Michigan. *Southern Economic Journal, 54*(4), 863–878.

Gyimah-Brempong, K. (1987). Economies of scale in municipal police departments: The case of Florida. *The Review of Economics and Statistics, 69*(2), 352–356.

Gyimah-Brempong, K. (1989). Production of public safety: Are socioeconomic characteristics of local communities important factors? *Journal of Applied Econometrics, 4*(1), 57–71.

Harrad, L. (2006). Are larger police forces better than smaller forces? *Police Professional, 44*, 24–26.

Hatry, H. (1975). Wrestling with police crime control productivity measurement. In J. Wolfe & J. Heaphy (Eds.), *Readings on productivity in policing* (pp. 86–128). Washington, DC: Police Foundation.

Hawley, M. (2004). *Civilianization of police department functions.* Memorandum to Berkley City Council. Retrieved on April 17, 2015 from http://www.ci.berkeley.ca.us/citycouncil/2004citycouncil/packet/110904/2004-11-09%20Item%2016.pdf.

Heaton, P. (2010). *Hidden in plain sight what cost-of-crime research can tell us about investing in police. Issues in policing.* Santa Monica, CA: Center on Quality Policing, Rand.

Her Majesty's Inspectorate of Constabulary. (1998). *What price policing? A study of efficiency and value for money in the police service.* London, U.K.: Her Majesty's Inspectorate of Constabulary.

Her Majesty's Inspectorate of Constabulary. (2004). *Modernising the police service. A thematic inspection of workforce modernisation—The role, management and development of police staff in the police service of England and Wales.* London, U.K.: Home Office.

Her Majesty's Inspectorate of Constabulary. (2005). *Closing the gap. A review of the fitness for purpose of the current structure of policing in England and Wales.* London, U.K.: Her Majesty's Inspectorate of Constabulary.

Her Majesty's Inspectorate of Constabulary. (2010). *Valuing the police: Policing in an age of austerity.* London, U.K.: Her Majesty's Inspectorate of Constabulary.

Her Majesty's Inspectorate of Constabulary. (2011). *Adapting to austerity: A review of police force and authority preparedness for the 2011/12–14/15 CSR period.* London, U.K.: Her Majesty's Inspectorate of Constabulary.

Her Majesty's Inspectorate of Constabulary Scotland. (2009). *Independent review of policing in Scotland: A report for the Cabinet Secretary of Justice.* Edinburgh, U.K.: Her Majesty's Inspectorate of Constabulary Scotland.

Her Majesty's Treasury. (2006). [Delivering a step change in police productivity]. Unpublished paper.

Hilmer, F., & Donaldson, L. (1995). *Management redeemed.* Sydney, New South Wales, Australia: The Free Press.

Hilsenrath, J., Ng, S., & Paletta, D. (2008, September 18). Worst crisis since '30s, with no end in sight. *The Wall Street Journal,* p. A1. Retrieved from http://online.wsj.com/article/SB122169431617549947.html.

Hirschman, A. (1970). *Exit, voice and loyalty: Responses to decline in firms, organizations and states.* Cambridge, MA: Harvard University Press.

Home Office. (1983). *Circular 114/83: Effectiveness and efficiency in the police service.* London, U.K.: Home Office.

Home Office. (2004, November 9). *Building communities, beating crime: A better police service for the 21st century—Cm 6360.* London, U.K.: Home Office.

Home Office. (2006). Police reform and protective services. Letter from Tony McNulty MP, Minister of State, to all England and Wales Police Chiefs and Chairs of Police Authorities.

Home Office. (2010). *Policing in the 21st century: Reconnecting police and the people.* London, U.K.: The Stationery Office.

Hoque, Z., Arends, S., & Alexander, R. (2004). Policing the police service: A case study of the rise of new public management within an Australian police service. *Accounting, Auditing & Accountability Journal, 17*(1), 59–84.

Hughes, O. (1994). *Public management and administration: An introduction.* New York: St. Martins Press.

International Association of Chiefs of Police. (2011). *Policing in the 21st century: Preliminary survey results.* Alexandria, VA: International Association of Chiefs of Police.

John, P. (2003). Is there life after policy streams, advocacy coalitions and punctuations: Using evolutionary theory to explain policy change? *Policy Studies Journal, 31*(4), 481–498.

Jones, T., & Newburn, T. (1999). Urban change and policing: Mass private property re-considered. *European Journal on Criminal Policy and Research, 7*(2), 225–244.

Jones, T., & Newburn, T. (2002). The transforming of policing? Understanding current trends in policing systems. *British Journal of Criminology, 42,* 129–146.

Kaplan, R., & Porter, M. (2011, September). How to solve the cost crisis in health care. *Harvard Business Review, 89,* 46–64.

Katz, M. (2009). *Camden rebirth: A promise still unfulfilled.* Retrieved on March 11, 2015 from http://articles.philly.com/2009-11-08/news/24987941_1_state-takeover-sewer-sewage.

Ketchen, D., & Short, J. (n.d.). *Mastering strategic management.* Retrieved from the World Wide Web on February 17, 2014 from http://catalog.flatworldknowledge.com/bookhub/3085?e=ketchen_1.0-ch01_s02.

Kingdon, W. (2003). *Agendas, alternatives and public policies* (2nd ed.). New York: Longman.

Kirschner, J. (2012). *Northampton county regional police study Hellertown Borough and Lower Saucon Township.* Pennsylvania, PA: Governor's Center for Local Government Services.

Kocher, C. (2012). Sustaining police operations at an efficient and effective level under difficult economic times. *The Police Chief, 79*(3), 28–33.

Koepsell, T., & Girard, C. (1979). *Small police agency consolidation: Suggested approaches*. Report prepared for the National Institute of Law Enforcement and Criminal Justice. Washington, DC: Department of Justice.

Koper, C., Lum, C., & Willis, J. (2014). Optimizing the use of technology in policing: Results and implications from a multi-site study of the social, organizational, and behavioural aspects of implementing police technologies. *Policing, 8*(2), 212–221.

Kraska, P. (1996). Enjoying militarism: Political and personal dilemmas in studying police paramilitary units. *Justice Quarterly, 13*(3), 405–429.

Krimmel, J. (1997). The Northern York county police consolidation experience: An analysis of the consolidation of police services in eight Pennsylvania rural communities. *Policing: An International Journal of Police Strategies and Management, 20*(3), 497–507.

Kurdzuk, T. (2014, December 6). New police force brings hope to Camden as crime drops after years of bloodshed. *The Star-Ledger*. Retrieved on March 11, 2015 from   http://www.nj.com/news/index.ssf/2013/12/new_police_force_brings_ hope_to_camden_as_crime_drops_after_years_of_bloodshed.html.

Kushner, J., & Siegel, D. (2005a, Summer). Are services delivered more efficiently after municipal amalgamations? *Canadian Public Administration, 48*(2), 251–267.

Kushner, J., & Siegel, D. (2005b, Spring). Citizen satisfaction with amalgamations municipal amalgamations. *Canadian Public Administration, 48*(1), 73–95.

La Grange, R. (1987). The future of police consolidation. *Journal of Contemporary Criminal Justice, 3*(1), 6–16.

Lacasse, T. (1986, October). An alternative approach to investigations. *FBI Law Enforcement Bulletin, 55*, 9–12.

Laday, J. (2014a, June 3). Camden County Police Department adds 70 officers as new academy class graduates. *South Jersey Times*. Retrieved on March 11, 2015 from http://www.nj.com/camden/index.ssf/2014/06/camden_county_police_ department_adds_70_officers_as_new_academy_class_graduates.html.

Laday, J. (2014b, September 3). County releases Camden crime stats for January through to August. *South New Jersey Times*. Retrieved on March 11, 2015 from http://www.nj.com/camden/index.ssf/2014/09/county_releases_camden_ crime_stats_for_january_through_august.html.

Langworthy, R. (1986). *The structure of police organizations*. New York: Praeger Publishers.

Laycock, G. (2001). Research for police: Who needs it? *Trends and issues in crime and criminal justice* (No. 211). Canberra, Australian Capital Territory, Australia: Australian Institute of Criminology.

Leishman, F., Cope, S., & Starie, P. (1995). Reforming the police in Britain: New public management, policy networks and a tough old Bill. *The International Journal of Public Sector Management, 8*(4), 26–37.

Lewis, R. (1976). *A force for the future: The role of the police over the next ten years*. London, U.K.: Temple Smith.

Lewis, R. (2009, July 15). 70 deputies jobs saved. *Sacramento Bee*. Retrieved on January 1, 2013 from www.sacbee.com/2009/07/15/2026680/70-deputies-jobs- saved.html.

Liederbach, J., Fritsch, E., & Womack, C. (2011, February). Detective workload and opportunities for increased productivity in criminal investigations. *Police Practice and Research, 12*(1), 50–65.

Lithopoulos, S., & Rigakos, G. (2005). Neo-liberalism, community, and police regionalization in Canada: A critical empirical analysis. *Policing: An International Journal of Police Strategies and Management, 28*(2), 337–352.

Littlechild, S. (1983). *Problems of controlling state enterprises. State enterprise and deregulation* (Special Study No. 5). Melbourne, Victoria, Australia: Centre of Policy Studies, Monash University.

Loizzo, L. (1994). *Community oriented policing—One step beyond major crime problem solvers—The evolution of investigations for the 21st century.* Tallahassee, FL: Florida Department of Law Enforcement.

Loveday, B. (1995a). Reforming the police: From local service to state police? *The Political Quarterly, 66*(3), 141–156.

Loveday, B. (1995b). Contemporary challenges to police management in England and Wales: Developing strategies for effective service delivery. *Policing and Society, 5*, 281–302.

Loveday, B. (2006a). *Size isn't everything: Restructuring policing in England and Wales.* London, U.K.: Policy Exchange.

Loveday, B. (2006b). Police reform in England and Wales: Producer-driven or consumer-led? An evaluation of the current police reform programme. *The Police Journal, 79*(3), 200–213.

Loveday, B. (2006c). Basic command units (BCUs) and local authorities: Future mechanisms of police accountability and service. *International Journal of Police Science and Management, 9*(4), 324–335.

Loveday, B. (2007). Re-engineering the police organisation: Implementing workforce modernisation in England and Wales. *The Police Journal, 80*(1), 3–27.

Loveday, B. (2008). Workforce modernisation in the police service. *International Journal of Police Science and Management, 10*(2), 136–144.

Loveday, B. (2015) *Police management and workforce reform in a period of austerity.* Retrieved on May 14, 2015 from https://policinginsight.com/analysis/police-management-and-workforce-reform-in-a-period-of-austerity/

Loveday, B., & McClory, J. (2007). *Footing the bill: Reforming the police service.* London, U.K.: Policy Exchange.

Maciag, M. (2014). *Can a new police force turn around Camden, N.J., one of the nation's most violent cities?* Retrieved on March 11, 2015 from http://www.governing.com/topics/public-justice-safety/gov-camden-disbands-police-force-for-new-department.html.

Maguire, E. (2003). *Organizational structure in large police agencies: Context, complexity, and control.* Albany, NY: State University of New York Press.

Marnoch, G. (2009). *Intent and execution in the construction of performance stories by police services—The Annual Reports of the Police Services of Northern Ireland, New Zealand, Chicago and London Compared,* Saint-Julian's, Malta. Paper presented to EGPA Annual Conference SGII 2009.

Martin, R. (1997). *Policing in Canada: Issues for the 21st century.* Auroro, Ontario, Canada: Canada Law Book Incorporated.

Mazerolle, L., McBroom, J., & Rombouts, S. (2011). Compstat in Australia: An analysis of the spatial and temporal impact. *Journal of Criminal Justice, 39*(2), 128–136.

Mazerolle, L., Soole, D., & Rombouts, S. (2007). Drug law enforcement: A review of the evaluation literature. *Police Quarterly, 10*, 115–153.

Mayo, L. (2012). Moving beyond the myths and misdirection impeding community policing success. In D. Cohen McCullough & D. Spence (Eds.), *American policing in 2022: Essays on the future of a profession* (pp. 33–36). Washington, DC: Community Oriented Policing Services U.S. Department of Justice.

McDavid, J. (2008, Winter). The impacts of amalgamation on police services in the Halifax Regional Municipality. *Canadian Public Administration, 45*(4), 538–565.

McGrath, M. (2011). Taking a closer look at the New Zealand model. *Public Sector Magazine*, pp. 76–77. Retrieved on November 10, 2012 from http://download. pwc.com/ie/pubs/2011_public_sector_reform_with_margarete_mcgrath.pdf.

McKenna, H. (1996). Ethical dilemmas in an entrepreneurial public service. In J. Wanna, J. Forster, & P. Graham (Eds.), *Entrepreneurial management in the public sector* (pp. 208–222). Melbourne, Victoria, Australia: Macmillan Education Australia Pty.

McLaughlin, P., Atherton, M., & Morrison, K. (2009). *Legislative approaches to right-sizing municipal services*. Philadelphia, PA: Institute for Public Affairs Temple University.

Melekian, B. (2012a). Policing in the new economy: A new report on the emerging trends from the Office of Community Oriented Policing Services. *The Police Chief, 79*(1), 16–19.

Melekian, B. (2012b). Car 54: Where are you? In D. Cohen McCullough & D. Spence (Eds.), *American policing in 2022: Essays on the future of a profession* (pp. 89–93). Washington, DC: Community Oriented Policing Services U.S. Department of Justice.

Mellors, J. (1993). The commercialization of common services provided by the Department of Administrative Services: Outcomes and emerging issues. *Australian Journal of Public Administration, 52*(3), 329–338.

Middleton-Hope, J. (2007). *Challenges in contemporary police leadership*. International Police Executive Symposium and Geneva Centre for the Democratic Control of Armed Forces (Working Paper No. 3). Geneva, Switzerland: DCAF.

Miller, R. (2006). Regionalizing police services. *Borough News Magazine, 6*(6), 1–4.

Ministry of Justice. (2012). *Delivering better public services: Reducing crime and re-offending result action plan*. Wellington, New Zealand: Ministry of Justice.

Mintzberg, H. (1978). Patterns in strategy formation. *Management Science, 24*(9), 934–948.

Moore, M., & Stephens, D. (1991). *Beyond command and control: The strategic management of police departments*. Washington, DC: Police Executive Research Forum.

Morgan Quitno. (2015). *America's most dangerous (and safest cities)*. Retrieved on March 11, 2015 from http://www.morganquitno.com/xcit06pop.htm.

Morris, N. (2010). *Home office: 20,000 police officers predicted to lose jobs*. Retrieved on March 12, 2015 from http://www.independent.co.uk/news/uk/politics/ home-office-20000-police-officers-predicted-to-lose-jobs-2112209.html.

Moynihan, D. (2006, January/February). Managing for results in state government: Evaluating a decade of reform. *Public Administration Review, 66*, 77–89.

Murphy, C. (1998). Policing post-modern Canada. *Canadian Journal of Law and Society, 13*, 1–22.

Murphy, C. (2002). *The rationalization of Canadian public policing.* The Police Futures Group (Electronic Series No. 1, pp. 12–40). Canadian Association of Chiefs of Police, Kanata, Canada.

Murray, T. (2000). Are the police destined for postmodern oblivion? A practitioner's view of present and future policing in Canada. *Journal of Police Research and Practice: An International Journal of Policing, 1*(3), 373–406.

Myers, P. (n.d.). *Consolidating police services: Local control vs. Financial choice.* Retrieved on October 30, 2012 from http://www.fdle.state.fl.us/Content/getdoc/258b0143-2da0-4dfd-b9e6-37979df84528/Myers-Rick-research-paper-pdf.aspx.

National Advisory Commission on Criminal Justice Standards and Goals. (1973). *Police—Report of the national advisory commission on criminal justice standards and goals.* Washington, DC: U.S. Department of Justice.

National Institute of Justice. (2014). *Coming together for Camden.* Retrieved on March 11, 2015 from http://www.nj.gov/governor/news/news/552014/pdf/20140924b.pdf.

New Jersey Office of the Attorney General. (2006). *Final report of Attorney General's Advisory Commission on Camden's public safety.* Retrieved on March 11, 2015 from http://www.state.nj.us/lps/com-report-camden.pdf.

New Jersey State Association of Chiefs of Police. (2007, March 27). *Police Department regionalization, consolidation, merger and shared services important considerations for policy makers.* Retrieved on October 30, 2012 from www.njsacop.org.

New Zealand Institute of Economic Research. (2007). *De-merging traffic enforcement from police: Analysis of information to review costs and benefits.* Wellington, New Zealand: State Services Commission.

New Zealand Police. (1989). *Annual report.* Wellington, New Zealand: Government Print.

New Zealand Police. (1992). *Strategic plan 1992–1996.* Wellington, New Zealand: Government Print.

New Zealand Police. (1993). *Corporate plan 1993–1994.* New Zealand Police.

New Zealand Police. (1994). *The annual report of the New Zealand Police to Parliament 1993–1994.* Wellington, New Zealand: GP Print.

New Zealand Police. (1996a). *Briefing to the incoming government: Issues, strategies and directions.* Wellington, New Zealand: GP Print.

New Zealand Police. (1996b). *Corporate profile.* Wellington, New Zealand: GP Print.

New Zealand Police. (1997, November 19). [A strategic assessment for New Zealand Police. Draft #4]. Unpublished.

New Zealand Police. (2001). *Annual report.* Wellington, New Zealand: Government Print.

New Zealand Police. (2010). *Statement of intent: 2010/11–2012/13.* Wellington, New Zealand: Government Print.

New Zealand Police. (2011a, October 12). [Policing excellence presentation.] Unpublished. Wellington, New Zealand: Police National Headquarters.

New Zealand Police. (2011b). *The New Zealand police deployment model: Right people, right place, right time, right result: Prevention first—National operating strategy 2011–2015.* New Zealand Police.

New Zealand Police. (2011c). *Prevention first: National operating strategy 2011–2015.* New Zealand Police, Wellington, New Zealand.

New Zealand Police. (2011d). *The New Zealand police deployment managers guide: Right people, right place, right time, right result: Prevention first—National operating strategy 2011-2015*. New Zealand Police, Wellington, New Zealand.

New Zealand Police. (2012, November). [Policing excellence report card.] Unpublished.

New Zealand Police. (2013). *Prevention first: National tactical plan 2013-2015*. New Zealand Police, Wellington, New Zealand.

New Zealand Police. (2014). *Annual Report 2013/2014*. New Zealand Police, Wellington, New Zealand.

New Zealand Police. (2015). *Annual Report 2014/2015*. Retrieved on 2 May 2015 from www.police.govt.nz.

New Zealand Police Association. (2013, November). Policing excellence and beyond. *Police News, 46*(10), 259.

Neyroud, P. (n.d.). *Cost effectiveness in policing: Lessons from the UK in improving policing through a better workforce, process and technology*. Retrieved on October 30, 2012 from www.eso.expertgrupp.se/Uploads/Documents/Neyroud.pdf.

O'Byrne, M. (2001). *Changing policing revolution not evolution*. Dorset, U.K.: Russell House Publishing.

Oliver, W. (2004). The third generation of community policing: Moving through innovation, diffusion, and institutionalization. In Q. Thurman & J. Zhao (Eds.), *Contemporary policing: Controversies, challenges and solutions* (pp. 39–54). Los Angeles, CA: Roxbury Publishing Company.

Oppal, W. (1994). *Closing the gap. Policing and the community. The report*. Victoria, British Columbia, Canada: Policing in British Columbia Commission of Inquiry.

Orde, H. (2012, August). The fog of transition in U.K. policing: Major changes abound. *The Police Chief, 79*, 72–76.

Ostrom, E. (1973) On the meaning and measurement of output and efficiency in the provision of urban police services. *Journal of Criminal Justice, 1*(2), 93–112.

Ostrom, E., Parks, R., & Whitaker, G. (1973, September–October). Do we really want to consolidate urban police forces? A reappraisal of some old assertions. *Public Administration Review, 33*(5), 423–432.

Ostrom, E., Parks, R., & Whitaker, G. (1978). Policing: Is there a system? In J. May & A. Wildavsky (Eds.), *The policy cycle* (pp. 111–144). Beverly Hills, CA: Sage Publications.

Oxford Online Dictionary. (2013). http://www.oxforddictionaries.com/.

Pachon, H., & Lovrich, N. (1977, January/February). The consolidation of urban public services: A focus on the police. *Public Administration Review, 37*, 38–47.

Pallot, J. (1991). Financial management reform. In J. Boston, J. Martin, J. Pallot, & P. Walsh (Eds.), *Reshaping the state: New Zealand's bureaucratic revolution* (pp. 198–232). Auckland, New Zealand: Oxford University Press.

Palmer, D., & Cherney, A. (2001). 'Bending granite'? Recent attempts at changing police organisational structures in Australia: The case of Victoria Police. *Current Issues in Criminal Justice, 13*(1), 47–59.

Palmer, M. (1994). Managing a hierarchical para-military organisation. In K. Bryett & C. Lewis (Eds.), *Un-peeling tradition: Contemporary policing.* (pp. 84–94). South Melbourne, Victoria, Australia: Centre Australian Public Sector Management, Macmillan Education.

Pallot, J. (1991). Financial management reform. In J. Boston, J. Martin, J. Pallot, & P. Walsh (Eds.), *Reshaping the state: New Zealand's bureaucratic revolution* (pp. 198–232). Auckland, New Zealand: Oxford University Press.

Parks, R. (1985). Metropolitan structure and systemic performance: The case of police service delivery. In K. Hanf & T. Toonen (Eds.), *Policy implementation in Federal and Unitary States*. Dordrecht, the Netherlands: Martinus Nijhoff.

Peak, K. (1993). *Policing America: Methods, issues, challenges*. Englewood, NJ: Prentice-Hall.

Pennsylvania Governor's Center for Local Government Services. (2012). *Southern York County regional police study: Borough of Stewartstown*. Philadelphia, PA: Pennsylvania Governor's Center for Local Government Services.

Phillips, P. (1999). De facto police consolidation: The multi-jurisdictional task force. *Police Forum, 9*(3), 1–6.

Police Executive Research Forum. (2009). *Violent crime and the economic crisis: Police Chiefs face a new challenge* (Critical issues in policing series, Part I). Washington, DC: Police Executive Research Forum.

Police Executive Research Forum. (2011). *Is the economic downturn changing how we police?* (Critical issues in policing series). Washington, DC: Police Executive Research Forum.

Police Executive Research Forum. (2013a). *Civilian staffing in policing: An assessment of the 2009 Byrne Hiring Program*. Washington, DC: Police Executive Research Forum.

Police Executive Research Forum. (2013b). *Compstat: Its origins, evolution and future in law enforcement agencies*. Washington, DC: Police Executive Research Forum.

Policy Exchange. (2011). *Cost of cops: Manpower and deployment of policing*. London, U.K.: Policy Exchange.

Popp, D., & Sebold, F. (1972). Quasi returns to scale in the provision of police service. *Public Finance, 27*(11), 1–18.

President's Commission on Law Enforcement and Administration of Justice (1967). *Task Force Report: The Police*. Washington, DC: U.S. Government Printing Office.

Preston, P. (1996). *Economic reform: The New Zealand experience*. South African Property Owners Association Annual Conference, Sandton, South Africa. Retrieved on December 10, 2012 from http://www.nzbr.org.nz/site/nzbr/files/speeches/speeches-96–97/preston-sud-afrika.pdf.

Queensland Police Service. (2010). *Annual report 1999–2000*. Retrieved on January 15, 2013 from www.police.qld.gov.au.

Queensland Police Service. (2011a). *Annual report 2011–2012*. Retrieved on January 15, 2013 from www.police.qld.gov.au.

Queensland Police Service. (2011b). *Strategic plan 2011–2015*. Retrieved on January 15, 2013 from http://www.police.qld.gov.au/Resources/Internet/services/reportsPublications/documents/StrategicPlan2011-15.pdf.

Reaves, B., & Goldberg, A. (1998). *Census of state and local law enforcement agencies, 1996* (Bulletin NCJ 164618). Washington, DC: U.S. Department of Justice, Bureau of Justice Statistics.

Reaves, B., & Smith, P. (1995). *Law enforcement management and administration statistics, 1993: Data for individual State and local agencies with 100 or more officers* (NCJ 148825). Washington, DC: U.S. Department of Justice, Bureau of Justice Statistics.

Reiner, R. (1986). *The politics of the police.* Brighton, U.K.: Wheatsheaf Books Limited.

Reiner, R. (2010). *The politics of the police* (4th ed.) London, U.K.: Oxford University Press.

Reiss, A. (1992). Police organization in the twentieth century. *Modern policing: Vol. 15. Crime and justice* (pp. 51–97). Chicago, IL: The University of Chicago Press Stable.

Report of Independent Reviewer. (1998). *Review of police administration and management structures.* Wellington, New Zealand: New Zealand Police.

Rigakos, G.S. (2000). The significance of economic trends for the future of police and security. In J. Richardson (Ed.), *Police and security: What the future holds* (pp. 176–179). Ottawa, Ontario, Canada: Canadian Association of Chiefs of Police.

Rigakos, G.S. (2002). *The new parapolice: Risk markets and commodified social control.* Toronto, Ontario, Canada: University of Toronto Press.

Rogers, B., & Lipsey, C. (1974, Fall). Metropolitan reform: Citizen evaluations of performances in Nashville-Davidson County, Tennessee. *Publius, 4,* 19–34.

Rogers, C., & Gravelle, J. (2012, March). UK policing and change: Reflections for policing worldwide. *Review of European Studies, 4*(1), 42–51.

Rose, N., & Miller, P. (1992). Political power beyond the state: Problematics of government. *British Journal of Sociology, 43*(2), 173–205.

Rutherford, B. (1983). *Financial reporting in the public sector.* London, U.K.: Butterworths.

R. W. (2014). *Lessons from Camden.* Retrieved on March 11, 2015 from http://www.economist.com/blogs/democracyinamerica/2014/12/police-and-people.

Salamon, L. (2000). The new governance and the tools of public action: An introduction. *Fordham Urban Law Journal, 28*(5), 1611–1674.

Savage, S. (2007). *Police reform: Forces for change.* Oxford, U.K.: Oxford University Press.

Schafer, J. (2012). Rethinking 'business as usual'. In D. Cohen McCullough & D. Spence (Eds.), *American policing in 2022: Essays on the future of a profession* (pp. 109–112). Washington, DC: Community Oriented Policing Services U.S. Department of Justice.

Schieder, M., Spence, D., & Mansourian, J. (2012). *The relationship between economic conditions, policing, and crime trends an addendum to the impact of the economic downturn on American police agencies.* Washington, DC: Community Oriented Policing Services U.S. Department of Justice.

Schnobrich-Davis, J. (2010). *Regionalization of selected police services through a law enforcement council: Is it worth the cost?* (Unpublished Doctoral thesis). State University of New York, Albany, NY.

Schwartz, A., Vaughn, A., Walker, J., & Wholey, J. (1975). *Employing civilians for police work* (Paper Number 5012-03-1). Washington, DC: Urban Institute.

Scott, G., Bushnell, P., & Salle, N. (1990). Reform of the core public sector: The New Zealand experience. *Public Sector, 13*(3), 11–24.

Scott, K. (2012). A single Police Force for Scotland: The legislative framework (1). *Policing: A Journal of Policy and Practice, 7*(2), 135–141.

Scottish Government. (2011a). *A consultation on the future of policing in Scotland.* Retrieved on February 20, 2014 from http://www.scotland.gov.uk/Resource/Doc/341417/0113500.pdf.

Scottish Government. (2011b). *Police reform programme: Outline business case.* Retrieved on February 1, 2014 from http://www.scotland.gov.uk/Resource/Doc/357534/0120783.pdf.

Scottish Government. (2011c). *Police reform programme: Outline business case.* Retrieved on February 2, 2014 from http://www.scotland.gov.uk/Resource/Doc/357534/0120783.pdf.

Scottish Government. (2012, January 16). *Police and fire reform (Scotland) bill: Policy memorandum* (SP Bill 8-PM). Edinburgh, U.K.: Queen's Printer for Scotland. Retrieved from http://www.scottish.parliament.uk/S4_Bills/Policc%20and%20Fire%20Reform%20(Scotland)%20Bill/Policy_Memo.pdf.

Seagrave, J. (1997). *Introduction to policing in Canada.* Scarborough, Ontario, Canada: Prentice Hall Canada.

Shearing, C., & Stenning, P. (1983). Private security: Implications for social control. *Social Problems, 30*(5), 498–505.

Sheptycki, J. (1998). Policing, postmodernism and transnationalisation. *The British Journal of Criminology, 38*(3), 485–503.

Sherman, L., Gottfredson, W., MacKenzie, D., Eck, J., Reuter, P., & Bushway, S. (1997). *Preventing crime: What works, what doesn't, what's promising?* Washington, DC: U.S. Department of Justice.

Shernock, S. (2004). The MJTF as a type of coordination compatible with both the Police Consolidation and Community Policing Movements. *Police Practice and Research: An International Journal, 5*(1), 67–85.

Simper, R., & Weyman-Jones, T. (2008). Evaluating gains from mergers in a non-parametric public good model of police services. *Annals of Public and Cooperative Economics, 79*(1), 3–33.

Skogan, W., & Frydel, K. (2003). *Fairness and effectiveness in policing: The evidence.* Washington, DC: The National Academies Press.

Small, F. (2000). *Ministerial inquiry into INCIS.* New Zealand Government, Wellington, New Zealand.

Snow, C., & Hambrick, D. (1980). Measuring organizational strategies: Some theoretical and methodological problems. *Academy of Management: The Academy of Management Review, 5,* 527–538.

Spitzer, S., & Scull, A. (1977). Privatization and capitalist development: The case of the private police. *Social Problems, 25,* 18–29.

Stockdale, J., Whitehead, C., & Gresham, P. (1999). *Applying economic evaluation to policing activity* (Police Research Paper 103). London, U.K.: Home Office.

Sullivan, R. (1998). The politics of British policing in the Thatcher/Major State. *The Howard Journal, 37,* 306–318.

Sustainable Policing Project. (2011). *Phase two report: Options for reform.* Retrieved on February 2, 2014 from http://www.scotland.gov.uk/Resource/Doc/254432/0115237.pdf.

Sustainable Policing Project Team. (2010, November). *Sustainable policing project: Interim report.* Retrieved on February 20, 2014 from http://www.scotland.gov.uk/Resource/Doc/254432/0110858.pdf.

Terpstra, J., & Fyfe, N. (2014). Policy processes and police reform: Examining similarities and differences between Scotland and the Netherlands. *International Journal of Law, Crime and Justice, 42,* 1–18. Retrieved from http://www.sciencedirect.com/science/article/pii/S1756061614000226#.

The Institute for Public Policy and Economic Development. (2010). *Regional polic-ing: The case for increased police service levels and accountability in Luzerne County*. Philadelphia, PA: Pennsylvania Economy League.

The Treasury. (1996). *Putting it together: An explanatory guide to the New Zealand public sector financial management system*. Wellington, New Zealand: New Zealand Treasury.

Thomson, J. (2012). A 'back to the future' paradox'. In D. Cohen McCullough & D. Spence (Eds.), *American policing in 2022: Essays on the future of a profes-sion* (pp. 85–88). Washington, DC: Community Oriented Policing Services US Department of Justice.

Thurman, Q., & Zhao, J. (2004). *Contemporary policing: Controversies, chal-lenges and solutions: An anthology*. Los Angeles, CA: Roxbury Publishing Company.

Tilley, N. (2003). Modern approaches to policing: Community, problem-oriented and intelligence-led. In T. Newburn (Ed.), *Handbook of policing* (pp. 373–403). Cullompton, U.K.: Willan Publishing.

Treverton, G., Wollman, M., Wilke, E., & Lai, D. (2011). *Moving toward the future of policing*. Arlington, VA: Rand Corporation.

Trueblood, M., & Honadle, B. (1994, April). *An overview of factors affecting the size of local government* (Staff Paper P94-7). St. Paul, MN: Department of Agricultural and Applied Economics, University of Minnesota.

Tully, E. J. (2002). *Regionalization or consolidation of law enforcement services in the United States*. Retrieved on December 8, 2012 from http://www.neiassociates.org/-consolidation-law-enforcement/.

United Kingdom Audit Commission. (1990). *Organisation of provincial police forces*. London, U.K.: Audit Commission.

United States Department of Justice. (2009). *Crime in the United States 2009*. Retrieved on January 7, 2013 from http://www.fbi.gov/about-us/cjis/ucr/crime-in-the-u.s/2009/crime-in-the-u.s.-2010/tables/10tbl01.xls.

United States Department of Justice, Federal Bureau of Investigation. (1951). *Uniform crime reports, 1950*. Washington, DC: U.S. Government Printing Office.

United States Department of Justice, Federal Bureau of Investigation. (1971). *Uniform crime reports, 1970*. Washington, DC: U.S. Government Printing Office.

United States Department of Justice, Federal Bureau of Investigation. (1991). *Uniform crime reports, 1990*. Washington, DC: U.S. Government Printing Office.

United States Department of Justice, Federal Bureau of Investigation. (2007). *Crime in the United States, 2006*. Retrieved on March 14, 2015 from http://www.fbi.gov/ucr/cius2006/.

Vancouver Police Department. (2008) *Options for service delivery in the Greater Vancouver Region: A discussion paper of the issues surrounding the regionalization of police ser-vices*. Vancouver, British Columbia, Canada: Vancouver Police Department.

Vickers, M., & Kouzmin, A. (2001). New managerialism and Australian police organizations: A cautionary research note. *The International Journal of Public Sector Management, 14*(1), 7–26.

Votey, H., & Philips, L. (1972, June). Police effectiveness and the production func-tion for law enforcement. *Journal of Legal Studies, 1*, 423–436.

Walker, S., & Katz, C. (2008). *The police in America: An introduction* (6th ed.). New York: McGraw-Hill.

Waltzer, N. (1972). Economies of scale in municipal police services: The Illinois experience. *The Review of Economics and Statistics, 54*(4), 431–438.

Wanna, J., O'Fairchealliagh, C., & Weller, P. (1992). *Public sector management in Australia.* Melbourne, Victoria, Australia: Macmillan.

Weisburd, D., & Eck, J. (2004). What can police do to reduce crime, disorder and fear? *The Annals of the American Academy of Political and Social Science, 593*, 42–65.

Weisheit, R., Falcone, D., & Wells, L. (1996). *Crime and policing in rural small town America.* Prospect Heights, IL: Waveland Press.

Willis, J. (2011). Enhancing police legitimacy by integrating compstat and community policing. *Policing: An International Journal of Police Strategies and Management, 34*(4), 654–673.

Willis, J., Mastroski, S., & Weisburd, D. (2007). Making sense of compstat: A theory-based analysis of organizational change in three police departments. *Law and Society Review, 41*(1), 147–188.

Wilson, J. (2012). Articulating the dynamic police staffing challenge: An examination of supply and demand. *Policing: An International Journal of Police Strategies & Management, 35*(2), 327–355.

Wilson, J., & Grammich, C. (2012, February). *Police consolidation, regionalization, and shared services: Options, considerations, and lessons from research and practice.* Be On The Lookout (BOLO). Washington, DC: Community Oriented Policing Services.

Wilson, J., Weiss, A., & Grammich, C. (2012, February) *Public safety consolidation: What is it?* Be On The Lookout (BOLO). Washington, DC: Community Oriented Policing Services.

Winnipeg Police Service. (2012, October). *Civilianization audit.* Retrieved on April 26, 2015 from http://www.winnipeg.ca/audit/pdfs/reports/2013/WPSCivilianizationAudit.pdf.

Wood, D. (2007). To regionalize or not to regionalize? A study in the politics of policing in the Greater Vancouver Regional District. *Police Practice and Research: An International Journal, 8*(3), 283–297.

Wood, S. (2014, April 1). *Crime plummets in Camden in 1st quarter.* Retrieved on March 11, 2015 from http://www.philly.com/philly/news/new_jersey/Crime_plummets_in_Camden_could_a_city_recovery_be_underway.html.

Zernike, K. (2012, September 28). To fight crime, a poor city will trade in its police. *The New York Times.* Retrieved on March 11, 2015 from http://www.nytimes.com/2012/09/29/nyregion/overrun-by-crime-camden-trades-in-its-police-force.html?_r=0.

Zimring, F. (2012). *The city that became safe: New York's lessons for urban crime and its control.* New York: Oxford University Press.

Index

A

Abstraction, 105
Accountability, 21, 119, 157
Accounting system, 54
ACCPS, *see* Advisory Commission on
        Camden's Public Safety Accrual
        accounting, 54
Active police governance, 89
Ad hoc collaboration, 67
Advisory Commission on Camden's Public
        Safety (ACCPS), 201–203
Age of austerity, policing in an, 113–114
Alliances, 68–69
Amalgamation, of police agencies
    advantages and disadvantages, 36
    cost reduction, 72, 221
    definition, 14, 16
    Halifax, 99
    philosophical problem with, 98–99
    reasons to consider, 69
    recommendations, 70
    supporters of claim, 25–26
    United States, service delivery in,
        131–132
APS, *see* Australian Public Service
Association of Chief Police Officers in
        Scotland (ACPOS) Council,
        150, 157
Audit Commission, 50
Austerity
    adapting to, 114–115
    policing in an age of, 113–114
Australian Public Service (APS)
    commercialization, 81–82
    globalization, 82
    NPM and, 80–81
    Victoria, reforms in, 82–83
Australia, service delivery in
    APS, changes to, 80–82NSWPF (case
        study), 84–85
    police forces, 79–80, 87
    QPS (case study), 85–87

B

Basic Command Unit (BCU), 106
BPR, *see* Business process reengineering
British Columbia Province, 94–95
Bureaucratic organizational structures,
        49–50
Business process reengineering (BPR),
        180, 183, 192
Byrne Grant Program, 60

C

Camden city
    crime, 204, 214
    murder rate, 199
Camden City Council, 201, 205
Camden Commission on Public Safety
        (CCPS), 198, 200–201
Camden County Police Department
        (CCPD)
    CCPS and, 198, 200–201
    draft plan (*see* Draft plan, CCPD)
    establishing, 198, 207–209
    high-level plan, 208
    performance 2012–2014, 213–214
    proposal to establish, 205–207
Camden County Police Department
        (CCPD) Metro
    CoPD, 212
    crime prevention, approach to, 215–217
    establishment, 198
    Operations Bureau, 211
    performance 2013, 214
    performance 2014, 214–215
    responsibility, 205
    RT-TOIC, 210–211
    SAU, 211
    in 2014, 212–213
Canada, service delivery in
    British Columbia Province, 94–95
    civilianization in, 61–63
    GVR, 95–98

Halifax City, 99–100
Ontario Province, 92–93, 98–99
police agencies and police services,
   90–92
policing in, 90
regionalization of police agencies, 92–93
CCPD, *see* Camden County Police
   Department
CCPS, *see* Camden Commission on
   Public Safety
Central/federal government, 18
Central government, policing policy in
   Scotland, 149
Change management programs
   NZP, analysis framework, 176–178
   organizational changes, 175–176
   Policing 2000 (*see* Policing 2000)
   Policing Excellence (*see* Policing
      Excellence)
   Prevention First (*see* Prevention First)
Chief Constable, 150
Civilianization
   in Canada, 61–63
   definition, 16
   implementation program, 107
   of sworn positions, 58–59, 127
   in United Kingdom, 63–64
   in United States, 60–61
Cobb–Douglas function, 81
Collaboration
   advantages and disadvantages, 67
   and multijurisdictional task forces, 221
   outsourcing and, 64–65
   spectrum of, 65–67
   stages, 67–68
Command and Control, 129
Commercialization, 81–82
Community approach, 11
Community-Oriented Police Services
   (COPS), 130
Community-Oriented Policing, *see*
   Community Policing
Community Policing
   in Canada, 37
   in CCPD Metro, 216
   Compstat and, 55–56
   development stages of, 130
   implementation, 180, 213
   MJTFs, 136
   organizational structure and, 51, 52
   police forces in Scotland, 146–147
   police service delivery, 3, 10, 23, 141

Problem-Oriented and, 129
U.S. police agencies and, 60
Community Policing Division (CoPD), 212
Community Service Officer (CSO), 61
Comprehensive strategic plan, 180–182
Compstat, 55–56
"Compstat Plus", 56
Conservative Government, 103
Consolidation
   approaches to, 16
   definition, 9, 14
   examples, 136–137
   forms, 14–15
   inconsistencies of, 132–134
   Pennsylvania, 137, 139–140
   programs and initiatives in other states,
      138–139, 140
   supporters of regionalization/
      amalgamations claim on, 26
Consultation on the Future of Policing in
   Scotland, 162
Contracting services, 16
Control of crime, 5
CoPD, *see* Community Policing Division
Core product/service management, 44
Corporate planning, 121–122
Corporatization, 118
Cost–benefit analysis (CBA), 31
Cost-effectiveness analysis (CEA), 31
Cost of Cops report, 115
Cost-reducing strategies, 3, 7
Costs, measuring, 12–14
Councils and municipal governments, 27
Crime control, 5
"Crime control effectiveness", 10
Crime prevention, CCPD Metro approach
   to, 215–217
Critical command information, 187–188
Cross-subsidization, 12

D

Data envelopment analysis (DEA), 84, 85
Day Patrol Division, 211
DCCs, *see* District Coordination Centers
DCED, *see* Department of Community and
   Economic Development
DEA, *see* Data envelopment analysis
Deliberate strategy, 177
Delivering agency outputs, 21
Demand for police services
   efficiency and effectiveness, 4–5

management methods, 7
role and responsibilities, 6
situational factors, 6
Department of Community and
        Economic Development
        (DCED), 133–134
Deployment model, 187–189, 190
Deregulation, 118
Detectives in policing, 52
District Command Centers (DCCs), *see*
        District Coordination Centers
District Coordination Centers (DCCs),
        189–190
Draft plan, CCPD
        expenditure of city, based on, 209–210
        Metro, pivotal components, 210–212
        proposed structure for essential
                functions, 211
        staffing by position type, 210
Drivers of crime, 187, 192

E

Economic operating environment, 128
Economic Opportunity Act (EOA), 218
Economy, United States, 128–129
Effectiveness
        definition, 12
        efficiency *vs.*, 10
        police services, delivery of, 4–5, 9,
                106–108, 167
Efficiency
        definition, 12
        vs. effectiveness, 10
        options, 41
        police services, delivery of, 4, 9,
                106–108, 167
Emergency Response Division, 211
Emerging strategies, 176–177
Engineering/accounting approach, 26
England and Wales, police service in
        adapting to austerity, 114–115
        current structure of policing, 110–113
        efficiency and effectiveness, 106–108
        manpower and deployment in
                policing, 115
        police reforms in, 102–103
        policing in age of austerity, 113–114
        role, management, and
                development, 110
        structure and size, 103–106
Executive functions, 14

F

Federal government, 18
Financial backdrop, 156–157
Financial management of public sector,
        20–21
Flatter organizational structures, 47, 50–51
Full integration of services, 15

G

General Police Act, 147
Glasgow Police Act, 147
Globalization, APS changes, 82
Government funding, theory of, 20–21
Greater Vancouver Region (GVR)
        criminal offending, influences
                impacting, 95–96
        problems with police structure, 97–98
        regional police agency, 96–97
Gross National Product, 17
GVR, *see* Greater Vancouver Region

H

Halifax City, 99–100
Her Majesty's Inspectorate of Constabulary
        adapting to austerity, 114–115
        civilianization of police, 107
        current structure of policing, 110–113
        manpower and deployment in
                policing, 115
        police force, efficient, 104–105
        policing in an age of austerity, 113–114
        VFM, 108
        Workforce Modernization program, 110
Her Majesty's Inspectorate of Constabulary
        Scotland, 150, 153, 157
High-end policing, 68
Hot Spot policing, 57

I

ILP, *see* Intelligence-led policing
Integrated National Crime Information
        System (INCIS), 123, 181
Integration, 14
Intelligence-led policing (ILP), 56–57,
        129, 175
Intended strategy, 177–178
Intentional and unintentional
        strategy, 176–177

Internal consolidation, 16
Investment in technology, 184

J

Justice sector performance targets, 187

K

Key performance indicators (KPIs), 107
Knowledge/quality management, 44
KPIs, *see* Key performance indicators

L

Larger-sized municipalities, 25
Larger-sized police agencies, 28, 35, 71, 92
Late-twentieth-century, service delivery
        strategies in, 42–43
Law Enforcement Councils (LECs), 136
Layered template to policing functions, 155
Local government, 18
    policing policy in Scotland, 149
Local Government in Scotland Act, 2003,
        150, 152
Local government reform, theory of
    cost of production, 25
    determination scale methods, 26–27
    Traditional Reform, 24
Locally driven agency collaboration, 65–67
Local merger, 16
Local police agency, advantages and
        disadvantages, 36
London Metropolitan Police, 190
Lower-level managers, 50–51

M

Managing for Outcomes, 119
Memorandum of understanding
        (MOU), 207
Merger, of police agencies
    advantages and disadvantages, 35–36
    alternatives, 166
    assertions, 70
    definition, 14
    large number of, 36–37, 92
    local government reform and (*see* Local
        government reform, theory of)
    plan for implement, 166–167
    planning, elements considered
        during, 69–70

of police forces, 165–166
    problems, 170–172
    regionalization and, 27–29
    United States, 131–132
Metro Division, CCPD, 205, 210–212
Metropolitan policing, 180
Mixed Economy Teams (METs), 63
MJTF, *see* Multijurisdictional task force
Modern accounting tools and
        techniques, 46
Modern police reform, theory of, 21–23
MOU, *see* Memorandum of understanding
Multijurisdictional task force (MJTF),
        136, 221
Multiproduct translog cost function, 71
Municipal budgets, in New Jersey, 205
Municipal governments, 27
Murder rate, 199

N

National agencies, 18
Neighborhood Resource Officer (NRO), 212
New Jersey Division of Criminal
        Justice, 199
New Jersey, municipal budgets in, 205
New Public Management (NPM)
    defined, 37–38, 118
    effects on police agencies, 46–47
    features, 38
    implementation, 52, 219, 220
    introduction of, 22–23, 80–81
    performance framework, 39
    performance management system, 53–55
    police reforms based on, 101
    purchaser/provider model of, 87
    strength of, 142
    supporters, 40
    in UK police forces, 220
New South Wales Police Force (NSWPF)
        (case study), 79, 84–85
New York city, murder rate in, 199
New Zealand Police (NZP)
    analysis framework, 176–178
    budget, 189
    change management programs (*see*
        Change management programs)
    corporate planning, 121–122
    culture, profound change in, 184
    investment in technology, 184
    response to environment (*see* Response
        of NZP to environment)

service delivery, 194–195
  strategic planning, 122–124
New Zealand, service delivery in
  government reforms, 118–119
  NZP, 175, 179, 183, 184, 194
  performance and accountability
    framework, 119
  public sector reforms, 178
  reorientation, 119–120
Night Patrol Division, 211
Northern York County Regional Police
  Department, Pennsylvania
  (NYCRPD), 29
NPM, *see* New Public Management
NRO, *see* Neighborhood Resource Officer
NSWPF, *see* New South Wales Police Force
  (case study)
NZP, *see* New Zealand Police

O

OB, *see* Operations Bureau
Ontario Province, regionalization
  programs, 92–93, 98–99
Operations Bureau (OB), 211
Organizational output, 10
Organizational structures
  component, 52
  flatter structures, 47, 50–51
  paramilitary bureaucratic
    structures, 49–50
  problems with, 50
  shape and size of, 45, 51
Organization for Economic Cooperation
  and Development (OECD), 118
Organization of police agencies, 69
Other public sector entities, police services
  and, 220
Outline Business Case
  high-level framework, 160
  ranking options, 161
  reform options, 159
  single service, benefits of, 162
  weaknesses within, 173
Outsourcing, 16
  and collaboration, 64–65

P

Paramilitary bureaucratic structure,
  49–50
Partial integration of services, 15

Pennsylvania, consolidations of police
  agencies in, 137, 139–140
Performance and accountability
  framework, 119
Performance management system
  components, 53
  Compstat, 55–56
  difficulties experienced, 53–54
  measurement, 54–55
  NPM program, implementing, 52
  quantitative and qualitative methods, 43
  supporting elements, 44
Personnel costs, 50
Planning and performance management, 44
Planning, programming, and budgeting
  (PPB), 33–34
Police (Scotland) Act 1967, 149, 150
Police agencies
  amalgamation (*see* Amalgamation, of
    police agencies)
  Canadian, 61, 62, 74, 92–93
  challenges, 6
  collaboration, spectrum, 65–67
  consolidation, 15, 136–137, 140
  funding allocations to, 127
  mergers (*see* Merger, of police agencies)
  NPM, 46–47, 53
  organization of, 69
  in Pennsylvania, 137, 139–140
  performance measurement framework,
    43–45
  and police services, 90–92
  regionalization (*see* Regionalization, of
    police agencies)
  staffing of, 130–131
  U.S., 60–61
Police and Fire Reform (Scotland)
  Act 2012, 163
Police–citizen relationship, 10, 46
Police–community relationship, 11, 46
Police Community Support Officers
  (PCSOs) program, 63
Police culture, change in, 184
Police decision-makers, 129
Police effectiveness, 10
Police employees, tasks for, 187
Police governance, tripartite structure of,
  149–151
Police interagency collaboration
  outsourcing and, 64–65
  spectrum of, 65–67
  stages, 67–68

Police operating costs, reducing, 4–5
Police patrol, 51, 85
Police, Public Order and Criminal Justice
        (Scotland) Act 2006, 149
Police reform
    elements, 101
    in England and Wales, 102–103
    factors led to, 33
    government approach to, 32–33
    high-level objectives, 152, 153
    highlights of report, 153, 154
    issues leading to, 152–153, 173
    program, Outline Business Case (see
        Outline Business Case)
    SPP, 153, 155, 157–159
    theory of, 21–23
Police resources, 221
Police service delivery, improvement in, see
        Service delivery, improvement
Police services
    demand for (see Demand for police
        services)
    efficiency and effectiveness,
        106–108, 167
    merging, 109
    and other public sector entities, 220
    police agencies and, 90–92
    regional, 135
    single, benefits of, 162
    structure and size of, 103–106
Policing 2000, 175
    aims of, 190
    creation, 183–184
    investment in technology, 184
    Policing Excellence, and Prevention
        First, 191–194
    projects, 182–183
Policing Excellence, 175
    Policing 2000 and Prevention First,
        191–194
    work streams, 124–125, 185–186
Policing functions, layered template
        to, 155
Policy analysis framework, 172–173
Political interference, 19
POP, see Problem-Oriented Policing
PPB, see Planning, programming, and
        budgeting
PPPs, see Public–private partnerships
Prevention First, 175
    deployment model, 187–189
    operating strategy for police, 186

Policing 2000 and Policing Excellence,
        191–194
    tasks for police employees, 187
Private industry values and strategies, 45
Privatization, 118
Problem-Oriented Policing (POP),
        57, 129, 175
Public choice theory, 24, 118, 172
Public good, 81
Public–private partnerships (PPPs), 68
Public sector management, 19–21
Public sector organizations, 18
Public sector reform
    New Zealand, 178
    reason, 18–19

Q

QPS, see Queensland Police Service
        (case study)
Qualitative methods, 43
Quantitative methods, 43
Quantitative performance measures, 10
Queensland Police Service (QPS)
        (case study), 79, 85–87

R

Rational choice theory, 24, 172
RCMP, see Royal Canadian Mounted Police
Real-Time Tactical Operations and
        Information Center (RT-TOIC),
        210, 211, 217
Reform Bill, 163
Regionalization, of police agencies
    advantages and disadvantages, 36
    ambiguities, 134–136
    Canadian, 92–93
    contention regarding, 69
    definition, 14, 16
    examples, 136–137
    local government agency, 24
    reducing expenditure, theory of, 35
    strength, 206
    supporters of claim, 25–26
    theory of, 27–29
    in United Kingdom, 72–73, 220
    United States, 37, 131–132
Regionalization of the Canadian police
        (case study)
    British Columbia Province, 94–95
    GVR, 95–98

Halifax City, 99–100
Ontario Province, 98–99
Regional Law Enforcement Councils
        (LECs), 136
Regional law enforcement restructuring
        program, 206
Regional/national agencies, 18
Regional police agency
    advantages and disadvantages,
        134–135
    GVR, 96–97
Reorientation, 119–120
Resilience", 51–52
Resource management, 44
Response of NZP to environment, 120–121
    police officers and nonsworn staff and
        officers, 179
    Policing 2000, 182–183
    strategic plan, 180–182
Restructuring, 127
Royal Canadian Mounted Police (RCMP),
        90, 94
Royal Commission, 103

S

SAU, see Strategic Analysis Unit
Scan, analysis, respond, and
        assess (SARA), 57
Scotland, police forces in
    challenges, 170
    consultation document, 162
    elements of improvement, 168
    financial backdrop, 156–157
    future improvement, 169–170
    high-level objectives, 152, 153
    highlights of report, 153, 154
    history, 147–149
    issues leading to police reform,
        152–153, 173
    merger, 145, 163, 165–167
    Outline Business Case (see Outline
        Business Case)
    police governance, tripartite structure
        of, 149–151
    policy analysis framework, 172–173
    reform, background to, 146–147
    Reform Bill, 163
    reform, measures of, 168–169
    single force, challenges to
        implementing, 167
    SPP, 153, 155, 157–159

Scottish Crime and Drug Enforcement
        Agency (SCDEA), 149
Scottish Drug Enforcement Agency
        (SDEA), 149
Scottish Police Board, 150
Scottish Police Services Authority
        (SPSA), 149
SDEA, see Scottish Drug Enforcement
        Agency
Semistructured interview for research, 164
Service delivery, improvement
    in Australia (see Australia, service
        delivery in)
    in Canada (see Canada, service
        delivery in)
    effectiveness (see Effectiveness)
    efficiency (see Efficiency)
    England and Wales (see England and
        Wales, police service in)
    ILP, 56–57
    late-twentieth-century, 42–43
    measuring, 11
    New Zealand (see New Zealand, service
        delivery in)
    organizational structures (see
        Organizational structures)
    performance measurement (see
        Performance management
        system)
    in United States (see United States,
        service delivery in)
    value improvement model, 13
Shared services, 16
Sheehy Inquiry, 101
Single police service
    benefits, 162
    objectives, 168–169
Smaller-sized municipalities, 24–25
Smaller-sized police agencies, 35, 70, 93, 140
Social choice theory, 24, 172
Social market approach, components of, 23
Social outcome, 10
Softer approach, 194
SPSA, see Scottish Police Services Authority
Staffing of police agencies, 130–131
State-owned enterprises, 18
Statistical approach, 11
Strategic alliance, 68
Strategic Analysis Unit (SAU), 211
Strategic plan, 122–124, 180–182
Strategy formulation and implementation,
        176–177

Sustainable Policing Project (SPP), 153, 155, 157–159
Sworn positions, civilianization of, 58–59

T

Target Operating Model (TOM), 155, 160–161
Tasking and coordination, 187–188
Technology
    investment in, 184
    use of, 74
Traditional police managers, 7
Traffic Offence Notice, 192
Tripartite structure of police governance, 149–151
2012 Act, 168–169

U

Unintentional strategy, intentional and, 176–177
United Kingdom
    civilianization in, 63–64
    efficiency and effectiveness, 106–108
    merging, 109
    regionalization in, 72–73
    structure and size, 103–106
United States, service delivery in
    amalgamation, mergers, and
        regionalization, 131–132
    civilianization in, 60–61
    Community Policing, 130
    consolidations, inconsistencies of, 132–134
    economy, 128–129
    management, 129–130
    reduced costs, 134
    staffing of police agencies, 130–131
Use of technology, 74
U.S. Marshals Fugitive Task Force, 204

V

Value for money (VFM), 47
    achievement, 48–49
    characteristics, 49
    objectives, 108
    PPB, 33–34
    principal components of, 48
Vancouver Police Department, 96–97
Vancouver Police Service (VPS), 63
VFM, *see* Value for money
Victoria, reforms in, 82–83
VPS, *see* Vancouver Police Service

W

Wales and England, *see* England and Wales, police service in
Winnipeg Police Service (WPS), 62–63
Workforce management, 188
Workforce Modernization, 109, 110
Work streams, Policing Excellence
    program, 124–125